I0494255

Sex As Symbol: The Ancient Light in Modern Psychology

By Alvin Boyd Kuhn

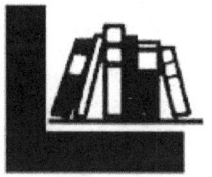

ISBN: 978-1-63923-224-6

Printed: July 2022

Cover Art By: Amit Paul

Published and Distributed By:
Lushena Books
607 Country Club Drive, Unit E
Bensenville, IL 60106
www.lushenabooksinc.com/books

ISBN: 978-1-63923-224-6

SEX AS SYMBOL

The Ancient Light in Modern Psychology

BY

ALVIN BOYD KUHN, Ph.D.

"We have only just rediscovered the precious stone; we have still to polish it. We cannot yet compete with the intuitive clarity of Eastern vision."—C. G. JUNG: *Integration of the Personality*, p. 41.

"All that can be said concerning the gods must be by exposition of old opinions and fables: it being the custom of the ancients to wrap up in enigma and allegory their thoughts and discourses concerning nature, which are, therefore, not easily explained."—HENRY O'BRIEN: *The Round Towers of Ireland*, p. 302—quoted from Strabo.

ACADEMY PRESS

227 MURRAY STREET ELIZABETH 2, N. J.

To

ALL THOSE

WHO STRIVE TO SEE

THE MIND OF THE CREATOR

IN ALL THE WORK

OF HIS HAND

THIS

VOLUME IS

SINCERELY DEDICATED

CONTENTS

CHAPTER I

THE BRIGHT LEXICON OF DEITY

IN a very venerable document, *Records of the Past* (XII, 68) we read that in remote days of antiquity geographical mapping and local naming were instituted according to a plan which has almost totally escaped recognition in our search for understanding of archaic culture. It is said there that the names and localities were derived from the features of an original uranograph, or chart of the heavens, and were transferred from it to earth and applied to the geography of a country, with a distribution of the names already localized in the empyrean amongst the places to be named, according to a scheme of correspondence or analogy. It is declared that "the mapping out of Egyptian localities according to the celestial Nomes and scenery is described in the inscription of Khnum-hept, who is said to have 'established the landmark of the south, and sculptured the northern—*like the heaven.* . . . He made the district in its two parts, setting up their landmarks, like the heaven.'" In obvious corroboration of this method we have the injunction given by deity to Moses in the Bible: "See that thou make all things after the pattern shown thee in the Mount . . . the pattern of the heavens."

Charts of the "Holy Land of Canaan" have been uncovered in early Egypt with evidence of their existence as much as three hundred years *before* the alleged Israelite exodus, which would add presumptive evidence that this promised land of peace and abundance was allegorical before it was historical. Hundreds of pages of data strengthening the case for the prevalence of this customary schematism in archaic religion are assembled in Godfrey Higgins' notable old work, *The Anacalypsis.*

That this systematic procedure back of primeval naming and topography had any remotest connection with two such widely separated domains of human ideation as theology and modern psychoanalysis has of course not been known. Yet it now looms on the horizon of intelligence that the roots of these sciences are grounded in that ancient practice. The connection appears superficially remote, but is in reality close and direct.

It inheres in the basic cosmic constitution of the creation, wherein the universe of total being, for the purposes of manifestation or becoming, bifurcated into the duality of subjective and objective, or spirit and matter. This is the procedure stated precisely where it ought to have been, as the very first step in cosmic creation—in the first verse of *Genesis*. Here it is proclaimed that the first act in universal creation was the splitting apart of the unity of being into its two facets or components, consciousness and objective reality. Most aptly these two segments of whole being were allegorized under the terms "heaven" for consciousness, or spirit, and "earth" for the opposite node, matter. We have here the philosophical dichotomy of being, the substrate of all life in the cosmos. Without the separation and opposition of cosmic mind and cosmic body there could be no existence and no awareness of it. Being would remain the Absolute, would remain asleep, if it did not rend apart its totality into the twoness of polarity. Spirit and matter spring into activity by concomitant stages of emergence from blank unconsciousness, and each, so to say, generates itself and its opposite by mutual counteraction or "hostility." For each is the counterfoil, the countervalence and by reflection the counterpart of the other. Each is the fulcrum against which the other can lift itself into reification. Hence intelligence is in the first step of understanding instructed by the item of knowledge that spirit and matter, or heaven and earth, mutually balance and mutually interpret each other.

Mind is the active agent, the creator, and matter, the opposite energy, is the plastic substance of creation. The two spring simultaneously into existence, the first impressing and shaping the second according to its original or archetypal ideas. Hence all material creation is formed over the patterns of heavenly or spiritual ideation. Divine thoughts may be said to be the molds into which the energies of divine will pour the fluid essence of substance in order to shape the universe projected in mind and purpose. Poured in while liquid or plastic, the matter of substance crystallizes, solidifies, hardens and thus brings into manifest existence the things of the visible worlds. Therefore each created object bears the image of the thought that shaped it. Even man was made in the image of his creator. The universe is the Logos of God, for it reveals the form of the logical structure of the cosmos. It is that logical structure concreted in matter.

If, then, the pervading oversoul of the system wishes to communicate with the intelligences of gradated ranges of lower being brought into function by its own initial activity, it is perforce constrained, if not confined, to speaking in the language germane to and commensurate with the lower ranges of consciousness addressed. For the enlightenment of inferior by superior intelligence, such a language must be constituted in the character and nature of symbols known or knowable to the lower. Therefore higher intelligence must speak to lower in the language of concretely known objects in the latter's world. Thus it is that the objective world of any creature's life furnishes the characters and alphabet of the language it is capable of comprehending. It is the office of the physical world to provide the symbols which constitute language, for all language must be concrete at base. There is not a word of remotest abstraction that does not take its roots in some simple physical or mechanical process. As Carlyle says, "Thy very *attention,* is it not merely a stretching toward?" To express spirit itself, the terms used are all in the meaning of breath or air. The human mind can conceive of abstractions, such as principles, laws, ideas, realities of superphysical nature, only with the help of sensually known objects or phenomena.

One of the most instructive truths of all time was announced by the great hierophant Hermes Trismegistus of Egypt in the inscription on the famous Emerald Tablet:

"True, without falsehood, certain and most true, that which is above is as that which is below, and that which is below is as that which is above, for the performance of the miracles of the One Thing."

Well had it been for the race of man if the pertinence of this wisdom-laden pronouncement of the ancient sage had not been obscured and lost when ignorance smothered sagacity in the third century of the Christian era. For it embodies the basic principle of all human culture. There goes with it as its corollary and necessary involvement the great truth that an immediate analogy subsists between things seen and realities unseen. It becomes in its primary cogency the key, as it is the starting point, of all religion, philosophy, morality and psychology, not to name such ancillary manifestations as mythology, anthropology, poetry, drama, ritual, folk-lore and celebratory festivals.

The modern world has witnessed, if somewhat stolidly, a remarkable phenomenon. It has seen, perhaps not strictly the renaissance, but at any rate the recrudescence, of three long buried and discredited ancient sciences. These are alchemy, astrology and symbolism. Neither of them has come back to vogue in the same aura of understanding in which they were esteemed of old. They have reappeared in the modern day resting on foundations that are for the most part pseudo or spurious. Their true nature and rationale are by no means known as formerly they were. They rest now on partial and imperfect theorization. Whatever they possessed of legitimate worth before their repression has not been reintegrated in their recent resurgence. Indeed it may be said with reference at any rate to astrology and symbolism that whereas in olden times they stood grounded on scientific theses of positive value, they now flourish largely through supposititious motivations. Their original high science has not been resuscitated with them.

Our concern is definitely with symbolism. While the rehabilitation of this primary science is still in its infancy, there are cheering signs that it is on the way to be given more adequate recognition of its pivotal importance. It is one of the indices of the waking of the modern mind out of the still-lingering obfuscations of Medieval-ism that a new science of "semantics" is well started toward a cen-tral place in mental procedure. Yet it is evident that current under-standing has far to go before it will have regained the ancient in-sight that discerned in symbolism the prime methodology by which the mind can be given any substantial degree of realistic grasp of the realities of higher worlds. Nationalistic languages, with their fixed signs and coins of mental imagery, are local and temporary. They come and go, and serve a partial segment of humanity, lock-ing each unit off in cultural isolation. *Symbolism is the one univer-sal and omnipresent language, significant and meaningful every-where.* For its alphabet is the world of ubiquitous nature. The tree, the seed, the leaf, the serpent, the beetle, the cow, the fish, water, earth, fire, the flower, the sun, the star and the dragon-fly deliver the same oration to penetrating perception in any land. "Nature never did betray the heart that loved her," sings Wordsworth. And again he adjures us: "Let nature be your teacher." She can not mis-teach, for she can not tell two varying stories of truth. She may indeed have a wide variety of ways of telling her story, but they all converge eventually upon the one monogram of truth. Life, or God, has but one law, as ancient sapiency affirms. But it deploys its manifestations out to concretion in a practically limitless play of variation or differentiation in the worlds of form. If there is unity, it is a unity behind or beneath an endless variety. No single expres-sion violates the canons of true meaning. All things in their several ways illustrate and exemplify the universal, the eternal. Truth in the absolute may be one. As such it has little serviceableness for man, who is no dweller in the absolute, but is still a citizen of the relative. Truth, in manifestation, is many-sided, has many facets, comes to an epiphany or showing forth at many levels. Strictly, man's concern is not directly with truth. His prerogative is to deal with the many truths that confront him, doing his best to rationalize them into an organic structure that approximates a vision of truth from his level.

As man, made in the image of Creator God, reflects the dual constitution of all being in his two aspects of mind and body, consciousness and instrument, function and organism, there is immediately at hand the ground of understanding the play of psychic forces in and through his world. Psychology has stumbled along a dark path, blindly trying to find a formula that would elucidate psychic phenomena in the life of man. Its failure heretofore has been due to its ignorant insistence on taking man as a unit, or as possessing a consciousness with but one single focus. It has not known that it has to take man for what he is,—a generically dual creature, of soul and body, each with a distinct life of its own and lived on its own plane. Scripture has well indicated this broad differentiation of his two elements, when it says that at death the body returns to dust, but the soul to God who gave it. St. Paul adds his declaration of light and truth when he dissociates man into two entities, a "first man" who, he says, is "of the earth, earthy," and a "second man" who—and here it is that modernity has not been able, to its profound confusion, to follow the Apostle—"is the Lord from heaven." Again he posits the existence of two men in us in his statement that "the first Adam" was made (merely) a living soul, an organic breathing animal creature, while "the second Adam," or the Christos, was made a far more vital thing, "a quickening spirit." Then comes Plato with his trenchant declaration that man is twofold: "Through body it is an animal; through intellect it is a God." And crowning all we have Heraclitus' significant definition and description of the human: "Man is a portion of cosmic fire, imprisoned in a body of earth and water." Also out of the majestic wisdom of Grecian Orphism, the foundation of the whole later structure of Hellenic light and philosophy, comes the ringing proclamation of the Initiate in the Eleusynian Mysteries,—the soul of man speaking: "I am a child of earth *and* the starry skies; but my race is of heaven alone." This predicates for man a dual constitution, asserting that his body is a product of earth and that his soul, or spirit, is from the empyrean, with the unforgettable reminder that he is intrinsically, by virtue of the part of him that subsists perennially whether in or out of fleshly body, of the race of the dynasty of imperishable souls, fragments of God's own integral being.

The early Egyptians symbolized the dual nature of mankind by a dramatization that is one of the sublimest and most revealing of all ancient hieroglyphs, and whose relevance we should no longer miss. They depicted man under the symbol of the sun standing, now at morn, now at eve, on the line of the horizon. Masterly dramatic genius represented man by the sun, because he has a portion of the sun's identic light, energy and intelligence in his own being. "Every man has a little sun (of intelligence) within him," was the averment of the Medieval "Fire Philosophers," the Illuminati and Therapeutae of occult wisdom. Rather it should be said that a part of man's constituent nature *is* a fragment of the dynamic life of the sun. Precisely like the sun, too, he stands in incarnation exactly on the horizon line in the evolutionary situation, at the place where he is half in the heaven world of high consciousness and half in the lower kingdom of matter, or on earth. "Head in heaven, feet on the ground," was again the statement of the position occupied by man as formulated by sage Egyptian knowledge. "Soul in heaven, body on the earth," was a variant of the same description. Virtually man shares the life of heavenly creatures whenever he lives in the uplands of his consciousness, for heaven is a state of exalted consciousness and not a locality spatially dimensionable. He need not be detached from his body to enter that superior condition of reality. In the same way the bodily part of his being partakes of the life of earth. He inhabits earth through the connection established with it by his senses. Verily man stands on the horizon line that divides heaven from earth, where also, conversely, the two segments of his nature are linked together. He enjoys the lofty prerogative of standing in two worlds at once, and he can pass over the borderline from one to the other by the simple measure of focusing his consciousness upon the body, or upon the world of noumenal unseen realities. "The horizon is covered with the tracks of thy passing," declares the Ritual of the great *Book of the Dead.* This is a reference to the continued aeonial passing of the soul back and forth between body and incorporeal existence for its incarnations. In variant Hebrew figure, but with kindred meaning, we are the angels ascending and descending the Jacob's ladder that links earth and heaven, as we emerge from the empyrean, or fire-land of spirit, to enter earthly body, or reascend thither at the end of each excursion into actual being. Also in minor relevance, there is implicit here the meaning that we pass up and down over the boundary line every time we shift the focus of consciousness from bodily, earthly, physical things to the interests of ideality.

Standing on the frontier between the two kingdoms of life, consciousness and objectivity, man is at the most strategic point of vantage occupied by any creature in evolution. It is deeply significant that Norse mythology locates man in *Midgard,* where from his seat on middle ground he is able to be the two-faced Janus of Roman mythicism, who stands thus at the opening door (*janua*) of his evolution and can look backward over the yesterday of his past, stored in the basement of his unforgetting subconscious mind, and forward prospectively to his oncoming future. The Egyptians were not ignorant of this situation, for they make the eternal pilgrim, the reincarnating soul, the bearer, collector and husbandman of all the values gained in living experience, utter this terse statement descriptive of its nature and its task: "I am Yesterday and I am Tomorrow. The things that have been and the things that will be are in my womb." Again the soul declares the fact of its everlasting perigrination through the realms of matter and being when it exclaims, "I am the persistent traveler on the highways of heaven." "Eternity and everlastingness is my name," it says again. "The name of my boat is Millions of Years."

But from his midpoint of strategic position he can, as intimated, gaze out upon two worlds at once, that of mind and soul in the higher reaches of his conscious life, and that of sense and feeling in the bodily half of his constitution. Again Egypt does not lack the aptest of figures to portray this advantage, for it says of the soul, "He cultivates the crops on both sides of the horizon." "He cultivates the two lands." Verily man is all too busy cultivating the wheat and the tares, or the crops sown by the higher mind and the random weeds that spring up voluntarily from the lower sense nature. Little wonder that it is enjoined in Biblical allegory that he must let both crops grow until the harvest. The *Book of the Dead* expands the figure into one of the most illuminating asseverations of man's true work and function in the world, when it says: "He cultivates the two lands; he pacifies the two lands; he unites the two lands."

Here indeed is the substance of spiritual ethics, and at the same time the genius and the rationale of modern psychoanalysis. The unification of the two natures, allegorized as "the two lands," in man is the entire sum, gist and essence of the effort of religion in the world. It springs directly out of the basic situation that sets the religious problem,—the duofold constitution of the human being, involving a perennial warfare between the two elements, to end in an ultimate reconciliation or atonement, symbolized by the "wedding" of Old and New Testament representation, and the birth of the divine child of Christly consciousness from the marriage. The age-long conflict waged between them till the consummation of their alliance is the grossly misconceived Battle of Armageddon, which, says the *Book of the Dead*, "is fought at midnight," and again, "is fought on the horizon." Midnight is the "horizon" between one day and the next, and obviously the battle must be fought on that line of both division and contact between the two natures. That frontier runs directly through the central point of man's being and his organization. He stands astride that line, with one foot, so to speak, in the kingdom on either side. He is the channel or pathway by which the forces of either the spiritual or the carnal nature can cross the line and affect the conscious life of the opposite compartment. Man is thus the only creature in whose life there is the equal admixture of sense and soul. And, as Browning has so well said—for the benefit of those who decry all things material—

> Nor soul helps flesh more now
> Than flesh helps soul.

Soul and flesh must battle each other through the aeon, for only by such mutual resistance are both able to generate their potential energies into functional development. But the great battle must end in mutual accord, since in the happy denouement of victory they find themselves merged in each other's arms.

The great Armageddon battle, dragged down from intelligible meaning as allegoric typism of human experience into the nonsense of supposed objective history in the form of a titanic war of nations on earthly fields of battle, has been contorted into a sorry caricature of its true reference. It has held, and always must hold, a central place in any great system of philosophy, being in Plato's system the mighty conflict between *dianoia* and *doxa,* or true knowledge and "opinion," or between the soul's unforgettable instinct for truth and the outer mind's mere notion of things, governed by sense and external influences. Not only in the dominant Greek philosophies was the struggle centrally related to the entire ethical and spiritual life of man, but it was vividly depicted on the stage boards of the Mystery Religions of the ancient world. There the Sun-God, or the Christ-Messiah, was arrayed in battle with the Titanic or Satanic character, temporarily overcome by him, to emerge as final victor in the end of the drama. This outcome typified the eventual triumph of spirit over the thraldom of matter. Nor is the great struggle less prominent in the Christian scriptures. In great measure it pervades the whole context of Bible literature, in drama, apothegm, parable and allegory, but is found in express statement in the Epistles of St. Paul and elsewhere. The Apostle launches his spear of attack against the "fleshly lusts which war against the soul." And he appears to lament his "wretched" human condition, subject to the sway of evil propensity, when he fain would do good. He perceives "in his members a law which wars against the law of" his mind, so that he cries out "Who shall deliver me from the body of this death?" For, he has argued, "to be carnally minded is death," and man is "dead" in his trespasses and sins. "The interests of the flesh meant death; the interests of the soul meant life and peace," he again admonishes. He lists the weaknesses or vices of humankind as those predominantly which spring from the promptings of the fleshly side of human nature, with sexual lust, concupiscence, at the very head. And in his list of virtues that redeem the soul to her heavenly estate he places continence and chastity at the summit.

CHAPTER II

DRAMA BEARS MISSHAPEN OFFSPRING

AS said, the ground of moral conflict in the dual nature of man has long been recognized in theology as the war between Christ and Satan. Even in the form of the promised reciprocal bruising of the head of the serpent and the heel of the Son of the woman, it was understood as Christianity's historical moral battle in the inner nature of man. But what has not been seen is the recognition that this same ancient depiction of internal conflict in the bosom of mankind is at once the ground condition for the comprehension of determinative phenomena in the realm of psychology. Theology, had it stepped aside from mere intellectual approach and formulations to investigate the phenomena of moral struggle on the side of their symptomatic and clinical manifestations in individual reaction, would have anticipated modern psychoanalytic purview and adopted its technique and methods of treatment. Or, looking back from the present, modern psychoanalysis would from the start have known itself to be but an extension of the legitimate scope and range of theological influences. It amounts to saying, then, that psychology, when adequately envisaged in relation to the basic content and nature of its practice, is just a branch of theological religion.

Whereas moral stress, with its concomitant emotional and intellectual strain, had been esteemed only a province of religious influence and only loosely and unscientifically subsumed under that head, being ascribed to motivations such as piety, faith, conscience and authority, now it is being taken in hand by a secular interest, or science, and brought under systematic investigation by a religiously neutral psychology. What would have been—perhaps in a measure really was—a true science under ancient priestly control, was lost out of religious manipulation during the fifteen hundred years of the Dark Ages and is only now, in the hands of profane agency, regaining its pristine scientific character. Healing in general has had much the same history, having been in antiquity a purely religious function, but in later centuries emerging as a secular profession, retaining a fringe of original religious flavor. Dreams, visions, trance, speaking in tongues, "prophecy," were all formerly matters of religious afflatus, esteemed generally as emanating directly from God, the gods or daemons. While they are still accorded a semi-religious characterization, they have become an integral part of profane science and are removed from the realm of phantasy religionism, holding a place in the open field of scientific research.

Religion has done mankind little service—rather a great disservice —in attempting to mark off his life in two mutually hostile areas, one the holy ground of religion, and the other the profane territory of worldly interest. The criterion of "holy" and "sacred" thus employed to introduce a precarious standard of worth-value in all of man's activities, has vilely misled and hallucinated the mass mind of many generations. A true philosophy would confer on humanity the inestimable boon of sanctifying the whole of its life.

This obliteration of a false evaluation would by no means wipe away the keen intellectual differentiation that subsists between man's two natures. The perception of difference in nature, function and rank between the two components of human being need not entail an unbalanced judgment of values. Unfortunately this is exactly what has come to pass. The whole science of theology indeed is based on the relation of the two natures in man to each other. The divine and the worldly elements are commingled in his constitution, and no interpretation of scripture is possible without a reference to the fact. Man is a soul and that soul is attached to a body. But the ascription of "sacred" to the one and of "sinful" to the other, however naturally it resulted from the premises, came only by default of sage philosophical insight.

The mistake, which confused and vitiated the whole view, came from holding the opposite characterizations as absolute and not merely relative within the total picture. Here lay the germ of an error which has erected its ugly head to warp and harry the thinking of millions for sixteen centuries. The body was conceived as absolutely evil, worldly, sensual, devilish, apart from any consideration of its obvious utility and beneficence, indeed its indispensability, for all the purposes of normal evolution. The body was condemned as the parent and ground of all evil in despite of the knowledge that life could not exist without it. The soul received the accolade of good character, while the body reaped the contumely of evil. Spirit was acclaimed the all-good, matter its enemy. The entire enormity of the ascetic fanaticism that swept early Christianity like a pestilence arose out of these philosophical aberrancies.

Drastic correction of misguided assumption in the case is pressingly needed. Neither matter nor body is to be flouted as evil. They are not even relatively evil. They are essential parts of the total good. They are equally as necessary to the ultimate aims of evolution as is soul itself. Each side of the polarity is impotent without the countervalence of the other. The evil ascription is only the shadow of erroneous thought falling upon a thing the function and the ultimate beneficence of which have been misconstrued through the sheer warping of vision and the mis-reading of ancient drama. The secret of this gigantic folly comes to light when it is known that ancient ritual dramatism and allegorism, in order to portray matter and body in their role of evolutionary service, had to represent them in their function of providing polar opposition to the force of spirit-consciousness. For they are the opposite node to spirit-mind. They form the negative cathode to spirit, the divine anode. Hence they had to play the dramatic role of the "opposers" of constructive and creative mind. But—and here is the core of the miscalculation which led to their aspersion and disparagement as evil forces—ignorance later construed their polar opposition in the terms of absolute enmity. As intelligence flew out of the window, calamitous misconstruction flew in at the door, and there it has dwelt ever since, defiling the hall of man's mind in religion with its vile contempt for matter. The stabilizing and balancing power that holds spirit to the performance of its function was foully besmirched with philosophical disdain. Shallow minds could not grasp matter's function as the twin of spirit without falling into the error of imputing evil to it. Because body had to stand at the opposite side and counterbalance spirit to give it localization, focus and a *point d'appui* for the exercise of its own positive qualities, narrow insight held it in depreciation as the opponent or enemy of spirit. From being represented dramatically as the necessary foil or balance of spirit, it became the hostile force, the enemy of soul. And down on its innocent head tumbled the whole weight of obloquy of millions of fanatic minds in many religions, notably Christian and Hindu, piling on it the accumulation of their malignant derogation. Under the lash of this mad persuasion the poor body of man had to endure the agony of centuries of brutal crucifixion and mortification in the alleged interests of the divine soul, which, it was fatuously believed, could not unfurl its wings of ecstasy as long as the least tinge of bodily enjoyment glued them fast to earth.

When it is seen how the frightful corruption of understanding, occasioning the hallucinated folly and torture of millions over the centuries, could ensue as the result of a mere and seemingly slight misconstruction of the elements of a dramatic depiction of a philosophical principle, it behooves sincere scholarship to examine the point with searching care. The blunder was superinduced by the subtle requirements of dramatic portrayal. To represent the opposition of polarity, spirit and matter had to be pictured as at war with each other. To carry profounder esoteric meaning, they had to be outwardly represented as battling each other. They had to be shown as "enemies" seeking to overcome each other. The sad outcome, for less capable mentality, was that the opposition was remembered, and the less concrete truth of polarity was lost. The deeper significance of the opposition of matter to spirit, and its truly beneficent function in providing spirit with the resistance it needed in order to cause its latent powers to manifest themselves, were forgotten. The opposition of matter to the good purpose had never adequately or decisively been translated over into the terms of a salutary and beneficent service to the final goal of good. Spirit could not operate and evolve within the vacuum of its own unopposed inanition. It is by itself but one half of a polar duality, totally inactive until confronted by the necessity for active energization against its opposite tension. It could not deploy its own hidden powers until it was challenged to do so by the opposite pull of negative matter. Only when linked to matter do its latent energies come into action, and its own potentialities find overt expression. It remains wholly helpless or "dead" until the opposition of matter summons forth its divine qualities to their awakening.

But this intelligent conception of matter's utility was swamped in that avalanche of ignorance which swept over philosophy from the fatal third century onward, and was replaced by the sorry misinterpretation of its function which cast the dark shadow of religious folly over the whole Medieval mind for centuries. Drama had done its best to fortify the mind with the just conception of the true place and function of matter and body in the evolutionary scheme. But the educative purposes of drama miscarried when the representation ran afoul of massed ignorance and was shattered into gross misshapen forms. The religious mind lacked the acumen requisite to the task of understanding that matter had to play its role in the cosmic drama opposite to spirit without earning thereby the stigma of evil character. It was unable to discern the true good of matter's service beneath the outward disguise of spirit's opponent. The mistake made was exactly comparable to what would be the case if an audience, after witnessing a theatrical play, would continue to attribute to the actor playing the part of the villain the same permanent character which he merely personalized for the performance. The Christian world became so drugged with sin-consciousness that it forgot to redeem the ritual personifications of good's necessary opposition from the stigma of evil outside the drama.

It is now clear that the balanced relationship of the anima of the body and the ego of the man within its confines in one flesh is not only the ground determinant of the whole of man's religious interest, his philosophy and moral effort, but that it becomes specifically the basis of the great human problem of psychology as well. Even more particularly it becomes the central situation activating the play of the phenomena manifesting in the realm of psychoanalysis. In brief it can be stated that when there is mutual compensation, harmonious energization, involving constant accommodation and readjustment, between the two claimants for possession of man's body and faculties, there will be the highest degree of peace and happiness pervading the whole organism. And when there is a failure in the achievement of this harmonious relationship between the two, there will be a discord manifested in inner or outer neurotic conditions, psychic disturbances and eventual bodily disease. In fine, the practical outcome of all study of psychology, if such study is to save itself from futility, must be the discovery of the forces in both the physical and the spirito-intellectual sides of man's life that establish, or, conversely, mar the mutually harmonious accord in motive and purpose of the two natures composing the human. If Goethe has sounded a true philosophical note in his affirmation that "two souls, alas, contend within my breast apart," waging a warfare for dominance over the sphere of his interests and activities, then the point of ultimate knowledge and wisdom for mortal man is to discover the terms on which the two contestants can find a platform of agreement and happy mutuality. For in the end, as St. Paul asserts, "the wall of separation between us" will be broken down and the two will effect a final union, "making of the twain one new man, so making peace." This is the Hindu yoga (union), the Christian at-one-ment, or attunement, and at the same time it is the psychoanalytic "integration" of the diverse warring elements within the ego consciousness.

There comes forcefully to mind at this point that enlightening declaration of the Demiurgus, Jupiter Cosmocrator, or world architect in the Orphic Greek system, given in Plato's *Timaeus,* as rendered by Proclus in his majestic work on *The Theology of Plato,* as translated by Thomas Taylor. It is the recording of the speech made to the legions of angels who were being charged with the message and import of their prospective mission to earth to become the souls or egos in the highest animal creatures and to lead them across the area of human evolution to its culmination at the foothills of divinity in the end of the aeon. The World Framer outlines their aeonial task and assures them, as requital and consequence of their successful performance of it, that they will gain immortal status: "You shall never be dissolved." He instructs them as to the dual composition of their natures when in the body and says that in the mortal part there will be buried the seed of an immortal nature, through the growth of which they will achieve immortality. He tells them that he will himself furnish the "seed and the beginning" of the immortal part within them, and that it is then their business to do the rest, to cultivate, nourish and fructify this seed germ of the imperishable divine. Then occurs the phrase which elucidates with vivid succinctness what should have been the constant beacon-light to guide man's evolution throughout history, the clear manifesto of the mission of souls on earth: it is their task *"to weave together mortal and immortal natures."* This pronouncement should have rung with anvil clearness on the good hard intelligence of man on earth and should have galvanized his whole worldly striving into the crisp lines of conscious direction of effort to achieve this goal of a unification of the two contending beings within his own life. If it had been his common knowledge that he must ever strive toward this consummation of a reconciliation between his soul life and his sense life, surely there could have been entertained some sound expectation that he might have passed from blind groping along his path to a more skillful concentration of his endeavors upon the object of life. Could the great objective have been fixed in general knowledge and purpose, it may be assumed that the course of human history for the last two millennia would have exhibited something nobler than the nearly untamed sway of animal propensities in human affairs. Some actual gain might have been registered in the transition that must eventually take place from subjection of human conduct to brutish selfishness over to direction by reasoning mind, the Lord of Life. But the knowledge and the capacity to be thrilled to apply it conscientiously in history were alike swept away by the deluge of fanatical ignorance that submerged esoteric wisdom after the third century.

The Egyptian *Book of the Dead* states that the ego in the man will bring together "the two sisters of the two lands," that he "does away with the enmity which is in their hearts," and will unite them in the bonds of friendly union. St. Paul precisely matches this with his statement that the wall of separation between the two natures will be broken down, and the two will blend in "one new man," "having abolished the enmity" between them.

History is just the record of this "battle of Armageddon," in which the issues of the internal moral and spiritual conflict between the soul of the animal man and the infant Christ-mind in evolving humanity will be pitched from the subjective inner sphere of motivation out upon the plane of physical activity and event. The doings of kings, armies, legislatures, assemblies, mobs, parliaments, courts, tyrants and heroes are but the precipitation of the issues of the inner subjective conflict from the sphere of mental, emotional, sensual or spiritual origin out upon the stage of overt concrete act. History is the record and study of these myriad events in their collectivity.

Psychoanalysis works primarily and practically with the individual. But the problem and the situation are the same as in man collectively. His outward conduct is the crystallization of the elements of his inward conflict upon the surface of his life as manifest in his body and in his acts. Causation arises from the world within, but comes forth in response to provocation from external occasion. It proceeds from conscious, or unconscious, inner motivation outward to register its nature in a physical deed or formation. Plotinus has well phrased it when he says that the inner life of the soul "publishes itself by the beauty of its works." But likewise, during the period of its ignorance in infancy, and until it has gained the poise of wisdom and the love of beauty and goodness, it will also publish the whimsicalities of childish waywardness and crudity, by the ugliness of its works.

As man is a miniature replica of the universe, or what the ancient sages called the Heavenly Man, he, like the universe, is composed of soul and body in a conjunct relationship, the one, the soul, functioning within and sustained and nourished by, the other, the body, precisely as the fiery energy of the candle flame is fed and fueled by its power to transform the gross elements of its physical substrate into the likeness of its own glorious soul of fire. This is precisely what St. Paul says the Christ-soul in us will do to our "vile" bodies, changing them "into the likeness of his own glorious body." Pope in his terse couplet has well reminded us of this our basic constitution—if we are made in God's image:

> All things are parts of one stupendous whole,
> Of which the body Nature is, and God the soul.

God, considered for the moment apart from body and as spirit or mind, is the *soul* of the universal Being, and nature, the visible manifest universe, is his *body*. So man is a soul, and he, too, has his body. As man is thus a little or miniature cosmos (microcosm), having his being as one cell within the milieu of the larger cosmos (macrocosm), he is placed, as the Egyptians so well intimated, on the border territory, or horizon line, facing the world of nature, the *body* of the macrocosm, on the one side, and its invisible *soul*, the hidden mind and spirit of the universe, on the other side. And as the outer form reflects the nature of the hidden conscious creative idea, so, as says Emerson, "man stands midway betwixt the inner spirit and the outer matter. He sees that the one reflects and reveals the other, and he becomes a priest and interpreter of nature thereby." Nature is the mirror of the soul. Paul confirms this in his remarkable statement that that which may be known of God *is manifest.* For, he says, the "invisible things of Him from the creation of the world are clearly seen, being understood from those things which are made." You can read God's mind from the observation of his works. God's stupendous physical body took form over the lines of his primordial creative thought-forms. For body is formed from the final deposit of matter or substance in the matrix or mold constructed by divine mind. Soul builds, or as we should say, out-builds body. The soul, seated within the inner "ark" of finely attenuated bodies of sublimated matter—"spiritual bodies," as Paul assures us we possess—projects vibratory radiations outward, carrying the form and nature of her thought, and these impact upon plastic matter and throw it into the mold of the ideal pattern, where it later hardens. In *The Faerie Queen* Edmund Spenser puts this so clearly in his memorable distich:

> For of the soul the body form doth take;
> For soul *is* form, and doth the body make.

Both the macrocosm and man, the microcosm, are composed of soul and body. And in every case the body reflects the mood and mold of the soul that energizes it.

We now have the background to understand the function of symbols, the enormous part they are now again seen, as of old, to play in the developing culture of the creature man, as the amber of meaning preservation and the agents of meaning transmission from mind to mind.

CHAPTER III

AND GOD SPAKE UNTO MOSES

THE study is led, then, directly back to the primary formula of understanding which ordains that as cosmic creative thoughts shaped the objects of the physical worlds over their patterns or forms, each object is thus the concrete image of the archetypal idea originally projected in God's mind, but now manifest to the conscious creature man through his open senses. Every physical thing or phenomenon is then a symbol, or the symbol, of the ideation that shaped it. And the primal language, as well as all later language, is thus—symbolism. The concrete object must be the only true and perfect symbol of an idea, since it *is* that idea crystallized in visible substance before the eye. A picture presented to the eye is ever the most vivid form of bringing an idea or a distant scene before the mind.

Symbolism is the language of utmost clarity and impressiveness, since through a symbol one mind gives another the *physical picture* of the thought or idea to be conveyed. And the pronouncement of culminative importance in the elucidative introduction to valid determinations is the discernment that if mind on a higher plane, or the mind of a creature higher in evolution than another (as man above the dog, or the gods above man), desires to communicate intelligence to mind of lower rank, it must perforce use as its medium of conveyance the objects known to the lower intelligence in *its* world. Higher mind must employ the physical symbols drawn from the objective world of the lower creature, if it would represent the forms of the thought it wishes to transmit. Therefore the unconscious must employ in its efforts to speak to the lower conscious mind of man, the language of nature symbols. They would be in man's known world the starting point from which rudimentary meaning could proceed.

It is no overweening gush of perfervid imagination to assert that the modern re-discovery of the unconscious is a far greater event in world history than the invention of the airplane or even the radio. It marks one of the long strides western humanity must take to lift itself out of the dismal murks of the still lingering Dark Ages. All merely physical conquests, all acquisitions of mechanical control of cosmic forces, are both useless and dangerous unless accompanied by the equal enhancement of inner intelligence, self-discipline and moral refinement. Material forces become frightful menaces if their human manipulators are neither wise nor disciplined enough to direct their use into beneficent channels. Man's magnificent discoveries of nature's powers can all too readily be made the instruments of his own destruction. If his philosophical intelligence and discretion do not keep ahead of his discoveries, he may be doomed.

The scientific recognition of the unconscious is one of the steps necessary to be taken if human life is to be redeemed from the throes of haphazard ignorant groping along the evolutionary path to some larger measure of directed progress through knowledge and understanding. Appalling in its revelation of the bondage to superstition under which the human mind has labored through lack of this datum, the discovery is also heartening in the prospect it announces of escape from superstition in the future. A thousand obscure or darkly mysterious motivations of conduct of men and nations, which had to be ascribed formerly to animism, fetishism, possession, devil instigation, demoniac obsession, witchcraft, glamor and the like, may now be assigned to the operation of forces uprushing from the subterranean depths of the unconscious in the individual himself. And these forces may, as technical interpretative skill develops, be traced to their deep lair, brought out to observation and studied to the end of rectification and intelligent control. The restoration of the unconscious to knowledge is the harbinger of a brighter day for human culture, civilization and happiness.

But its discovery—good omen as it is—has not yet brought with it a full knowledge of its nature and function, its origin and place in the economy of human evolution, which would vastly increase the practitioner's adeptness in handling psychopathic cases. The professional knowledge of it in these respects is as yet hesitant, groping and tentative or hypothetical, in the main. The modern world of academic intelligence may be astonished to hear it said that the ancient sages and philosophers had ample knowledge of the unconscious and dealt more or less directly and scientifically with it in character stabilization. It was to them an aspect of philosophy, even religion, and was an integral ingredient of an overall philosophical attitude and practique, rather than a detached branch of psychology. The study and treatment of the psyche stood then in far more intimate relation to philosophy than it does now.

It has been intimated in a preliminary way that symbolism must be the language used by the mind of a higher being in the communication of ideas to a lower intelligence. It is this vital deduction that stands as the basis of the next great scientific announcement in the field of psychology: *symbolism is now known to be the language employed by the unconscious to impart its ideas to the conscious mind of the individual.* At once the inference from the premises inspires the question: Is the unconscious then the mind of some being higher than the personal human? Where is there such a being operating in relation to man? What is its nature, how is it placed in superior status to man, and how is man reduced to a position of subserviency and tutelage under it?

Psychoanalysis has deemed that the unconscious is an epiphenomenon of man's total functionism, an expression of his life conditioned to play a subterranean role in the area of motivation and conduct, and uniquely and specifically generated in pre-conscious childhood to be a life-long agent of underground influence upon the outer life. One theory, and that of the founder of psychoanalysis himself, is that it is composed of the native instincts of the animal-human psyche that have been driven underground by repression.

It is the compound of all that one would naturally like to do, but by conventional taboo, dare not. It is composed of the repressed motivations that the individual has put out of his mind, but which he can not put out of his deeper being, and which from time to time reach up from out those deeper wells of natural incentive in dream or trance.

The entire apprehension of the rationale of the unconscious has limped along in gross incompetence because the ancient knowledge of the essential dualism in man's constitution has been lost or ignored. It must now be realized that only in the light of that basic dualism can the nature, place and function of the unconscious be understood.

The Bibles of antiquity, venerated almost to the point of fetishism, have, strangely enough, received a meed of worship which they have hardly merited, yet failed to receive credit for containing truly supernal wisdom and the profoundest scientific knowledge. Accepted largely as books of superhuman origin and contents, they have fallen short of recognition of the sound principles of true philosophy which they present. They, for instance, deal voluminously with the element in man's psychic constitution which is now classified as the unconscious. Plato likewise discourses upon it, but both Paul and Jesus, speaking from an appreciation of Mystery dramatism, and even John, delineate its origin and status in the human economy of consciousness. Each has a statement which, with numberless others of similar import, outlines its basic character. Paul gave it in his statement of man's dualism: "The first man is of the earth, earthy; the second is the Lord from heaven." This is paralleled in its companion passage: "The first Adam was made a living soul; the second Adam was made a quickening spirit." John's averment that the Christos is "that bread which came down from heaven, that if a man eat of it he shall hunger no more" posits the higher personage in the dualism, the divine dweller within the body. Even the Christian creed speaks of the divine element in man, "who for us men and for our salvation, *came down from heaven,* and was made man." The Covenant—the "broad oaths fast sealed" between the Deity and his sons sent to earth—has been noticed in Plato's *Timaeus,* wherein the Demiurgus promised to plant a heavenly seed of immortal consciousness in the mortal self of man on earth. But Jesus himself comes forward with a decisive declaration that he, the Christos, is that seed of immortal life, that Lord from above, that spirit that descends upon man from the over-world, that heavenly bread of life that, he says, must be "eaten" by man if he is to be lifted to the race of the immortals and end by becoming gods. (All the mighty relevance and truth of these affirmations have been lost for centuries on western objective-mindedness by the application of them to the Christ as a man and not to the Christos as the saving principle of divinity gestating for its birth in human consciousness universally.) In an early chapter of John's Gospel in the New Testament the dramatic character of Jesus, speaking to his disciples in their character as natural human beings, and speaking of himself as that consciousness sent down from above to be their Immanuel, makes a pronouncement which should long ago have carried basic enlightenment to a Christendom groping in darkness. He says: "Ye are from beneath; I am from above." This is perhaps the most sententious and instructive verse in the scriptures, certainly the most definitive and clarifying. It tells mortals that on their human and bodily side they came up from beneath, from the animal orders through the long development of something approximating "Darwinian" evolution of forms and structure. And it adds to this the priceless datum that, while the body of man comes to the human estate through this upward line of development from simple to complex form, there is another part to him that did not reach its superior status through the experience of a line of growth in the present life of the race—surely not in unconscious childhood—but is an element that has become conjoined with the mechanism of the animal brain and nervous system, by a virtual "descent" from a loftier plane of being. This higher element did not come "up" from rudimentary state to unfolded powers in the short life of the individual now in body. On the contrary it was already "up" above the level of man's register of consciousness, and "came down from heaven" to tenant for seventy or eighty years the conscious world of the individual's experience. It did this for two reasons, as expressed by Plotinus: "to develop her own powers, and to adorn what is below her." In these words the philosopher means to say that she (the soul, treated as feminine) comes to earth to continue her own evolution through further experience in the concrete world, and conjoins with this effort for her own growth the undertaking to lift up the animal species by a tutelage of its members whose bodies it overshadows by an immanent attachment of its forces to the organism itself. Even modern biological science, particularly as stated by Sir Alfred Russell Wallace, co-discoverer with Darwin of the theory of evolution, has positively asserted that there has nowhere been discoverable in the life of any animal species on earth a body of experience which could have developed in animals the faintest germ of reasoning mind. Yet man, physical, tops the ladder of evolution on the planet and crowns the animal's development with its most complex and differentiated organs and functions. And in man there suddenly flashes out the light of memory, imagination and "godlike reason," with the outburst of human life. The circumstances confronting us in this situation force us to recognize the truth, heard in Greek philosophy, reiterated in our own scriptures, yet never solidly grasped, that the element that introduced intellectuality and spiritual aspiration into the motivations of the highest animal coming up "from beneath" was an imperishable nucleus of divine selfhood, a veritable Son of God, a unit fragment of God's own mind, that by vibrational and other capabilities of organization and nature could "come down from above" and be linked by a kinship of registry with the higher potential capacities of the human mind. Our revered, but latterly disdained and never capably understood, scriptures have been shouting at us greater truth than we have had the acumen to appreciate.

The Christos, coming first as "a little child," the *Krist Kind* of the Germans, the *Jesu Bambino* of the Italians, was born into the nature of man generically. He came to share our life, as all sacred books testify, and so he was that seed of immortal nature that the Demiurgus promised he would implant in us when the animal side had risen from beneath to the point of refinement of structure and sensitivity of feeling at which it could register the play of the vibrations of a truly spiritual, divine or Christly mind. At this point, reached when animal development had approximated the brain refinement of the first humanity, this seed of God's own mentality was implanted, linked, coalesced within the potential unfoldment of the animal's life. More and more of his inherent capacity for superior genius and goodness was to be developed into manifest expression as upward progress further refined and sensitized the mechanism of consciousness. Incubated at first as a mere seed of later growth, coming gradually to birth as the Christ-child, his powers and faculties slumbered long, as do the powers of the human infant. The analogy is perfect and quite illuminating; the infant divinity in us slumbers long in latency, in dormancy, in unconsciousness, before awaking to recognition of his own innate endowment. But experience in the outer world gradually evokes latent power into conscious expression. His faculties are awakened to activity and their keenness is sharpened. He becomes master of his powers and conscious of his high destiny. But long he dwells within the unconscious area of the individual personality, the unknown guest within the mortal house. And he is "the unconscious" of the psychoanalysts.

He comes to link his life with the human in order to continue his own quest of life more abundant, the eternal prerogative of all living creatures, and, secondarily, "to adorn," that is, to beautify, spiritualize, divinize, "what is below him," as Plotinus says. His Covenant oath, given at the time of his departure from celestial kingdoms, bound him to lift up the animal race. This feature of ancient teaching is clearly expressed in Jesus' statement, "if I be lifted up, I will draw all men unto me." Though he stands a full grade above the animal whose body he tenants, he, too, is marching along in the line of ongoing, and must dip again and again into the worlds of sense in order to grow further in stature. Indeed he expressly tells the animal human in the Biblical allegory, the mortal who comes first as his forerunner and way-opener, that he must come under the baptism of the lower nature. That is to say, he must undergo the carnal experience in a body which is seven-eighths water. And, be it affirmed with certitude at last, this is the only water of baptism ever referred to in any doctrine or ritual of religion! The animal human is that faithful servant-beast on whose back he is borne in the end up to and within the gates of the Holy City of full-blown divine consciousness, or "Jerusalem" above, while the multitudes acclaim his triumph with exultant hosannas.

It is not too strong an assertion to declare that the true renaissance of human culture has waited long, and still waits, upon the general recognition of the presence and the nature of the indwelling child of divinity within the core of conscious being. The thought and philosophies of modern man in the west are afflicted with the age's predilection for mechanistic theories of causation. It seems impossible that the tendency to view soul activity and phenomena as products of bodily function and therefore destined to vanish with the demise of the body can be overcome by the rebirth of ancient knowledge, which took the soul to be an independent entity that detaches itself from union with body at the latter's disintegration, retires to mansions of spiritual being and returns in due time to build up a body again. Recreant to this fundamentum of primeval wisdom, the modern age persists in maintaining its philosophical position on the wholly untenable ground of a veritable worship of ancient scriptures combined impossibly with a rejection of the basic anthropological datum on which alone the true interpretation of those scriptures can be made and their true meaning understood. Modern mentality thus stands on the precarious platform of attempting to use as its guiding light the ancient scriptures whose fundamental theses it stubbornly repudiates. Thus it has come about that for sixteen centuries the light that shines in those scriptures has been darkened and nearly extinguished. The holy writ of the sages of antiquity deals with the history of those fragments of the God-mind, those Sons of God who undertook the commission of becoming human souls on earth. And modern religious philosophy attempts to utilize this munificent literary gift as the prime inspiration for culture—by denying the very existence of those same souls. Meaningless is the reverence and hollow the worship paid the great scriptures, the true sense and message of which is completely blocked off from comprehension by the obdurate blindness of traditional view. While a veritable fetish worship is offered up to these venerable documents, it is insidiously undermined by the treachery that refuses acceptance of the fundamental theses and premises by means of which alone the full gospel of their truth-telling can be brought to the light of understanding. And this interior self-contradiction of attitude has stood, and will continue to stand until rectified, at the causative center of the world's delirium of philosophical confusion. When the world returns to sanity it will be achieved through the recapture by intelligence of the substrate of archaic wisdom which fortified the mind with the definite knowledge that there was in man a conscious entity distinct from the body, yet consubsistent with it, capable of accumulating and preserving to perpetuity the values won by living. Until this knowledge is restored there can be little more than a continuance of the world's groping and stumbling in the twilight.

CHAPTER IV

THE GODS DISTRIBUTE DIVINITY

IT is an axiom of Greek philosophy that in the vast hierarchy of beings and intelligences from supreme Deity down to man each god is as it were a cell unit of the life of one superior divinity and that the total company of such cells comprising the body of the higher lord multiplies, magnifies and "distributes" the life of that more exalted being, in seed form, out over a wider range of creative activity. In this formulation Greek philosophy quite fully agrees with St. Paul, who says that we are all members of one body, of which Christ is the head. It seems difficult for world thought to grasp realistically the cogent force of this teaching. All living creatures are the component atoms in the life or body of some tremendously greater being, who lives and moves in and through the activities of his constitutive elements. Precisely as the oak renews and expands its total life by the generation and distribution of the seeds of its own being, so a larger unit of life produces in potential form a multiple progeny of its own kind in order thus to expand its own measure of total being.

But each fragmented son of parent being must start from seed potentiality and through a long process of growth eventually bring its separate life back to the level and completeness of the progenitor. Thus it comes that life proceeds from the Father and returns unto him again. Obviously the life of the son is a part of and "in" the life of the parent, and equally the life of the parent is "in" that of the son. As the life and being of the progenitor is latent in the seed, until it is finally brought to awakened consciousness in the later stages of growth, there is implicit here the entire explanatory formula for understanding the presence and nature of the uncon-

scious in man. The unconscious is just the unawakened being of
the higher parental life and consciousness of whose unitary selfhood
the individual man is one organic cell.

There occurs in a sentence in an enlightening late work of psychoanalysis by a practicing clinician of wide experience and deep insight into the science a single word, which falls with the aptest,
though with perhaps altogether unsuspected, relevancy into the context and support of the thesis of the unconscious here expounded.
The work is *The Recreating of the Individual,* by Beatrice M.
Hinkle, M.D. Asserting that the unconscious can not carry through
any form of expression or activity that counters the rational judgment of the outer conscious mind, she writes that under the ban of
such repression "the individual remains unaware of the *ancient*
processes functioning in and influencing his present life and he
cannot evolve beyond them except through greater self-consciousness
or according to the immeasurably slow process of nature herself." [1]
This is to say that the present activities of the conscious mind over-
lay and keep buried under their constant play a body of innate and
generic motivations which would exercise a control in the direction
of the individual life if they were given free course in the conscious.
It may fairly be presumed that the word "ancient" in the passage
quoted carries far more significance than the author dreamed. This
word, used in description of "processes functioning in and influencing . . . present life" is *the* prime clue to the mystery of the unconscious. For *ancient* indeed is the unconscious. It is, in reference
to the human individual, that part of the man which is the "Ancient
of Days" of the Psalmist. Wordsworth caught the vision of it when
he wrote in his immortal Ode:

> The soul that rises with us, our life star,
> Hath had elsewhere its setting, and cometh from afar.
> Not in entire forgetfulness,
> And not in utter nakedness,

[1] This and the numerous other citations from Dr. Hinkle's fine work made in this
volume are reproduced with her gracious permission.

But trailing clouds of glory do we come
From heaven, which is our home.

"The sunshine comes and goes," he says—and so does the soul
of man. It comes into expression in the life and body of a human,
and at the end of its cycle goes back to celestial repose, and it does
this time and time again. It has had many births and "deaths," but
never death. It has garnered up the fruits of vivid experience in
the kingdoms of the world and in the bodies of men, and preserved
them in the indestructible treasure house of its inmost spiritual
body, which is safe from the rot of decay, the tooth of moth or
the loot of thieves. And it comes forth for each fresh sally into the
daylight of world experience, bearing the wealth of its deposits of
wisdom, knowledge and genius, not to be hoarded, but to be put
out to "usury" in further investment in living, for the endless enhancement of its own glory in the more abundant life promised
it by its Parent. The central phrase of old theology, "for the *glory*
of God," bears with more direct pertinence on pivotal meaning
than has been surmised. The onward march of progress does indeed
bring an increment of *glory* to the son of God within the body of
the man. For as the sun-fragment of divine soul in corporeal man
grows in self-consciousness, it increases the shining texture of that
"body of the resurrection," that "robe of glory" integrated of the
essence of solar light, which the soul weaves for itself in ever more
effulgent splendor to be its spiritual temple not made with hands
and in which it may dwell when the earthly tabernacle of this flesh
has been discarded. There is fathomless meaning in Paul's statement
that this mortal shall put on immortality and this corruptible shall
be clothed in incorruption. The climactic guerdon promised by
Deity to man is that the creature shall have immortal life. And to
be undying, man must have wrought for himself a body which
when he shall have put it on, will never decay. Hence the great
object of his coming to earth is, as Plato said, to "weave together
mortal and immortal natures," so that the mortal part can inherit

immortality through its partaking the life and nature of the immortal. By charity and wisdom, all the scriptures affirm, man shall transform, transubstantiate and transfigure his being until it glows in equal radiance with the glory of the gods whose raiment shines like the sun. Man will end his earthly career by casting off the "filthy rags" of fleshly vestments of decay, and come forth arrayed in the glory of the sun. "I shall clothe thee with light as with a garment," saith the Lord in the Old Testament. We are to be made "children of the light," he again says. We are adjured to let our light shine, since we "are the light of the world." The Christos is the "Lord of light," "the life and the light of men." This has all been killed in its thrilling meaning by being shifted away from humanity at large and allocated—and hence lost—upon the person of one man in history. It was to be the possession of all the sons of earth who achieved it.

The vital truth about this glory body, this house from above, with which Paul says he waits to be clothed upon, is that it is imperishable. Once formed—and Paul says he groans and travails in pain with us until Christ be "formed" within us—it does not die; it does not disintegrate. "You shall never be dissolved," promised the Demiurgus, once the garment of shining Christhood has been woven.

And now comes the denouement of mighty truth from out these ancient scriptures that becomes the open sesame for unlocking the hidden mystery of the rationale of the unconscious. The white raiment of the redeemed is not only composed of solar essence that is imperishable, but so close is it to the heart of eternal being, so changeless in its protogonic essentiality, that an impression made upon it is forever ineradicable. The unconscious never forgets!

Here is an item of cosmic truth that even the uncertain tentatives of psychological searchings have already brought out. An impression made upon the innermost part of man which stands nearest to true being is never erased. The substance of that holy of holies of real being is changeless first matter. It partakes of the ultimate nature of the real. It is the primordial mind-stuff. And so the Greeks had a beautiful word for that which this mind knows, truth. Truth in Greek is *aletheia,* from *a,* "not," and *lethe,* "forgetfulness." Truth is therefore that which is not forgotten, can never be lost. Once gained, it is stored up in the alcoves of indestructible mind-essence. What the soul has gained of truth, ,she brings with her when she comes anew into body. "Truth is from heaven," declares Jesus in one of the apocryphal gospels in answer to Pilate's derisive question, an answer omitted from the four canonical Gospels. Truth is indeed from heaven, from the overworld of diviner ideality. It is inscribed upon the imperishable tablets of cosmic mind. What the individual mind grasps of its eternal principles is never lost. But at each dip of the soul into incarnation it loses its paradise of knowledge and understanding as it plunges deep into the heart of matter and is buried in the underworld of sense. Paradise must be regained each time with the return of the consciousness to the levels of former development, and new glories won. And so we have the great Plato giving us the twin doctrines of "the loss of memory of divine things" and "reminiscence," or recovery of divine memory.

The unconscious mind never forgets; yet here is Plato saying it suffers the loss of its memory. Is it contradiction? The Platonic amnesia is only a forgetfulness which is paralleled and analogized in the life of the oak, which loses its eternal memory or conscious-ness when it goes as a seed of future growth into the soil, but regains its full awareness of life when it attains maturity in the new cycle. For life must die to be born again, must lose its life to repossess it, must suffer loss of memory to win eternal memory. Life ever passes from the highest stage of conscious unfoldment in any cycle back into the embryo of itself to begin a new cycle. As a seed it can carry, not the adult development of its powers, but the sheer poten-tiality of renewing those powers. It enters earth shorn of all that it had won in the last cycle's effort, save the capability of renewing and increasing all previous winning. It must start each cycle over again from beginning. It more quickly each time recapitulates the range of previous development, now become "instinctive," and then takes new strides forward into infinite being. Thus all evolution moves forward through what the sage ancient teachers everywhere called the "eternal renewal" of life. Life "dies" to be born again. And the wreckage and then the loss of the intelligible structure of the ancient wisdom came through the failure of philosophic thought to retain the true reference of the words "die" and "death." Life, poetized the wise men of old, "dies" when it goes under the trammels of the flesh in incarnation. "Death" in theology is then precisely that which goes by the name of "life" in our world. Says Paul in the seventh chapter of the *Epistle to the Romans:* "The command that meant life proved death to me." So the ancients regarded this life as the "death" of the soul under the sluggish waters of the river of the underworld, the river of forgetfulness—Lethe! But always it was a "death" from which there was the resurrection. Always the planted seed died and then germinated and lived again. And thus life went forward to its ever-expanding conquest of new glories, "through death to life eternal," as the Easter hymn sings it. For what the soul loses temporarily at the start of each cycle of growth, it regains and eventually holds in perpetuity. The unconscious never forgets!

The pursuit of truth through this channel leads to the open door of a revelation of one of the great Biblical allegories so sweeping in its magnitude and relevance that its disclosure may indeed promise a wholly new regeneration of scriptural interpretation. At first glimpse no two things would appear to be farther apart and remote from each other in significance than the unconscious in modern psychology and the ark and deluge story in the Bible. It happens, however, that the flood allegory in the Old Testament is the ancient esoteric glyph of the unconscious in the human constitution! Again this has never been seen because the narrative in *Genesis* has been taken as history, or at least quasi-history, and not for what it really is—the allegory of evolutionary method, as the *Genesis* story is the allegory of creational method.

Light is gained on this cryptic scriptural representation by tracing the pivotal words employed in it back to their archaic or basic meanings. These are "ark," "Noah," and "Ararat," as well as the numbers that crept in, seven and forty. Noah was given seven days in which to build the ark and collect numberless thousands of animals of every species from all over the earth, manifestly impossible as actual history, but immensely significant as allegory. It rained forty days and nights, covering the whole earth to the highest mountain tops,—again absurd as history. The ark floated on the waters till the flood subsided, and then the occupants emerged and landed on Mt. Ararat.

Who was "Noah"? It is evident that though Hebrew in origin, at least found in a Hebrew document of antiquity, the name "Noah" is built on the stem of the word which in Greek stood for the rock principle of the universe, Mind, the mental principle in mankind. Anaxagoras' theory that the world is the production of a cosmic Mind, or of *Nous,* is relevant to this determination. The root of the word is that basic Greek stem, *No,* and the Greeks called the intellectual principle in man *Noē.* It is important to notice that this is feminine in form and grammatical gender. This is so because, although mind and spirit are commonly typed under masculine symbolism, yet when the spirit descended into matter and became the soul of a living organism, it was regarded as feminized through its coming under the power of matter and body, which are symbolically feminine always. The feminine ending was placed upon it to indicate that it was mind involved in and energizing matter. The ancients always affirmed that the soul entered its "feminine phase" when it incarnated. The Greek feminine ending is the long *ē, eta.* When the Hebrews used the word they substituted on the *No* stem their own feminine singular ending, which is *-ah.* This gives *No-ah,* the principle of mind in body.

It is next to be noted that, in perfect accord with all ancient philosophy, the mental principle, Noah, was given three sons. In the arcane allegorism the intellectual ray from God's mind suffered differentiation from its primal unity into a triplicity when it established its connection with physical organisms on three linked planes of higher consciousness. It has been lost out of studentship that terms corresponding pretty closely to our three words, spirit, soul and mind, expressed this differentiation. In one Hindu system they were named *atma, buddhi* and *manas.* In astrological pictography they were represented by the three stars, most significantly known for ages as "the three kings," in the belt of Orion. They were the lower trinity of spirit, the reflection in the human microcosm of the cosmic trinity above. Mind is ever triple in its manifestation. Modern theology posits little difference between mind, soul and spirit, but the early philosophical and anthropological systematism knew of the gamut of distinct gradation subsisting among the three. Spirit held the topmost rank, more ethereal and sublimated in its nature than the other two, being the pure energy of intuitive knowledge. Soul was a further projection of that energy into matter, manifesting one step lower, and standing midway between pure intuition and concrete thinking. Mind was a still deeper injection of spirit into matter, coming to expression as the glowing rational power of conscious thought directly conditioned by the mechanistic function of the brain.

The mind-body problem has been a perplexing conundrum for human understanding, entangled in the difficulty of perceiving how an immaterial force can lay hold of and utilize a physical mechanism. But no longer should this problem offer difficulty to the modern mind that understands even remotely how the radio wave can blare through its instrument. It has been said that the repeated note of a violin string, properly attuned, could destroy a steel bridge. Really the secret of the mind-body relation has been opened to our unthinking minds ever since a piano note has been known to rattle a cup in its saucer on the old parlor mantel across the room. Caruso, the tenor, demonstrated it when, having lightly struck a delicate drinking glass with a tuning fork to get its pitch, he then shattered it with the same tone sung from his powerful vocal cords. A thought is just the registry of a vibration in ethereal matter of great tenuity, projected by that root energy known as will, and carried by an electric play of force generated by the chemical constitution of the blood. The human blood has in it the components requisite for the production of battery current. A modern scientific pronouncement states that the brain contains four quadrillions of minute dynamos, and these are charged by electricity carried by the blood and drawn by it out of the vast sea of static electricity in the air. Each cell of the brain is the seat of the flash of electric current between the positive and negative poles within it. These tiny currents can catch and carry the energies of primal will and thought, as the voice carries the structure of an idea. Life energizing as will or thought is at once the generator of electric force that can carry into expression its creative forms of ideas. Immaterial energy such as that of the mind can lay hold of and move matter and body, for the simple reason that its every impulse can stir the vital currents that are themselves constitutive of the very being of matter.

Understanding of the problem was thwarted as long as the blind conception prevailed that matter was inert, lifeless substance. Now that it is known that matter is itself a composition of purely etheric energies, really no longer to be conceived as matter at all, but spirit itself held in static bondage, the fundamental kinship between mind and body is readily intelligible. If lines of immaterial force can move the iron filings around the head of a magnet, it should no longer be a task to know how life works to accomplish its purposes. There is needed only the mathematically correct adaptation of structure to vibration rate and wave length to produce motion. Life manifests through an infinite gradation of such adaptations, be it in coarse substance or in finer ethereal or "spiritual" matter. And we have spiritual bodies, more than one of them, archaic science asserted. Each of these registers energy in its particular form and expression, each one conditioned by the fineness or coarseness of the material composing its organism. Sound, as the old philosophers argued, is one; yet it manifests in a million different *sounds,* determined by the quality and structure of the instrument sounded through. Man's very "personality" is based on this hoary knowledge, since his "person" is the physical instrument *through* (Latin, *per*) which the higher rates of conscious vibration *sound* (Latin, *son-*) out their tones in the manifest world. The personality is the physical instrument through which the soul sounds its characteristic note of spiritual being in the world. The spirit deep within, being a ray of changeless being which is eternally one—however it manifests in variety—is not subject to division. Hence it is the "individuality," the regnant king within the personality. It is further instructive to recall that *persona* is the Latin word for "mask." This item illuminates intelligence with the important knowledge that the physical personality is the mask which the divine individuality puts on and through which it can sound out its proper keynote in the total symphony of being.

If the allegory was to be kept true to profound wisdom it was necessary that "Noah" should have three sons. The intellectual principle in cosmic operation must manifest in triple form. This is the explanation of the many figures of triform gods, the Trimurti of India and the gods with three heads or three faces so often found. It is likewise the lost meaning behind the legend of the three "Magi" who come with the Christos in the Christian Gospel narrative. For whenever divine Mind deploys its forces into creative expression, it generates its three distinct aspects which stand behind the great doctrine of the Trinity.

And their wives? Not even divine Thought can create worlds of manifest existence without uniting its energies with the physical power hidden in the atom of matter. Spirit must "marry" matter if it is to create concrete universes. The subjective side of life may know what it wishes to create, but it can not build structures until it has the material with which to build them. It must therefore link its directive energy with the latent power in the atom. This is its *shakti,* or spouse, through whose motherhood spirit alone can procreate. It became his wife, his sister, eventually his mother and his daughter, and it is pictured under all these characters in mythology.

But the great enlightenment comes with the elucidation of the recondite significance hidden under the symbolism of the "ark." Here again it is the language root that brings lost intelligence to view. The "ark" was, last and least of all things, *not* a boat or floating structure, save, of course, in a purely figurative sense, as the "flood" was *not* a deluge of water. It is all arcane allegorism, and this is established beyond any possible question. The true meaning of the "ark" is to be found in its derivation from the Greek noun, *archē*, "beginning," which is in turn from the Greek verb *archo*, "to begin." It is past all understanding how the scholars of many centuries have failed to discern either the etymological background of the "ark" or its implications for the Biblical interpretation. The fact that it is the first word in the Bible (preceded by its preposition "in") should in itself have gone far to open blind eyes to obvious meaning. The Bible thus starts from the point of proper departure —"in the beginning." The Greek word *archē* means beginning, primal state, aboriginal condition of being. It is seen in our words *archaic, archangel, archetypal*. God's archetypal ideas were the original ideas projected in and by his mind to give shape to the universe. So the "ark" is the primal or beginning state of a thing. For anything of objective existence to "go into the ark" is, then, its retirement back into the stage from which it emanated in the beginning of its cycle.

Next, what is the "flood" or "deluge"? Grievously has ignorance plunged into shameful asininity over this aspect of the representation. It has nothing actually to do with water, or rain and water have nothing to do with it. But it has much to do with flooding, or washing, or washing away, in the sense of a trope. For the scriptural "deluge" (found in some fifty national mythologies!) is nothing more or less than the figurative washing away of all created things by the flood-tide of *dissolution* which cyclically ensues at the end of each age of creation. The flood figure of description is imaginative, a trope; but the washing away through dissolution is an actual event. It is the dissolution of the worlds and universes at the end of the age (Greek: *teleuten aion,* so tragically mistranslated "end of the world" in the Christian texts of the Bible), when infinite being absorbs back into its capacious bosom the disintegrated forms of its last cosmic manifestation, when concrete existence dissolves back into sheer be-ness. Matter disappears or is washed away from palpable existence, and spirit retires into the interior core of being. The cosmos and all its formations dissolve as the creative energy that threw them into shape runs its given course and subsides into motionlessness and silence. For life works cyclically, after the analogy of the heart beat and the life breath. It awakes, and energizes its creative effort in building. In the evening of its cycle it tires of its labor, and like us made in its image, it withdraws it energies and rests. When the animating and supporting energy of creation is withdrawn, the universe it shaped collapses and disintegrates. It dissolves. Where does it go?—since there is no "place" for it to go save where it is. It goes where a handful of salt goes when you put it into a basin of water. It goes into solution. And as the capability of bringing the salt back from invisible subsistence into visible material form again is always present, in like fashion can the dissolved universe be recreated in the beginning arc of the next cycle. The "deluge" is the tide of dissolution that washes away all forms.

Against this philological and philosophical background there is now the possibility of seeing at last the stupendous significance of the ark and flood story. When the structure of solid substance that housed and gave play to the energies of the life principle during its active period of creation is washed away—like the giant oak that has fallen and gone to decay and disappeared in dust—where, if life is *not* to come to an end along with the disintegration of its containing vessel, does it go to be tided over the period of dissolution and "death" till it can live again in new forms? Whither can it retire to ride out the flood? What can hold it in integration, or the possibility of new integration, when it has no mechanism, no organism of manifestation, no point of support in the realm of space? Life and nature have been confronting us with the clear answer to this central query through the ages and we have been too obtuse to see it. We always miss the meaning of the things that are most common in our belief that the great meanings are to be found in the extraordinary, the supernatural. Nature and life have shown us where the immaterial immanent principle of being goes when its physical embodiment disintegrates. For life provides every one of its creatures with a mechanism by which it can insure the renewal of its existence after its body dissolves. It withdraws into its beginning stage, its *archē!* And this is all included in our small but stupendously pedagogical reality, *the seed.* The seed is the "boat" in which, safe from extinction, the soul of life is tided over the flood of disintegration of form. Obviously expressed life can not be preserved in the form of its organic structural fullness of stature, in its adult body. It can not be preserved in existential embodiment, since body is dissolved. It must perforce be preserved, then, in purely *potential* form. Not it, but only the possibility of it in new form survives. It goes back to reside again in the *ideal* form and essence from whence it issued in the first instance. As it was projected thence once before, or many times, it can be sent forth again in the round of the cycle.

Here indeed is the answer to many aspects of life's great riddle. When the worlds of form dissolve away life goes back into its *archē,* its beginning. From thence it will begin all over again, enriched, to be sure, with the capital it has acquired in all previous adventures. Any student of ancient systems learns to know that the grandiose view of all life process is that based on the prime fact that life does nothing but endlessly renew itself. Says the soul of life in the Egyptian scriptures: "I die, and I am born again, and I renew myself, and I grow young each day." ("Day" is the term for any period, cycle or age of manifest existence; "year" is used similarly.) No more majestic passage than this stands anywhere in the "sacred" literature of mankind. It is the one assured fact that the human mind *must know,* to maintain its sanity and balance, its equanimity and courage under the press and stress, the strain and pain, of existence in body.

If the revived voice of ancient wisdom, that is fortified with the concepts of the most sagacious revelation of truth to man, dare speak to the distracted modern mind and tell it how it has come to such chaos and wreckage of its philosophy, it can be broadcast in categorical terms that the seed of all world fatuity was planted in the soil of uncritical human thought when about the third century of the Christian history the great crucial doctrine of the eternal renewal of life, as applied to the human soul, was lost under the sweeping tide of fanatic ignorance that converted the allegories and mythologies of sapient philosophical wisdom into alleged literal sense and historical event. Clement, Origen and the learned philosophers of the early Church treated the scriptures properly as allegories. St. Paul declares that the Abraham story in the Old Testament "is an allegory." But philosophical light gave way to pietistic zealotry misguided by ignorance, and the world's ancient knowledge that would have stabilized the human psyche in its course through history was extinguished. The knowledge that a nucleus of conscious life—the human soul—can retire into its *archē* and subsist in latency, and thus be tided over the period of its non-existence in the inmost depths of immaterial being, to emerge again and pursue its forward course into the realities of ever more abundant life,—this is the salt that has lost its savor, the preservative without which man's psyche must lie in the foul odor of corruption.

As the intellectual principle is the first to emerge from out the ark of being onto the stage of physical existence, so it must be the last to re-enter as all things retire into the bosom of non-being. So Noah enters the ark, after the animals, and his sons and the sons' wives with them. All living creatures, be it noted, must re-enter the ark.

As to the final term, Ararat, the lost meaning is simple, once the other clues are found. If life comes to manifest expression in its day cycles in visible matter, it must be localized somewhere in visible worlds. Such worlds are planets, primarily. So, in our case, it is "earth." When life retires to ride out the flood in its ark, the worlds disappear. The ark is lifted above the earth. Earth vanishes. But when the flood is over and the dawn of the new day-cycle swings around, where must the *archē* land if it is to take hold of matter again and build of it a new house to live in? Obviously it must come back to earth, it lands again on earth. And *most* significantly a study of symbolism and of language discloses that the cryptic meaning of the word "mount" ("mountain") in the arcane typology of the Bibles, is precisely the earth. Time and again the earth is referred to as "the mount of the earth." Much data of studentship can be presented to verify this item. It is by no means a mere guess, stretching the meaning to fit a preconceived rendering, in Procrustean fashion. It *is* the meaning of the term. And it needs but a moment's glance at the Hebrew language to see that "Ararat" is itself the word for "earth," juggled a bit. The present Hebrew word for "earth" is *arets*. An older form, states an authority, is not *arets*, but *areth*. Practically here is the English word "earth" itself. The ark lands on the mount of the earth, and the seeds of life emerge to be planted once more in the garden of the world.

If a touch of personal reference may be pardoned in this connection, it is worthy of mention, for the sake of showing how the interpretation of symbols is the true key to scriptural sense, and how unerringly its guidance will lead to true meaning, that when, from the side of symbolism purely, we had worked around to the rendering just elucidated, and felt that a startling discovery involving considerable "originality" had been made, imagine our surprise and very intense amazement when, happening to go over the text of the seventh chapter of *Genesis,* we found that the third verse of the story told us precisely the thing we thought had not been grasped before, and used in doing it the same word that contained the kernel of our whole abstruse conclusion,—the seed! The verse runs to the effect that Noah and his household, the animals and fowls, were herded into the ark "to keep *seed* alive upon the face of all the earth." Had the clear implications of these words—or that word "seed"—been followed out to evident conclusions, there would have been no need of our remaining in gross benightedness as to Biblical meaning for sixteen centuries. The situation here unfolded must glaringly illustrate the devastation and havoc wrought upon the Western mind and its culture by the obsessions of ignorance which imposed a literal or physical meaning upon archaic symbols of recondite truths. Under this incubus no mind for sixteen hundred years has had the strength of imagination to rise above the conception of seed as just grains of corn, beans, larkspur and male fluid. The figure of "seed" as being the glyph for all renewal of life in evolutionary or cosmic sense, or the mental graph for the cyclical re-existence of the human soul, was entirely washed away by that fatal third-century deluge of philosophical doltishness, when Christianity passed from the hands of the philosophically capable Greeks into those of the practical-minded, but ignorant, Romans, who soon closed up the last of the Platonic Academies and doused the ancient gleam of world intelligence under stupid literalism.

But what has the restored light of Biblical allegorism to do with psychoanalysis and the unconscious? Pretty nearly everything vital. It puts a known history behind the unconscious, explains its origin, its presence in the human psychic constitution, and its nature and function. It reveals the important part it plays in evolution. It enlightens with the knowledge that the unconscious is the divine soul itself in the human, pursuing the course of its cyclical recurrence in the world and preserving the continuity of its unfoldment throughout the whole. It tells us where the unconscious got what it possesses, where it found or acquired its present content and where it gained the higher wisdom that it flashes in dream symbol, in moments of rare afflatus or intuitive insight, or in subtle intimations of many types, down upon the conscious mind. And ancient sagacity, supplying us also with many points of knowledge of concomitant life phenomena in its postulation of spiritual bodies interpenetrating the more substantial physical in the depths of man's make-up, provides us with the rationale for understanding both how an ego can keep its impressed accruement of wisdom gained from experience and project it forward into the present existence, as well as how a "sub"-consciousness can be an actuality of man's possession apart from and in addition to his normal consciousness.

CHAPTER V

LOST DATA OF ANTHROPOLOGY

NOT many years ago there could have been no conception more unintelligible and more impossible of credibility than the suggestion that man could possess and be influenced by a consciousness that he was not conscious of. Sheer abstract logic seemed to forbid the predication of an unconscious consciousness. It was like saying "dark light" or "wet dryness." But the discovery of the unconscious has come, after the radio and the true nature of the atom had opened the bound mind of the age to the possibility of "the impossible."

It may be worth the citation of a paragraph or two of contemporary expression to accentuate for our dullness of mind the admitted importance of this discovery in psychology. There occurs a passage in the work of Dr. Hinkle, already referred to, *The Recreating of the Individual,* which states the case from an interior point of view with great appositeness. She is speaking of the upsurge of interest in psychoanalysis (p. 422):

"In my opinion the significance of this popular espousal lies in the unconscious recognition that in the psychoanalytic technic we have an instrument which for the first time makes possible that further individual human development or creation of self by self which formerly depended upon the 'grace of God,' and was entirely bound up with religious creeds."

Here is an intimation based on years of positive empirical testimony that this new science is one of the greatest of historical advances from ignorance to knowledge, releasing the human ego from the stultifying sway of blind belief and giving it the knowledge of a workable technique for further liberation. Whenever actual

48

knowledge has come to hand, the former boundless area that had to be covered by religious pietism and helpless trust has been diminished and the portion recovered from credulity and its victimization has been happily enlarged. No dissertation is necessary to demonstrate the value of such a gain. It is the liberation of human life from former bondage to the unknown.

A recent testimonial manifesto issued to commemorate the life and work of Sigmund Freud states that his discovery of the unconscious is close to being the most momentous revelation in the history of civilized man. To the deep student its preciousness resides in the fact that it restores to modern thinking that item of the priceless wisdom of the ancients which postulates the existence and persistence of the divine soul in humanity. The functioning of soul wisdom and faculty within man but beneath the surface of his ego consciousness, and "unconscious" because resident in one of man's interior "spiritual" bodies, the connection of which with the outer brain and nerve mechanism was generally, but not wholly, cut off by the play of the outer consciousness, and could at times, as in sleep, be established and communication set up, was the central item of archaic knowledge that enabled the ancient mind to ground itself in assured philosophies of positive value. On top of hundreds of quotable testimonials to the brilliance of ancient intelligence, one comes to hand in a recent book, *The Crisis of Faith,* by Stanley Romaine Hopper. A passage from it will serve well to introduce the argument for the soul, to which some space must be given. On page 206 he writes:

"The early humanism of the Greeks, . . . attained a view of man that was sane, balanced and 'human.' . . . This wholeness and health of the Greek perspective was grounded on wonder and in wisdom. . . . With sure intuition the Greek mind turned to this element of per-manency which everywhere transcends the flux or founds it, and estab-lished there its wisdom." [1]

---

[1] This citation from *The Crisis of Faith,* by Stanley Romaine Hopper, and others taken from the same volume, are used with the permission of its publishers, The Abingdon-Cokesbury Press, Nashville, Tenn.

This tribute to the sanity and wholesomeness of Greek philosophy is not overdone; possibly it is even modest. And it lays the finger directly upon the point where lurks the crux of human understanding of the meaning of life. Of all the ineptitudes and failures of the philosophic mind the greatest would appear to be that which has blocked a clear and certain recognition of the truth that no solution satisfactory to human thinking can ever be worked out on any other basis than the assured knowledge of the continuing existence and cyclical rebirth of the divine soul in man. Unless the intelligence of the mortal is fortified with the dependable conviction that the gain he struggles to achieve in a life will be held for all the future and become capital in further cycles of existence, he must despair. This assurance, even the postulation of it, lacking, despair is precisely the ultimate note already sounded as the only philosophy possible in the view of a scientifically enlightened thinker like Bertrand Russell. Knowing nothing of the possibility of the integral part of man's constitution possessing a means of survival in the inner "ark" of its spiritual nature, he envisages the ultimate destruction of the race of mortals with the decay of life on the planet. Uninstructed by the profound ancient philosophy which knew of an inner core of being that can carry and hold values won, he sees only futility as the aim and outcome of the evolutionary effort on whose tide man moves forward. On the grounds of his suppositions life has no purpose beyond the play of the hour, or of the longer hour of the cycle. At the end of the aeon its work will indeed be washed away in the flood of dissolution, with no ark to retire into to betide the deluge. This is the supreme upshot of the modern scientific envisagement of life's great movement.

Unless man is strengthened by the certitude that while one part of him, the physical, obviously "returns to dust," as the Preacher says in the book of *Ecclesiastes*, another part, joined temporarily with it, is indestructible and provides a bank of deposit for all values earned by effort, in which they can be preserved in permanence, his mind *must* run out in despair and his heart sink, beyond the help of any power of hope or faith. Unless the modern mind can disentangle itself from its helplessness in the spider-web mesh of its own inadequate presuppositions, due to its lack of knowledge of basic anthropological elements, and will follow the light of clear intimation of truth as the ancients did, it can have no hope of sanifying and sustaining positive understanding. Even modern psychology now avers, from clinical observation, that unless a mind is philosophically fortified in affirmative values, it will deteriorate into neurosis and wreckage. The most important thing in all life, after physical necessities, is philosophy. There is some evidence that at long last the light of this perception is breaking on intelligence. In *The Crisis of Faith,* quoted above, the author states (p. 203) that

"Scheler holds that the problem of a philosophical anthropology stands today at the mid-point of all the philosophical problems. Berdyaev goes further and asserts simply that philosophy is primarily the doctrine of man. It is easy to see that ethics depends upon an understanding of the nature of man, and that the civilization of any particular period is largely determined by it. . . . We are searching today for a new humanism—for the recovery of an understanding of man in his wholeness and completeness. In this larger and more intimate sense we need desperately to be humanized."

It is doubtful whether by extensive searching a passage could have been found which sketches the form of our real need in more appropriate terms. Here at last is the modern recognition of what might have been supposed to be seen by simple facing of the problem of human life at any time, namely that the attempt to rationalize the world and man's adjustment to it must proceed blindly until man's own nature and constitution are known and understood. Universal tragedy and suffering on an enormous scale have come, over centuries, from the effort of Western mind to take attitudes and initiate action, or frame policies and institute systems, in total ignorance of what was once known as to the basic composition of man's organic nature. Thousands of tomes of Occidental lucubration on history, philosophy, religion and ethics have fallen far wide of the mark and totally missed true guiding light from the sheer fact that they were not grounded upon or framed in reference to the constitution of the creature they were to serve. If Scheler holds that the problem of a "philosophical anthropology" stands at the center of all thinking, it is indeed a good augury for a more humanized rationale. It might perhaps do better, however, to say that our need is for an anthropological philosophy, one based upon more competent knowledge of anthropology. Naïvely it can always be asked how a working program for the most favorable human progress can ever be formulated when a knowledge of the nature and reaction potential of the creature for whose welfare it is to be applied is not known. How can a system of outer or inner life be framed to bear man most happily forward on the stream toward his high goal, if neither the goal nor the equipment and endowment of the traveler is known? How can a workable formula for the greatest happiness of man be constructed if the measure and dimensions, the shape and habitudes, of the man himself are not known? Kant indeed attempted to interpret the world in the terms of man's psychic constitution. But his knowledge was wanting in particular data, such as the ancients possessed, and stopped far short of specific relevance to the actual situation.

Without knowledge all endeavor is haphazard. There may be faith and hope in ever so large measure. And, oddly enough, it is not an inch outside the pale of natural causality in the psychological history of Europe over sixteen hundred years that the religion that crushed out former knowledge came to insist, as the main reliance for its millions of purblind devotees, on "faith." It was as inevitable as geometry. In want of wisdom and knowledge there is nowhere for a mind to go save to faith, hope and prayer. And just this unfortunate trend took its evil course to fatal fruition in spite of the adjuration of the most astutely philosophical writer in the cult's own scriptures, St. Paul, who says that faith is not enough. "To your faith add knowledge." Plato and Socrates acquiesce in this declaration of the Apostle.

The egregious and fatal error made by the theologians, and still perpetrated from a thousand pulpits every Sabbath, is in holding up faith as a high Christian virtue to be attained by a victorious Christian apotheosis. It is indeed not so. On the contrary Paul starts the gamut at its bottom tone, its lowest range,—with faith. Why? Because faith is instinctively omnipresent in all minds not demented. It is no attainment; it is given, it is inevitable. In the finale, what can any thinking creature do, confronting life, but have faith? There is nothing else one can do but trust the universe of life to be beneficent. If one can not do that, and do it effortlessly, all other aspiration and striving is of no avail. And in lieu of any overwhelming demonstration that life is malevolent or malefic, faith is as natural as sunshine. We start with it, as does the Apostle. We do not end with it. But it is only the ground platform we stand upon. If we are to build the structure of our evolution we must proceed from the foundation and move upward. And to know how to build the superstructure we must have knowledge. From that will grow wisdom, and from wisdom will blossom virtue and godliness. Here is a simple item of religious homiletics that has been lost for ages, and the loss has traced its direful consequences in many a page of appalling religious history, blotted with bigotry, persecution and slaughter.

From anthropology the ancient sages drew their basic data on which religion and philosophy could proceed to build structures of thought and behavior that would accommodate man commodiously to the play of the forces making for his growth. With such knowledge man could align his effort harmoniously with the stream of evolutionary life and win true happiness. The supreme datum supplied by anthropology to ancient thought was of course the fact that man is a composite creature of two natures, a divine soul and

an animal body,—a god in the body of an animal, as Plato puts it.
The conscious soul of a human is an amalgam or product of the
god and the animal natures in wedding or conjunction. This consciousness stood on the midground—the "horizon" of the Egyptians,
the "cleft in the rock" of the Hebrews—between them. That position gave it its "human" characterization. As human it was engaged
in traversing the ground of evolution reaching from the summit
of the animal's position to the foothills of the mount of divinity.

The Greek wisdom which Hopper has justl" extolled, he adds
(p. 211),

"is basically maieutic, a criticism of life, teaching men that if they are
to care rightly for their souls, as Socrates says, they must know *what*
they are—what it is to be *human*. They must come to know their true
condition; they must be made to recognize as their first task the task of
existing as human beings."

Here, it may be said, is the concentrate, the essence of the problem of philosophy. Obviously the problem of man can not be confronted, much less solved, as long as the nature of the human being
remains unknown. Ancient teachers imparted this basic datum of
anthropology; the modern mind distracts itself futilely in want of
it. As Hopper again well affirms (p. 203),

"philosophy *as it has been practiced* has been one of the best ways of
avoiding the issue. . . . Philosophers have ceased to be *philosophiae*,
lovers of wisdom *in the ancient sense,* and in so far have stunted their
true work in the world through diminishing wisdom to science. Their
work has become . . . detached. It touches the surfaces of life as little
as possible, rebounding into the speculative the moment it does so, like
a toy balloon. Life is severed from thought." [Perhaps it would be better
to say that thought is severed from life.] "Philosophy has become what
Nietzsche said it was—thought husbandry—a trade in thought."

To this Nicholas Berdyaev adds:

"Philosophers and scientists have done very little towards elucidating
the problem of man," in the medieval and modern periods, it should
be specified.

In these periods, as it only too evidently appears, the thinking mind had sunk below the power of comprehending the heights and depths of ancient sapiency.

In the ancient day philosophy was denominated "divine," for the reason that it supplemented the feeble efforts of human wonder and speculation with a body of assured knowledge vouchsafed by perfected men, graduates of this or a previous human evolution, who has mastered the range of human capability and become Illuminati. The tradition of the existence of such exalted men standing not at the bottom but at the summit of the human mountain path is too universal in archaic lore of all nations to be flouted as childish. Besides we have the age-long regnancy in the whole world of sagacious writings, or Scriptures, which were never discredited as tomes of infallible wisdom until the sophomoric intellectuality of the modern age began to judge them in total incomprehension of their cryptic methodology and in utter ignorance of their majestic argosy of forgotten truth and reality. These came from consummate knowledge.

Ancient philosophy was "divine philosophy" because it established the certitude of the presence of a divine element in man which would ultimately redeem his life from the unintelligence and rapacity of the beast to the lordly rulership of truly divine wisdom and charity. As this element was the agent of human transition to godhood, philosophy concerned itself primarily with its origin, nature, struggle and victory in the arena of incarnate life. This history, presented allegorically and dramatically, makes up the content of the scriptures. These tomes of "Holy Writ" deal with the career of the divine fragment, a portion of God's own imperishable unity of mind, after it had migrated from "heaven" (acceptably understood as a "locale" of exalted types of consciousness in non-physical states of being) and taken lodgment in the bodies, distributively, of the most highly evolved animal, to take that creature across the gulf of humanity up to the feet of divinity, the while it accomplished its own advancement to more godlike stature. Its coming introduced into the merely animal-human constitution the seed germ of a deific nature, at once imperishable and potentially omniscient. It brought the god down to share the animal life of mortals, coming into "bondage," coming "under the law" of sin and death (of the body), until the task was done.

Fortified with the knowledge of the presence of this all-gracious guest in the human constitution, minds nourished in so adequate a philosophy could bend their life effort to conformity with the terms of the living problem. They could co-operate intelligently with evolution. They could build on the solid foundation of a workable philosophy, having under their feet the ground of positive attitudes and the bases of fortitude. They could aim at character formation on the strength of the cheering assurance that no effort was ever wasted or cheated of its count in the final score. And again philosophy was "divine" in that it linked the life of man the human with an arm of living deity not outside himself, not in distant heavens, but immediately at hand in the depths of his own being. It brought heaven close and set up a Jacob's ladder of accessibility to it. Man could ascend into celestial glories by the sheer effort to cultivate the companionship of the divine Friend who had come to earth to be his Emanuel.

While mawkishly driveling over the "infallible truth" of Holy Writ in Sabbath habitudes of hypnotized pietism, we have at the same time fallen into actual doubt of the real existence of the divine soul as the eternal pilgrim through the kingdoms of nature, the persistent traveler on the highways of heaven. For the most part our unctuously mouthed averment that the Christ is within us has frittered out into a pretty poetization, since we invariably end by looking across the distances to clutch at its localization in the person of the Galilean peasant. Indeed the central iron rib of Christianity's structure is not that the Christ mind came to be incorporated collectively in humanity, but that it came and was incorporated solely in one man, Jesus of Nazareth. Long buried and lost out of general knowledge is that prime datum of anthropology on which a religious philosophy alone could build its mansion securely. Until that forgotten item is restored human thought can not pursue the path of truth through the jungle of modern guesses and speculations to positive ends. Dr. Hopper sees clearly that we must turn back and catch up with the ancients. Our vaunting presumption of superiority over past ages, in which we approach the study of the relics of antiquity with a condescension veiling a real disdain or contempt, has cost us dearly in the prolongation of our own sojourn in ignorance from which ancient sapiency could all the while have rescued us. A pretty clear discernment of this situation has dawned upon the mind of our eminent psychologist, Jung. His vigorous statement on the point will bear quotation:

"It would be an absurd and entirely unjustified self-glorification if we were to assume that we are more energetic or more intelligent than the ancients—our materials for knowledge have increased, but not our intellectual capacity. For this reason we become immediately as obstinate and unsusceptible in regard to new ideas as people in the darkest times of antiquity. Our knowledge has increased, but not our wisdom. . . . Unfortunately we acquire in school only a very paltry conception of the richness and immense power of life in Grecian mythology."

Our entire study of ancient life and culture and our search for the origins of human constructions in past times have been contorted out of all semblance of truth by our addiction to the word "primitive." Strong books have lately been written to open our minds to the sheer tyranny of words and shibboleths. Here is one calamitous example of it. To be sure, mankind passed through its infantile period in remote days, and it is legitimate to speak of its earliest dawning of intelligence and its efforts to interpret life as primitive. In so far as it was left to itself to grope its way through blind stumbling to incipient knowledge the word "primitive" is applicable to its products. But there is a phenomenon presented by antiquity that finds no explanation through the formula of childish "primitivism." It has been divined at times and the haunting sense of it has disturbed and confused the academic mind. But it has never been honestly and logically faced. It is the significant fact that side by side with the evidences of real primitivism in many ancient peoples there are found books or scriptures containing bodies of wisdom and ethical and philosophical systems transcending even our own maturest attainment. The attribution of infallible truth and sublimest wisdom to the sacred scriptures of the world, which are of *remote ancient origin,* has never been accounted for on any hypothesis consistent with the universal presumptions of "early primitivism." How could the products of the most exalted culture and intelligence have come out of primitive childishness? The presuppositions of the "primitive" theory are shattered into absurdity by the ghostly presence of the tomes of supernal wisdom found in the hands of still "primitive" peoples. Egypt is perhaps the best example. Its *Book of the Dead,* its *Books of Thoth,* its *Pyramid Texts* and its massed inscriptions, doubtless extant thousands of years before a period in which the scholars have been pleased to style Egyptian civilization primitive and even barbaric, stand to this day unapproachable in the majesty of their truth and sagacity. They are now found to be the fountain source of the Hebrew and Christian scriptures and the whole construction that has become modern religion of the Occident. We have not yet risen to any just or full apprehension of their sublime message. Truly it is, as Massey named it, "The Light of the World." And it is light that to us, because of our imperfect vision and blind conceit, is still largely darkness. The children of humanity—but they come bearing the products of perfected maturity! They already carry what humanity will produce at its acme of evolved culture. "Primitive ignorance" comes carrying the structures of perfection! The beginning stage presents to us the end product! The tomes of Egypt's golden wisdom—thanks to the Rosetta Stone—have shattered at last the "primitive" theses of ancient study and rendered obsolete the thousands of books tracing cultural origins through their elaborations. In the shadow of Egypt's sage profundity *we* are found to be the babbling children. Why does the world in its present vaunted maturity cling to the books produced in its childhood? When the world was a child it spake as a child. Now that it has grown up why does it not put away its childish things—the "primitive" scriptures? Because it could not re-create them and can produce nothing even remotely equal to them. Evidently when the world was a child it spake not only as a child, but also in the amazing fullness of matured evolution. Struck nearly dumb by its own discovery, modern psychoanalysis, and Jung, have begun to touch the hem of the garment of the mighty wisdom that brooded over the ancient mind of child humanity. And they begin to perceive that virtue is flowing out to them from the touch, the virtue of truth, wisdom, understanding. For they perceive now that the "primitive" was transfused already with the pervading radiance of the great "unconscious." More truly than we could have dreamed, Wordsworth was right: "The child is father of the man."

For Freud has gone back to childhood to find the origin and explanation of adult behavior, and Jung has gone back to the childhood of the race to find the origin and explanation of the adult behavior of present humanity. And as the sacred scriptures of the race, written in its childhood, still dominate and guide the life of the world, so Jung finds that the instincts of the race motivating its life in its childhood still dominate human conduct, welling up from the depths of the unconscious in dream and phantasy, even when denied a place in consciousness by the inhibitions of tradition, social custom and cultural restraint of any sort. And in those revered scriptures from the race's childhood is found the same lexicon of symbols employed as that same unconscious still uses to speak in dream and phantasy to adult humans today. The discovery of the correlation between man's "unconscious" and the childhood of the race is indeed one of the most epochal in human history.

Having brought the charge of error against the ubiquitous theses of "primitivism," we will be challenged to announce the corrections. The nub and kernel of the mistaken view are to be located in the assumption that the great and lofty scriptures of most remote antiquity were written *by* primitive people. The truth is that they were composed *for* primitive people, but not *by* them. Primitive people *could not* create literature of the exalted character which the great scriptures reveal. They are the creations not of childish immaturity and wonder, but of the most consummate genius ever displayed in world literature. They are not works of speculation, but productions of certified knowledge and confirmed wisdom, of matchless profundity and piercing insight. As moral, intellectual and spiritual norms they have been measured against the run of human experience for some thousands of years, and never has that test supported a single successful impeachment of their veritude. Their message is timeless, their truth is ageless.

But if they were not written *by* primitive people, who in the primitive age possessed the supernal genius to edit them? No answer to this query is possible as long as we imprison our minds in the narrow presuppositions of academic orthodoxy. We must break loose from these fetters and accredit truth instead of "superstition" to the great universal tradition of antiquity. Omnipresent throughout the ancient world is the legend that in the golden dawn of humanity's existence divine kings and "mighty men of renown," yea, the gods themselves, consorted with mankind in its innocent childhood, and taught it arts and cultures, giving it great books of wisdom as perennial guides and manuals for a safe treading of the path of human evolution. It has been assumed that this is a legend, arising out of the roseate phantasy-producing mind of the racial childhood. Yet even legends are not created out of total mental vacuity. There is substance behind every legend. The presence over the whole earth of a universal tradition bespeaks a certain amount of veridical truth at its fountain source. Besides, there stand the scriptures which, appearing in the world's childhood, are not the works of children. It has been assumed that humanity alone, of all life's progeny, was left without parental guidance, protection and tutelage. Everywhere life is parented. Its infantile period is carried through by the adult guidance of parents, guardians and mentors. Is it to be assumed that man alone is left to shift through his infancy as a race with no help from the carriers and products of antecedent development? In a school system an earlier generation turns back to teach the children of its successor. Wisdom accruing to a grown generation is handed down for the benefit of the next generation at its start. All the scriptures of the past are at one in their claim to have been indited by sages and wise ones of super-human stature. Here is the invincible evidence that surpassing wisdom and intelligence presided over the construction of these books. One thing is certain—they are not the products of primitive ignorance. They are the creations of consummate genius and majestic artistry.

And if knowledge is an accumulated acquisition and wisdom an ingrained deposit of the fruitage of right action, then the authorship of the divinely inspired scriptures must have been the product of minds that had traversed a long course of evolution. Life never gratuitously dowers its creatures with qualities, powers or genius that they have not themselves earned and developed in *their* experience. It has limitless largesse to pour upon us, but insists that we prepare the ground and cultivate the growing vine before the intoxicating wine is ours to quaff. As Plato's *Timaeus* assures us, God has himself planted the seed of immortal divinity within us. Ours is the task of tending and cultivating it to its maturity. When it is full grown it is the deity-genius within us, guiding, instructing, enrapturing. It can then write sage scriptures to pass the torch of wisdom along to future children of the cosmos. Says Heraclitus in one of the most sententious utterances in all philosophy: "Man's genius is a deity." But it is a deity that comes at the start of human evolution as a divine infant and has to await the development of corporeal instrumentalities to give it full conscious expression in the outer world. To the degree that such conscious expression has not been implemented by the outer personality it is the "unconscious."

CHAPTER VI

"OLD CHILD" IS HIS NAME

"I DIE, and I am born again, and I renew myself, and I grow young each day." This is the utterance of the divine soul in man as voiced in the sublime literature of ancient Egypt. That literature depicted in forms and analogues of living reality the history of the god that comes to be the heavenly guest tenanting a human body for a season. This celestial visitant is no newcomer to try earthly hospitality; he has been here for similar visits many times. He has died and been born again, he has renewed his life and grown young as often as he has grown old. Indeed he is growing younger with each sally out into the adventure of life, for each excursion takes him deeper into the heart of eternal being, closer and ever closer to the Center of everlasting life where abides perpetual youth. Length of days is indeed in his right hand, for he is the Aged One of Heliopolis, the Ancient of Days. He comes each day as the infant, but he bears with him the wisdom garnered through his many cycles of birth, growth and death. He returns to earth until his wheel of birth and death has completed its turning, when he enters the kingdom of his Father, to go no more out. He is then a glorified Sahu, clothed in radiant body of solar light, and dwells among the gods. But antecedent to that climactic Day of the Lord he is the god in the becoming, hiding his growing light under the bushel of a human personality, toiling, striving, exhorting to right-eousness in the milling scene of earthly life.

The vital truth so long and disastrously lost, then, is that man, in his essential and indestructible selfhood, is a soul, which alter-nately animates physical bodies, gains through them experience in-dispensable to its continued evolution, and drops them for periods

63

of rest in ethereal worlds, during which it lives in a state of latency, or as the sheer potentiality of self-renewal.

The light this determination sheds on psychoanalysis is seen to be the substantial reification or hypostatization of the great new element of psychology, the "unconscious." Indeed it brings to this shadowy consciousness nothing less than a positive entification. It sets it up as a living individual entity, consciously pursuing its way through the labyrinth of evolution as actually as we conceive the mundane individual to be doing. It enables us to bring forth this nebulous presence from out its dusky habitat and to give it definitive form and character, as we recognize it to be a long familiar personage in our revered scriptures. For at last *the "unconscious" is seen to be the soul, the godlike part of the dual nature of man.* Only from the standpoint of our waking consciousness that functions directly through the physical mechanism of a brain is it fittingly denominated the "unconscious." On its own plane it is not unconscious, but more vividly and widely conscious than the earthly self can ever be. But it comes here in search of the offices of the outer personality of man to enable it to achieve an *actualization* of its capabilities of consciousness which it could not possibly gain by remaining continually in sublimated worlds. Consciousness, to be completely evolved, must be ground to a state of hard realism. This can be effected only in worlds of concrete experience. The soul must be centered in a physical body to win its growth. And once in body, it must await the slow evolution of the mechanical and physiological agencies of brain and nervous system before it can deploy its full forces outward to untrammeled expression.

From the standpoint of the open waking consciousness of the individual the soul within is the unconscious. For it is the Genius behind the scenes of the surface consciousness. It is the individual's own self—best spelled perhaps with a capital S—conditioned by the effects of its own long past history, standing in the shadow behind the curtain and appearing almost to play the part of a *deus ex machina* to the personal conscious self. To Socrates and the ancient philosophers it was their Daemon, or guardian angel, interposing at times of crucial exigency to warn the personality against making false or dangerous moves. To the poet it is the source of his higher "inspiration," the spring of his divine afflatus. To all it is the rock of character which so clearly marks the individual's status of high and strong, or low and weak, in evolution. It stands behind—rather one should say above—in the overworld of the personal man, and is the generator or holder of that body of fixed qualities and dispositions which distinguish one person's life from another's. The physical and emotional personality is, so to say, an antenna of it, extended outward into the world of factuality in order to help it fend for itself in the arena of experience. Through the personality it has sensuous contact with the world in which it is destined to play a notable part. It registers the experience impressed upon it through the outer instrument and digests in consciousness the moral substance thereof.

The reservoir of wisdom with which it stands to guard the outer mind is the accrued deposit of the moral value of all its past history. Wisdom can come in no other way than as the assimilated fruit of experience. If it comes otherwise it is unearned, and life bestows nothing without the expenditure of effort commensurate with the gains to be won. As a man soweth, *so* shall he reap. Wisdom is the rich harvest of seed sown, watered and tended. Modern thought has envisaged a near-divine, near-omniscient monitor residing in the over-area of man's constitution and standing ever ready to guard and counsel the personality, but has never even postulated for that monitor any known or unknown cycle of experience requisite to have dowered it with such a faculty or such a prerogative. Obviously nowhere in the present existence of the individual can there be found a body of experience qualified to endow an interior mind in man with such superior wisdom, as all experience comes through the personality. Biological science, through such a representative exponent as Sir Alfred Russell Wallace, has declared that there can nowhere be found in the line of evolving life from animal to man any chapter of experience sufficient to have developed human mentality in the highest animal orders. All observation of the stream of growth negatives the claim. Yet there exists in man's organization a grade of consciousness that manifests the highest knowledge and wisdom, exceeding always that of the conscious man himself, and deploying on occasions of his own strategic choosing resources unknown to the individual on behalf of the supreme welfare of the personality. And there is left no way for the mind to account for the presence and exalted genius of this inner mentor save by postulating for it cycles of living existence and experience in its past, such as the ancient seers allotted to it. So then for the first time in modern systematism both philosophy and psychology are confronted with the challenge of a thesis which, now as of old, can provide the mind with a formula adequate to rationalize the presence of a god in the life of man, and to account understandably for his divine status above the merely animal counterpart in the dual composition.

It is well to adduce several pronouncements from modern psychoanalysis itself that speak in confirmation of the diagnosis. One comes to light in the work on psychoanalysis already cited, *The Recreating of the Individual*. Says the author, Dr. Hinkle (p. 108):

"The unconscious proper is not formed or created by the individual *in response to culture,* but exists *a priori* behind all culture."

With the mere substitution, perhaps, of the word "experience" for "culture," no passage could hit and express the truth more pointedly. It is not any of Freud's Oedipus or Electra complexes generated by early infant reactions. It is not the product of a few years of odd idiosyncratic habits or circumstantial pressures, that warp the mind into unnatural and unwholesome fixations. These are of some account in the total, but they do not create or condition the unconscious. As the author of the citation says, that is already there as the old root out of which a new tree is to spring up. The *Book of Daniel* in its first chapters speaks of leaving the stump of the hewn tree in the ground, so that a new growth may start from it. Elsewhere Dr. Hinkle has noted that the conscious part of the individual remains "unaware of the ancient processes functioning in and influencing his present life." Nothing could be more revealing of ancient truth than such a statement, although its force is largely lost through default of the knowledge that the "ancient processes" that still function in and influence the present life of the individual were the past experience of the individual himself, as well as the collective experience of the race of his ancestry. The meaning is always made to embrace racial limits, when it should apply directly to the individual's own history. The same author says additionally that in the psychoanalytic talk of the unconscious as being composed of conscious motivations suppressed and driven underground, we are not here dealing with the "suppression of individual experience, but with the suppression of racial experience, belonging to an earlier phase of humanity."

This again reifies an ancient element in the makeup of present consciousness. But again the exposition advanced by modern psychology denies to the individual his own previous experience and the fruit of it, by ascribing his present deep-seated unconscious to racial heritage. Archaic philosophical acumen chose to believe that the individual was present anciently when the experience was acquired, that he indeed gained it for his own eternal possession. He did not come by it through a vicarious inheritance or through the transmitted blood of ancestry. They asked how justice could be meted out equably in the world if individuals were either exalted or saddled with a heritage other than that which they themselves had created. The human intuition of justice demands that no creature should be afflicted with the consequences of actions not his own. "The fathers have eaten sour grapes and the children's teeth are set on edge," observes a revered scripture. And it presents a harassing and disturbing anomaly to the reasoning mind which takes seriously the scriptural pronouncements of Deity as to absolute and impartial justice in the universe. Then, too, we recall that the same scriptures tell of "visiting the iniquities of the parents upon the children unto the third and fourth generation." If in any way these declarations are to be harmonized with the simple and direct human sense of justice, it must be assumed that the children involved in these visitations were in line, through previous faulty action, for the ill fortune that traces to parental dereliction. Otherwise the simple mind of man must give over the effort to vindicate the operation of clear justice in the law of inheritance. If you are afflicted with your forefather's sinful consequences, you will look doubtfully toward a God whose sense of fairness seems less rigorously true than your own. A morbid and sin-haunted Christianity has forever refused to face these corollaries of its announced Biblical canons with untrammeled logic or sincere intellectual probity. In the most godlike exercise of human judgment a Deity whose operation of living laws afflicts a soul from the very start of life with the iniquitous consequences of action not its own, must be categorized as outside the pale of what man must think of as justice. Since the early centuries of Christian history the logical and moral issue here involved has been sedulously evaded. But the ancient philosophers met it and they were able to maintain their predication of a God of total justice. This they did by virtue of their knowledge that souls come into an earthly heritage accurately suited to the needs of their own growth at their status. They could assume that a soul born into a malformed physical or material legacy inherited his own, and not his parents' past defects. He falls heir to his own mistakes, not another's. For he brings back with him into renewed expression—until they are at last obliterated—the germs of his own waywardness, to flower out afresh in the new embodiment. The forefathers' physical transmission through the outer line of descent merely provides the good or bad body conditioned to give the old soul its appropriate milieu and circumstantial influences which enable it to work ahead on its own ground.

Lending corroboration to the thesis that the unconscious is an element in us given *a priori*, and not the outgrowth of earthly experience in this life, is another excerpt from Dr. Hinkle's work (p. 39):

"But psychoanalysis is built entirely upon the theory of unconscious motives and purposes, different and antecedent to those known by man in consciousness and upon which his present conscious manifestations and symptoms rest."

This says in effect that there is in man, buried below his normal consciousness, another consciousness which knows more than the man and is greater than the man himself, but which has not been limited to this man's experience. It has the stored-up experience of all previous racial history, explains modern psychoanalysis. Well, then, the situation stands thus: there are two strata of consciousness in man's constitution, the personal open consciousness and the unconscious. Both carry the heritage of the past, yet one is conscious of it, the other is not. The one has it, the other possesses no memory of it. The one has it not, ostensibly because it is a totally new creation, never in existence before and having no link with the past. Then, if the other has it, the legitimate obvious inference is that it is not likewise a new first creation in this life, but that it has a link with its past, that it is a durable entity treasuring all its previous experience and that it was a participant in whatever experience it carries in memory. In a full, frank and fair envisagement of the elements in the situation this is the only channel of explanation open to logic. If there is in man a consciousness which retains the memory of the past, and another which does not have such a memory because it did not share the past, the inescapable inference is that the entity that does retain the memory did share the experience. It (or he) is verily "the Ancient of Days," the eternal pilgrim through the cycles of time and the kingdoms of nature, gathering up and holding the digest of all experience in faculties of supermind and higher consciousness which transcend the three-dimensional scope of man's open awareness. As far as he has not been brought out to expression in the brain consciousness of the outer personality, he dwells in covert position within the deepest recesses of the individual self, the silent guardian and watchful *daemon,* the "higher ego" of the person. In Dr. Hopper's work already cited, *The Crisis of Faith,* the author takes a dozen or more pages to present and support the thesis that the god whose influence molds the individual's life from the hidden depths is an *a priori* reality, given from the start, in relation to the present existence.

Dr. Hinkle likewise is insistent, as her chief ground of refutation of Freud's central presentments regarding the infantile sexual motivations of the child, that the main "drive" of the ego in man is of precisely that character which it would be presumed to be if the premises were granted that an aged, wise and benevolent soul occupied the place and performed the function allotted to the unconscious. That is to say that the unconscious is characterized by an incessant perennial urge toward the actualization of an ever-enlarging potential "divine" expression through the personality. She says (p. 31):

"He [man] bears within himself all the potentiality of individualistic development; the future claims him as well as the past."

She also quotes the words of Antigone:

"The moral law is sacred because it is not a thing of today or of yesterday, but lives forever, and none knows whence it sprang."

It needs no dramatic flourish, however, to declare that there is no unfathomable mystery as to the genetic history of the moral law. The ancient sages give evidence that they were not ignorant of it. The great Egyptologist, William H. Breasted, in his last work, *The Origin of Conscience,* traced its course of development back to remote Egyptian religious conceptions and cultures. The moral law is the deposit of the conscious resultant of all experience undergone by that fragment of the divine mind that tenants one physical body after another, building each in turn over the model of its inner nature, and carries the everlasting memory of its past with it. The moral law is framed in an indelible memory out of the impacts of the consequences of action perpetrated by a conscious perduring entity able to hold the lessons learned and create from their ensemble a code of determinative norms. It is just the fixing of the recognized values accruing from experience upon the consciousness of a spiritual entity which is able to hold them in perpetuity. For its "spiritual" body is imperishable, its substance indestructible. And that which is impressed thereon is retained forever.

The discovery and recognition of the unconscious in modern psychology is bringing out to open view the data which corroborate ancient scriptures in their predication of a divine consciousness in the upper reaches of man's life. Says Dr. Hinkle again (p. 4):

"It is this sense in the individual man of his potential but unfulfilled greatness that forces him to become aware of his incompleteness as a human being. It is this state of faulty development of his psychic capacities that psychoanalysis has brought so clearly into view, and for the improvement of which, to those interested in and capable of using its method, it offers a technic—an aid toward the conscious development of a greater self."

True indeed is all this, since, it is pertinent to ask, how would the personal entity man be able to register a sense of his imperfection and shortcoming in the first place if there was not resident and conscious within him a being possessing familiarity with higher norms of attainment and standards of perfection by contrast with which the present performance of the outer man exhibits faultiness and failure? If psychoanalysis is just discovering this inner mentor, it has taken just about two millennia for the world to regain what its ancient hierophants of religion possessed.

The Hopper claim that the divine element is as "given" a presence in man's make-up as is the body is again substantiated by a quotation from Dr. Hinkle's work (p. 43):

"Man possesses, independent of any frustrated pleasure aims, the capacity for individual development and the need for its fulfillment, as definitely as he possesses the physiological sexual desire."

This statement is part of her refutation of Freud's position that psychic neuroses and mental disturbances trace their genesis always to frustrations of the basic sexual instincts. Disturbances may of course arise from frustration of the life of the outer man; but it is to the credit of the Jung school and such psychoanalysts as Dr. Hinkle that they have recognized likewise something of far deeper import, namely that violent inner tempests will arise from the frustration of the evolutionary purposes and aims of the indwelling god-ego.

And Dr. Hinkle adds a most significant statement, which should carry the minds of both theorists and clinicians to decisive conclusions, when she adds to the above citation the results of actual empirical practice:

"When the obstacles to this forward movement are removed, when he is able to achieve some progress toward the inner goal of his being, then his neurotic symptoms and his psychic disturbances disappear."

Here, in short, is the specific empirical demonstration that if the mind of the outer personality of the individual is not measurably conducting the life so as to minister to the onward progress of the soul in the subterranean—or superior—recesses of the consciousness, the soul will register objection, dissatisfaction and disturbance by bringing the untoward condition to light through neurotic inharmony and unbalance, wretchedness or pain. Indeed some such situation is the nub and crux of nearly every drama and novel, representing the desperate or heroic efforts of the soul to break through a cordon of environing circumstances which have tangled it in a predicament threatening its expression of diviner qualities or thwarting its free growth. Lending corroboration of the very highest sort to Dr. Hinkle's conclusions regarding the voice of the inner god is Jung's repeated affirmation that people only come to the psychoanalyst if and when they have lost possession of a positive religious philosophy and that he has not been able to send them away cured unless he has been able to restore to them an affirmative mental grasp on basic life meanings.

Dr. Hinkle and Dr. Hopper unite in asserting that it is this disagreement, this default of the lower mind from the purposes of the inner, that constitutes the real essence of "sin," and in this they are substantially in accord with the early sage Greek philosophy. Jung is cited (by Dr. Hinkle) as interpreting the psychic discord or disturbance as a longing of the ego for "rebirth," "the desire for a necessary psychic birth which uses the symbols of physical birth to represent the psychological need." This again is startlingly in consonance with ancient theory. The Platonists, the Neo-Platonists and Jesus of the Gospels alike lay down the necessity for a new birth—a second birth—of the soul. Indeed it is general in all archaic religions. The soul can not tolerate stagnation too long. To be normal and "happy" it must have the sense of growth and progress, the assurance of making steady advance on the road it is traveling. This feeling is the perennial condition and prerequisite of its conscious well-being. The soul has needs that must be ministered unto through and by the external paraphernalia of the body,—and philosophies of ascetic religious tendency should never forget this. But also it has interests that reach to higher worlds and that no amount of sensual gratification can promote. St. Paul emphasizes that "the natural man" has no cognizance of the things of the spirit, "neither can he know them, because they are spiritually discerned." Rather the physical man is to the god within as soil is to the tree: the base and ground of its ability to expand its life in the air above. Like the tree the soul can not grow unless it is deeply and firmly rooted in the life of the physical, but its concern with the physical is in no sense an ultimate objective. It is but the necessary foundation and starting point of its own primary business, as it is that of every unit of conscious being, of advancing from the point of present attainment to wider consciousness and more abundant life. The soul sustains a relation to the body that demands its enjoyment of the body's strength, health, buoyancy, comfort and the fullest and freest flow of its elan. The failure of ascetic movements to recognize this fact has led to untold psychic disaster, warping into discord the lives of both the body and the soul and defeating the purposes of evolution. But the soul did not come to link its life with that of the body merely to indulge in that enjoyment. That would indeed be to take the downward path, to fall into "sin." Its way of growth runs through the exercise of its own potential powers and faculties in the development of a higher consciousness, to all of which its happy relation of harmony with the body is a primary and fundamental condition. The soul builds the body as the house in which it is to dwell and work, cycle after cycle. Its prime aim is to build it to be most commodious and comfortable for its tenancy and in such fashion that to live in it is a delight. But once built and ability to maintain it in good state established, it would surely be a mistaken philosophy to assume that the soul's chief business in life was to end with the fulfillment of its enjoyment of the house. It can not do its work in the world without a proper house to dwell in, but once the house is constructed, it can then turn its attention to the higher work it came here to do.

The job of constructing and accommodating itself to its house, however, is an integral part of its incarnational mission and takes on a larger measure of importance than might at first glance be assumed. Its work in spiritual worlds transcending bodily influences still is greatly affected and conditioned by the need of complete harmony with the instrument. As the body is the keyboard, so to say, of the soul's expression, it is essential that there be maintained at all times the most delicate balance and nicest adjustment of conscious motivation to organic reaction. And it is now the province of psychoanalysis to diagnose the conditions of maladjustment between the two factors. The discovery of such maladjustment and the location of its basic causes is indeed its high function.

The ancients, as is well indicated in the philosophy of Plato, adjudged virtue to be the individual knowledge of the art of keeping a perfect balance between the animal man and the indwelling god. Conversely they defined "sin" as the ignorance that stupidly permitted inharmony and discord to be generated in the interplay between the two. The soul, they said, stood at the point of middle ground between the divine spirit above and the animal body below, and its function was to mediate between the two in such fashion that a happy blending and merging of their forces was effected. Standing midway between the two, it could deploy its energies and center its interests and affections in either direction. It could cultivate the life of the higher spirit or devote itself to fostering the sensual expression of the animal. Its own intelligence, be it high or low, was the determinant. The destiny of the individual was the outcome of its decisions.

It is quite likely that the true definition of "sin" is to be reached by taking into account the terms of this philosophical situation. Surely "sin" is that which impedes the most felicitous and orderly flow of the stream of life forward to greater being. And obviously in the human world that which would most effectually block and thwart the movement of "the rivers of vivification," as the Greeks called them, would be the failure of the soul to perform with deft intelligence its high function of maintaining that just balance between the god and the animal in man upon which true growth depends.

"The soul that sinneth, it shall die," is the strong declaration of the scripture. Since all souls undergo death in its common meaning of the dissolution of soul from body, obviously another meaning of the word "death" is here involved. And this is of the greatest significance for all religious and scriptural interpretation. The entire understanding of the language of the Bible has been sadly warped out of line with truth by the failure to read into the words "death" and "the dead" in the scriptures the same meaning which was attached to them in the ancient Greek and Egyptian religions. The great lost light of antiquity comes out in glorious splendor when the original philosophical meaning is restored to these terms. By "death" is meant nothing less than what we call our "life" here!

And "the dead" of the scriptures are none other than ourselves, the "living." This is now established beyond question. For the ancients regarded the life of the soul in the body as its death, using the term of course in a figurative and relative sense. In the body the high life of the soul was so reduced in potential capacity by the sluggish vibrations of the corporeal nature that it lay inert as in death, and the body was poetized as its prison, grave or tomb. Indeed the body and tomb are identical in the Greek words for body, *soma,* and tomb, *sema.* The soul was said to go to its death when it "was united to the ruinous bonds of the body." Socrates says to Cebes that he has "heard from one of the wise that we are now dead and that the body is our sepulcher."

This construction is directly in line with what St. Paul asserts in his Epistles. "To be carnally minded is death," he says. "Ye are dead in your trespasses and sins," he adds. And again he states most pointedly that "the interests of the flesh meant death; the interests of the spirit meant life and peace." The death referred to in the old books of wisdom was that of the soul, occurring when the unit of divine consciousness made its descent into the body of man on earth, there to come "under the law" of birth, growth, maturity and decay. The whole import of sage writings of the past has been utterly lost by the ignorant exoteric assumption that the "death" spoken of was that of the physical body. A thousand irreconcilable perplexities of scriptural interpretation vanish, and one clear and consistent flash of illuminated meaning takes their place the moment one reads the old Greek philosophical meaning back into the terms under discussion. And the whole systematic structure of archaic theology is restored to glowing significance and the old rendition vindicated, when St. Paul says in the seventh chapter of *Romans:* "the command that meant life proved death to me." The "command" he is speaking of has never to this date been understood to be the command—which comes to all souls in the empyrean—to incarnate. What the Apostle says in the verse immediately preceding this statement is of the utmost elucidative value for all theology, for all understanding. He says: "When the command came home to me, sin sprang to life and I died." It gives us final certification as to what is connoted by "sin." Evidently it is an inclination in the soul that lies dormant so long as it remains in static suspension of its energies in the celestial spheres, but which springs to life and activity as soon as the soul is embodied in a fleshly organism on earth. "Sin" is that disposition of the mind which can be implemented only by union with the carnal self of the animal body, and awaits its opportunity to awake to expression when that union is consummated. Then Paul makes that correlation between "sin" and "death" which should not have remained a sealed mystery for hundreds of years, with this passage of his in front of our eyes. "Sin sprang to life and I died." His "death" was his descent into the world of carnal mind, the indulgence in which is at last seen as the terrible hobgoblin that has plagued the Christian conscience with entirely needless morbidity for these many centuries. "Sin"—be it proclaimed to all the world in clarion tones— is the soul's indulgence in the life of the flesh. Indeed, with "the mount" being a symbol for the earth itself, this globe is many times referred to in the scriptures as the "Mount of Sin." It is likewise "Mount Sin-ai." Now it is possible to see what the Apostle meant by saying that "the wages of sin is death." For if sin is the addiction of the soul to the lusts of the flesh, and residence of the soul in the flesh is "death" to its higher nature, then continued sin necessitates continued "death." The longer the soul clings to carnal affections the longer it must return to earth and body to give play to its desires—until they are burned out in the fires of purificatory suffering. And again can be seen in clearer certitude the meaning, so terribly mutilated, of Paul's apocalyptic utterance: "The last enemy to be overcome is death." Of a surety it now is obvious that when the soul has at last been entirely purged of its bent to sin, which drags it again and again back to earth where alone the instincts of a physical body can give channel to its carnal leanings, it will

have no further need to enter the "valley of the shadow of death."
It then need "go no more out," as *Revelation* puts it.

Modern psychology has at last got around to the vantage point
of envisaging the inner conflict in the area of human consciousness
in much the same light as that in which it was viewed by the ancient Illuminati. It has made discovery of the "Aged One," the
older soul hiding in the covert depths of the individual consciousness, and has seen the necessity of interpreting the phenomena of
psychic disturbance and mental illness in terms of the phases of
the mutual thwarting of the interests of higher soul by the instincts
of the flesh, and those of the flesh by the cultural restraints imposed
by the soul. And at last it stands and works on solid ground, the
title to the authenticity and validity of which is volubly attested by
ancient lore.

Nearly every word of the few fragments we have left of the writing of Heraclitus is an utterance of prime value. Among such is
his brief sentence: "For all human laws are fed by one thing, the
divine." And further than that, he grounds the roots of the divine
in man in no less high and immediate a ray of the Absolute than
the Logos itself:

"Go hence; the limits of the soul thou canst not discover, though
thou shouldst traverse every way; so profoundly is it rooted in the
Logos."—Fragment 45; Diels.

Clarity might long ago have supervened upon the mortal conception of divine things if the Occidental mind had been open to
receive the assertion of Greek philosophy that the Logos is a ray
or emanation from Supreme Deity, the spirit a further extended
ray from the Logos, and the soul a still further diffraction, through
the medium of matter, of a ray from the spirit. Use of this outline
graph enables thought to fulfill every requirement in meeting both
the theoretical and the empirical problems involved in the analysis.
As Plotinus so capably has blue-printed the scheme of the universal
construct. the emanation of divine energy from the heart of being,

proceeding farther and farther from initial impulse, pierces ever deeper into matter, losing force as matter grows denser out on the periphery, until the last wave is just sufficient to enable the soul to nucleate around its node of power the physical body. So that Plotinus says that "the soul suspends from it the mundane body," which is characterized as "the last of things" in the chain that reaches from spirit at the top to dense matter at the lower rung.

The outcome also of the great Kant's elaborated philosophical lucubration was the conclusion that what constitutes in his system the highest "spirit" in man, "the transcendental unity of apperception," is "a condition which precedes all experience and in fact renders it possible." Here is the soul "given," *a priori,* again.

Irenaeus, who is not often found admitting or expressing his agreement with the principles or teachings of the antecedent pagan philosophies, which in so far as they came into early Christianity fell under the condemnation of his pen as "heresies," puts general ancient philosophical understanding of the triplicity of spiritual elements in man in splendid clarity in the following (*Adversus Haereses,* V, ix, 1):

"The perfect man consists of these three, flesh, soul and spirit. One of these saves and fashions—that is, the spirit. Another is united and formed—that is, the flesh; while that which lies between the two is the soul, which sometimes follows the spirit and is raised by it, but at other times sympathizes with the flesh and is drawn by it into earthly passions."

This is admirable; and finds buttressing also in Plutarch:

"But in his [Plato's] *Book of Laws,* when he was now grown old, he affirmed, not in riddles and emblems, but in plain and proper words, that the world is not moved by one soul . . . but not by fewer than two; the one of which is beneficent, and the other contrary to it, and the author of things contrary. He also leaves a certain third nature in the midst between, which is neither without soul nor without reason, nor void of a self-moving power, but rests upon both of the preceding principles, but yet so as to affect, desire and pursue the better of them."

Indeed here is seen the basic formulation of that which became the doctrine of the "mediator" in Christian theology, the higher and the lower natures in man, with the soul standing on mid-ground between them, and functioning as the way or the bridge over which the two might ultimately effect their reconciliation and atonement.

From Erasmus comes an equally direct statement of the duofold man-god constitution, with the soul mediating between upper and lower:

"The spirit makes us gods; the flesh makes us beasts; the soul makes us men."—*Enchiridion* v. 20—D.

So definitely did ancient insight comprehend the tripartite division or gradation of man's nature that it typified the mediatorial function of the middle-man, the human, standing on the horizon or boundary line between the gross body below and the divine mind above, by the symbol of the bee, which became the living zoötype of the soul because of its function in fertilizing female ova in the flower with male pollen and thus effecting the new birth. The insect performed the mediatorial function of priest in the marriage of the opposite poles of the plant. So even the Christos in man was characterized as the High Priest, since he functioned in the union of male and female elements in man in holy marriage. The soul it is that mediates between spirit and flesh and unites the logos of the higher with the atomic mothering and nurturing capabilities of the physical. The soul is the agent and focal point of the interplay between the two natures.

Now psychoanalysis has discerned the forms and features of this interplay and speaks of it in the most direct terms. Here is Dr. Hinkle giving us her statement of it in the vernacular of psychology (*The Recreating of the Individual,* p. 50):

"As a matter of fact there is a constant interplay between the two aspects of human life—the external world and our own concrete objective tendencies and needs which are a part of it, and the subjective human creative and transforming processes lying entirely within the individual psyche."

This is of course likewise the conflict of the lower man with the higher god, who find themselves co-tenants of the same domicile. The words of Prof. N. Shaler apply most fitly here:

"It is hardly too much to say that all the important errors of contact, all the burdens of men or of society, are caused by the inadequacies in the association of the primal animal emotions with those mental powers which have been so rapidly developed in mankind."

It is the struggle between the emotions and the intellect! When has mankind not been keenly aware of it? It is so much the burden of every day's conscious life that it does not shape itself out as a concrete and specifíc problem. It is nearly the whole focus of the psychological activity of life. How much one should yield to the bent of the feelings and desires, or how much to check them; how far one should follow the clear voice of reason, when it counsels adversely to the instinctual propensities, and how far one should sacrifice obvious present advantage or pleasure in the interests of deferred greater good;—these are the unending skirmishes in the vast struggle waged between the animal and the god in the nature of man on earth. They are the daily combats in the aeonial Battle of Armageddon. And never have the issues and conditions of the battle been sufficiently clarified in the world's understanding. The vast and calamitous ascetic movement aimed at victory for the god by the curt and conclusive method of crushing out the animal with a tragically mistaken austerity. Epicureanism and naturalistic hedonism sought a resolution through a free rein to the instincts, tempered with aesthetic norms. As might always have been known since Plato's day, the only safe and perfect modus is to be found in the gradual blending of the two natures through the experiences of both parties in the give and take of earthly evolution. St. Paul has well indicated this denouement, when he speaks of the breaking down of the "middle wall of partition between us," and the making of "one new man" out of the amalgamation of "the twain." Only thus can the great cyclic conflict be fought out "on the horizon," as it is said to be in the Egyptian texts. And only thus can the engagement terminate in a manner to promote the ends of the evolutionary movement, so that both soul and body acquire the maximum amount of beneficial development from the complication.

CHAPTER VII

THE TWO SUBTERRANEAN GROTTOES

THE intermediate soul, therefore, is the meeting ground, the arena, of the conflict between soul and body. It is rent and torn by the tug and pull of opposing motivations, the animal tending downward toward sensuality and grossness, the spirit striving with the soul to raise it up out of the mire. The animal self reached upward to intrigue the soul down into its coarseness and brutish delights; the spirit wrestled valiantly to entice its lower brother upward by the desirable rewards of virtue. The great battle was on. All religions have so fully depicted the grim stress and the crucial issues of the struggle that it needs no considerable elaboration here. What is needed, however, is the orientation of relevance and pertinence from the purely theological purview over to its even more pertinent reference in the field of everyday consequence, particularly as the nub and core of psychoanalytic technique. It has not been known that the immediate categories of the psychoanalytic situation were all the while those time-hallowed fundamenta of the old theology and the Bible texts.

Dr. Hopper, in another passage from his *The Crisis of Faith* may be permitted to sum up what has been presented in the foregoing pages as to the three-ply constituency of our consciousness, and adduce for our consideration in psychology the practical outcome of the living action in the three-storied human structure (p. 249):

"It is true formally and structurally, that man may live his life on one of three levels: on the sub-human, the human, or the divine—*below* the level of the regulative control of reason, or within the regulative control of reason conditioned by existence, or under the regulative control of God's will. These levels of experience are conceived formally;

but they are lived dialectically. Each level when chosen is a commitment to a total end." (The italicizing of *below* is ours, for a purpose soon to be specified.)

Broadly this is precisely what the elaborate and recondite Greek Orphic, as well as its parent Egyptian Hermetic, wisdom promulgated in the ancient day in the arcana of the Mysteries. The sages of olden time knew of man's threefold composition, and it is obvious that they knew also the vast involvements of the triplicity for all phases of human conduct, thought and understanding. Their astute philosophy reveals their underlying recognition of the inter-related status of the three levels of conscious life, since indeed their systems and principles can not be apprehended dialectically without grounding the effort in these formulations. What they knew is that which has not yet dawned on modern mentation, namely, that as man lives on, or in, three levels of consciousness, he must have an organic equipment that will relate him, consciously, with the reality of each level, and that he must therefore have three separate "minds." He must possess a sub-human, a human and a super-human, or divine, mind!

Here is the mighty key to the modern psychoanalytic science without which it yet hobbles ahead in semi-groping. Circumscribing itself ignorantly within the limits of a twofold segmentation of con-sciousness, psychological science has hit and missed in its assumptions. Conjecture and confusion have come in because it prescribed but one realm of play for man's "unconscious," whereas there are two quite separate and different strata of unconscious content and influence. The one lies *below* (sub) the ordinary conscious, and the other *above* (super). The first is of the earth, physical; the second is "the Lord from heaven," spiritual. And the conscious human mind stands between its unconscious underling and its unconscious overlord. Here in Greek philosophy is the key to the scriptures. No less is it the key to psychoanalysis. For how can a thing which concerns the very constitution of mortal man be true in philosophy or theology, and then not be the actuality in the same mortal nature when it is studied through the eyes of psychic interest?

Man, the strictly human, stands as the conscious being between two areas of unconsciousness, one "below," the other "above." His little life is indeed rounded with—unconsciousness, which presses close in upon him from both above and below. He is a little gamut of sound and action between two immense silences. And just as his physical sight extends over only the narrow segment of the scene upon which his vision can focus, but his cognition can take in in a secondary awareness further areas on each side of the middle focus without the gaze falling directly upon them, exactly so his consciousness can reach upward and downward from his central ground of focus and cover in a secondary type of recognition some sections of the rim of the great unconscious domains stretching far below and far above his allotted range of being. His consciousness is therefore extensible some distance into both the subconscious, beneath his ordinary status, and the hyperconscious, or world above his vibratory range. Man's conscious being, then, is a little light set aglow between two great darknesses, but through the evolving powers of the mental genius within him he is able to penetrate some distance into both of the two environing border regions of outer darkness.

The interrelationship of the three minds in man has never been systematically diagnosed. It is all important. It is the structural anthropological key to the problem of man. Its exposition must be attempted. The three minds must be described and classified.

The first step in the elucidation is taken from a hoary volume, Egypt's venerated *Book of the Dead*. The "Speaker" is the soul and he says: "I am Yesterday, Today and Tomorrow." "I am what hath been, what is and what shall be." Again he dramatizes his three consciousnesses in saying: "I am Atum in the morning; I am Ra at noon; I am Khepr at evening." What is meant here is that of the three elements or conditions of consciousness, one is the deposit of his actual experience in his past; the second is his conscious present awareness; and the third is a higher consciousness supervening gradually for his future. We are thus instructed in the great truth that the subconscious mind is the hidden memory of our past; the conscious is our present awareness; and the superconscious is the mind that will function in our future. The last is only embryonic, potential, in seed state, as yet unopened to operative function. It can thus be seen that man's present consciousness is a point of transition from past to future, or equally from future to past, and that it is his effort to gain a state of stability at the neutral point between the two nodes of the movement of time. As his life and therefore his consciousness are a continuum, they must entail the union of all three experiences, or a union of the two end moments in the center. That is, the two end aspects that are not now in overt awareness must be integrally present, related and incorporated, essential components of the total deposit of experience in consciousness.

The past has teleological relation to the future and to the whole, since its meaning is determined by the nature of the ultimate goal at which the total experience is archetypally aimed. The future is conditioned by the past, as its ontological product, since it is built up on the past. The present moment is the resolution of the past into a mold that at the same time shapes the future.

All this brings out the important functionism of the three minds. As only one of the three grades of consciousness can fill the field of awareness, that is, occupy the mind's attention at one and the same time, owing to the finite limitations and the single dimensionality of the time concept as applicable to human mentality, it is both a logical and a practical necessity that the other two must lie in the unconscious sphere. The mind must retain the memory of its past experience, but that dare not occupy the field of consciousness at the cost of driving out the present,—or life would stop. Therefore the experience of the past, held in memory, must be stored out of the way, so to speak, in the halls of potential memory, to be available at any time if needed for present uses. This is just as understandable as that a person must have a room or attic in which to store things accumulated (in the past), so that while they may be available if needed, they are nevertheless out of the way to leave free space for present activities and uses. The subconscious, then, is the attic or storage room in which are packed away the gist of our past careers. The present is the new moment arising out of the past and receiving the influx from the future. The brain consciousness then is that poise in the flux, or that moment at which the content and essence of future development is registered in open awareness, to be dealt with by the initiative of the present, and passed back into the storehouse, an addition to what has been stored there previously.

But the purely temporal aspect of the movement must be oriented over into the concept of quality. The future can be, of course, just additional moments or events of the same kind of beads on the string of time. But it is proper to think of the future as bringing at least the potentiality of a higher grade of consciousness. It is just about an evolutionary instinct to count on the future to bring higher values to life than those of the past or present. What the mind of the future will bring is expected to be something richer and fuller. The play of consciousness for the coming time will be cast at a higher frequency and shorter wave length than those in the past. Man is, as it were, but very actually, walking up a gamut of values, climbing up a golden stairway of realities, much like a cat walking from left to right over the piano keyboard. Each forward step he takes strikes a higher-pitched string of consciousness and realization. He awakens from silence to sound in his world a new and higher note each time he can reach one key higher in the scale. At each step of advance in his evolution in time, be it slow or rapid, he is progressing from a lower to a higher tempo or pitch. The past has resounded or responded to the lower tones; the future will strike the higher ones. For evolution is tuning up the strings and refining the mechanism of the physical instrument at each step of ongoing. Present man can produce sweeter tones and manage completer harmonies than past man, and future man will be able to come ever closer to striking ineffable symphonies.

The past goes into latency—though it is always re-available—while the future awaits the slow development of the instrument in order to be brought forth out of latency and be registered on the surface of the actual. Until this moment it is only potential, awaiting the perfectability of the sounding board of brain and nerves. The future thus emerges out of unconscious potentiality to pass through the gate of the present moment of actualization into the storehouse of accumulated and partly digested reality. It is the birth moment of ever advancing stages or registries of real being. All life progresses from the potential to the actual, and the area of immediacy in consciousness is the necessary ground whereon that which has been held in conscious thought in the mind of the great Oversoul of creation can be projected from the superior plane above the range of man's conscious grasp down into the open field of actual experience. The superconscious is that segment of the gamut of God's graded values which lies or extends immediately above the highest arc of man's responsive reach.

God is the sending generator of waves of reality; man, as he perfects his instrumentalities of body, mind and soul, is a poor, a good or a better receiving instrument. The total harmonies of God's being are thrilling about us all the while. But we are bound in silence to all of them except those that we have grown able to match in vibration through the evolving capacities of our organisms. Only these are the limited though ever expanding glories of reality that we are able to make actual to ourselves. The Egyptians again solidly portrayed this basic truth by one of their sagacious "myths." They said that man was imprisoned in twelve dungeons, one after the other, and that he could only be liberated from each in turn as he learned to pronounce the name of the god who stood guard at each dungeon door, and who held the key but would not use it until the prisoner pronounced his name properly. *N*ame and *n*ature are identical in this situation, so that man's ability to utter correctly the name of a god is the same thing as being capable of manifesting that god's divine nature through the personality, the lower mind and self. This is brightly illuminating on the mental side. This is the meaning of "calling upon the name of the Lord" in the scriptures, a vastly different and far more demanding thing than a mere vociferation of the word-name of deity as understood in Christian rendering. We are, as the Egyptians poetized it, in prison to a faculty that is as yet unopened and undeveloped. We are freed from limitation only as potential faculty and power are opened to function through unfoldment. This is as clearly true as is the simple remark that we are blind until we evolve the faculty of sight through development of the organs of seeing. No wonder the ancients set forth man's life in the flesh as an imprisonment, a burial, sleep and death. We are the captives in a long exile here on earth. We are in bondage to matter, Hagar, the bondwoman, until brought up out of this land of Egypt, the abode of flesh and sense. That is what is entailed for the soul in its migration to earth, its coming "under the law" that prevails not in the world of spirit, but holds consciousness at low ebb in the realm of body and matter. This is what it means to be "crucified in the flesh." The Logos was made flesh—not only in one man, but in all men—and came and dwelt among us, hiding for the early time his grace and truth under a bushel of matter. This is our Immanuel, the god *imman*-ent in us. We are in prison under the limitations of our still undeveloped potentialities, and the Christos within us, who brings not only the stored-up capital of his former achievements, but the potentiality of vastly greater genius to be unfolded in the living process, is kept on the cross, in darkness and inanity, until we of the outer personality open the barred doors and let him out to freedom. He abides on the level immediately over our heads, a resident of a plane the life of which transcends ours, awaiting the chance to incorporate more and ever more of his unexploited capability in the world of the actual through the heightened mechanism of consciousness we slowly learn to provide. He dwells on the plane above us, but is eager to break through into our world and find thereby a greater actualization of his own powers, as we prepare the way in the wilderness for him.

This being understood, a glimpse can now be had into the inter-linked operation of the three levels of mentation in the human con-stitution, on its purely mechanical side. As Dr. Hopper has said, one can live in any of the three kingdoms, the sub-human, the human or the super-human or divine. We can step from one to the other of the two end realms across the connecting bridge of the human or conscious link. We can rise to divinity, or sink to animality, by a shift of the focus of interest, desire or will. The process by which true advance is constantly being made, however, is clearly to be seen and is the basis of a deeper understanding than has been gained hitherto. The present or human state of the con-scious mind is, as said, the point of meeting, and therefore the point of friction, clash and struggle between the two natures. It is to be set down categorically at once, however, that this clash and struggle *is not evil,* but only the exertion of the tension necessary to bring out to activity the latent energies of both soul and sense. (A whole prodigious segment of religious theory and practice has gone awry, with fatal consequences, as the result of regarding the contention of soul and body as evil.) It is here on the plane of ordinary daily struggle and effort, and not in ethereal palaces of mystical realiza-tion, that the battle is fought and the gains made. No bliss will ever be enjoyed in Nirvanic heavens that has not first been won on earth! For it is the function of the conscious mind, as the outcome of its insistent, perennial divine urge and aspiration, to reach up-ward toward the fuller and sweeter life of the supermind, to catch the purer tone of its more exalted radiation of divine character, and to bring it down into its lower station and hold it there. Ordinarily it is only at infrequent times that the human is able to vibrate consciously in rapport with that upper divine. These are the high moments, when we are wafted upward as by an afflatus, when inspiration flows and light flashes. We may thereafter sink back in dullness, the glory departed. But having had one touch and taste of paradise, we will not rest until we have more; and with each new one there comes a greater skill to impound and hold the illuminated moment.

That there is a mind in us pointing to the future is indicated by what the eminent psychologist, Carl G. Jung, has to say in a footnote (p. 493) of his profound study, *The Psychology of the Unconscious*. He here succinctly lays the foundation for the erection of the two unconscious minds:

"Just as traces of memory long since fallen below the threshold of consciousness are accessible in the unconscious, so too there are certain very fine subliminal combinations of the future, which are of the greatest significance for future happenings in so far as the future is conditioned by our own psychology."

He says it is impossible for analysis to concern itself with these intimations pointing to future happenings. That would be the task of "an infinitely refined synthesis, which attempts to follow the natural current of the libido." This, he says, is beyond us, but it "might possibly happen in the unconscious, and it appears as if from time to time in certain cases significant fragments of this process come to light, at least in dreams. From this comes the prophetic significance of the dream long claimed by superstition."

He adds that "the aversion of the scientific man of today to this type of thinking . . . is merely an over-compensation to the very ancient and all too great inclination of mankind to believe in prophecies and superstitions." There will be hearty agreement with the revulsion of the scientific mind from age-long superstition and the gullible credulity of uncritical masses, but the literature containing the authentic record of prophetic dreams and premonitions is too great for denial of the possibility of projections of the future into consciousness. We are not too well fortified with a clear rationale of their occurrence, but it is certain that the future touches us closely and now and again pictures from its panoramic screen

pierce the curtain and drop down into the area of present awareness.

Dr. Hinkle, too, speaks of the necessity of man's transforming
himself through the effort to follow the "transforming power within
life," resident in the unconscious. She says that man "has now
apparently for the first time arrived at the borderland of that supreme necessity, self-creation, and involved in his attitude towards
this task lies his answer to the great urgent question of the present
time and all time—the future of humanity itself."

The archetypal norms of divine thought implanted in the creation
and suspended above man's head, as it were, are to be projected
downward into conscious recognition in the minds of thinking
beings. The first reception of them is a matter of impression, much
like a photographic print. But the firmer fixing of them upon lower
mind is effected through the operation of a very wonderful law,
the law of repetition, engendering habit. The subconscious memory
is built of repetition. It gains and holds its possessions by means
of its power of retaining impingements made repeatedly upon it.
It is possible that it retains all impressions made upon it, even in
the slightest manner; but ordinarily, from the standpoint of known
powers of memory, several repetitions are required to fix an im-
print indelibly upon its sensitive slate. Repetition induces a sort of
automatism in the memory. It is entirely akin to the mind operating in children and animals, and is therefore not aided by the processes of conscious intelligence, reason or will. It is just the power
of sheer automatic memory. It is grounded on repetition. What it
hears or sees often enough stays with it, having carved its form
upon the "tablet of consciousness."

The rationale and the sum of all progressive growth for man
the human, then, is the effort of his superconscious, the god within
him, to project downward from above the ideal realities of the
noumenal world, the same being the thoughts of God's own creative
mind, stamp them upon the open consciousness of the individual,
and then fix them finally through the force of repetition upon the

subconscious level of habitude. The conscious mind, Prometheus-like, catches and draws down a light from out the upper chamber of the superconscious, ingrains it in its mentation by repetition, and thus finally plants it firmly in the soil of the subconscious. Man is in this manner slowly but constantly transferring bits of "heaven" down to earth, and holding them as his permanent possession. Habit (from the Latin *habere*, "to have") is the method by which we *have* something. But it is a matter of the gravest import, whether in the end, owing to the hypnotic power of mental action, it is not to be said that a habit is something that *has us!* "A slave to habit" is one of the commonest of phrases. The great majority of our actions in a day's time are the automatic impulsions of habit. The whole structure of tradition and custom is the product of habit, or the inertia that binds men to habits. The maxims of old-fashioned character building, and much in educational procedure, were based on the effort to form good habits or to cultivate the mind through memory work.

Evolution proceeds as the conscious mind exercises its mediatorial office of drawing down divine "fire" of wisdom and knowledge out of the heaven of the overworld, the ideal empyrean, and passing it on down to the custodianship of the subconscious, where it becomes automatized as part of the built structure of the human. Physiology falls in conclusively with this delineation, since it tells us that the autonomic nervous system, the organism of the subconscious, is the apparatus that holds the impressions fixed by habitual practice. It functions in the ganglia of the spinal cord, we are told. These take over what the brain consciousness builds up by repetition.

Man's advance in evolution, as far as the attainment of higher consciousness is concerned, consists, then, in the ability of the conscious self to capture more and more of the superconscious potential, to repeat it consciously, and so store it away as a permanent possession, an increment of living gain. Each time he becomes capable of registering a higher note in the scale of conscious values he takes a step up the ladder of evolution from man to god. He is climbing up the Jacob's ladder toward the heavens, the locale of more vivid reality.

There is a grand enlightenment for intelligence in the consideration of the habit phenomenon in the human economy. Through habit, more particularly and clearly noted in animals, in whom there is no free initiative of new action by the deliberative reason, but seen even very generally in humanity, life is able to achieve a close approach to invariability and uniformity in its normal procedures. These traits may be assumed to be requisite and indispensable in so far as the welfare of creature life may be dependent upon absolute regularity. At any rate the genius that orders the universe has evidently found it necessary to install regularity and uniformity into the operative scheme, since they are most amazingly in evidence. The constancy of life's procedures, movements, activities in periodicity and rhythm is the one element in the creation that has so powerfully enchained the human mind. The immutable repetition of cycles, the endlessly renewed alternation of activity and rest, the diastole and systole of all pulsations of living energy in the cosmos, have struck the thought of man with an overwhelming sense of the play of divine mind in the phenomena of the universe. It is the feature that the human mind builds upon in its determination that the universe is a cosmos.

Two items of knowledge, then, combine to instruct us further, both as to the nature of God and as to his laws. The first is man's constitution in God's image; the second is an immediate derivative of that, the corollary assumption that if man is like God, then man's composition and functionism supply to thought an analogical suggestion as to the make-up of God's being. The astonishing inference then rises to conception that, as man has the three minds or levels of consciousness, God must be constituted likewise! And a startling formulation arises out of the parallel. It is the determination that what we observe in the way of invariable natural procedure and style "the laws of nature" are just the fixed habitudes of God's subconscious mind! They are invariable in their regularity because sufficient of God's conscious energization has from the beginning been expended in establishing them to make them automatic. They have by habit of God become the actions of his autonomic "nervous system." Pope's astute discernment that God is the soul of the universe, while "nature" is its body, must be given the chance to register its full import here. Like us, God is spirit-soul-mind, and all three ranges of consciousness function in his great body, the universe. He, too, must be able to turn over the products of his present consciousness, if conscious mind is the creating and ever recreating power behind the worlds, to the automatic unvarying control of his "lower mind" resident in "ganglia"—the suns—so as to free his conscious self for ever new exercise of desire and will. The laws of nature, as to which we affirm poetically that the mind energies of God uphold and perpetuate them, and which we declare would crash in chaos the moment his mental concentration was relaxed, are evidently the established habitudes of his former conscious regimen of activity. They are immutable because they have, through repetition, come under the control of a segment of divine consciousness that holds an aptitude fixed upon it by initial impact and endless recurrence. It lies below the realm of freedom. It can not exercise choice. It obeys the will of the conscious part. It is the *anima,* the animal part of mind, and its universal function is to repeat automatisms ingrained upon it. When God says, in the Old Testament, that he will write his laws in our minds and hearts, he is announcing the great principle here discussed. Little by little he is able to communicate the transcendent principia of his exalted being from the higher vibrational key in the gamut to the next lower stratum of his organic being, and from that to the one below, until all creature life reflects his nature and in miniature repeats his procedures. Thus his law pervades the total creation. Our fixed systematic operations, such as pulse, respiration, food intake and elimination, metabolism, cell decay and renewal, are all operations that were once for a limited period consciously ordered and directed by intelligence, but were later turned to automatic actions, to free the conscious. These are the laws of nature operating in our bodies, as all larger procedures are the laws of nature operating in the spacious reaches of life beyond our little lives. In both cases they are under the control of the never-failing subconscious. We think of God so constantly as Mind or Spirit that we forget he has his body, which is the physical creation in the large. And that body provides him with the "nervous" apparatus for a subconscious activity.

This, in fine, elucidates to our puzzled minds why it is that God can give his *attention* to the inconceivably vast range and multitude of all his activities in all his worlds! They are under the control of his subconscious. They do not require his *conscious* attention. For whatever the word may conceivably connote when applied to the higher level of God's life and being, they are *automatic*. Our little, though still marvelous, automatisms are copies of his. We *are* made in his image. The profounder and more real implications of this datum in the scriptures have never been taken at obvious face value. It is the key to practically the whole science of human understanding of life and its processes and phenomena.

It is a subsidiary reflection that it is therefore a matter of inexpressibly serious consequence in the life of man, collectively and individually, what activities of body or mind he chooses to make habitual. He has the power of choice and initiative, and these are virtually the powers of a god. If, through ignorance, which is his handicap from the start and hobbles him in diminishing degree thereafter, he chooses the wrong kind of procedures, he fixes upon his subself an inharmonious, pain-engendering routine. The outcome must in all cases be suffering and misery. Human suffering has here its origin. The chains of a bad habit can be broken only by resolute correction of the addiction by conscious re-direction when the disease or corruption created in the organism has brought the intelligence and the will in line with a better run of conduct. Pain is the guardian angel that with inevitable certitude announces whether the ingrained habitudes produce in the organism a life-sustaining harmony or jangle a death-bearing cacophony. In the end, knowledge, requisite to the making of choices aright, is the indispensable warden of human happiness. Pain is both our chief protector and our ultimate educator. Without its timely signals we would be totally at the mercy of our own follies.

CHAPTER VIII

IN PLUTO'S DARK REALM

THROUGH lack of this dual departmentalization or segmentation of the unconscious by modern psychological science, vast confusion and much futile groping have characterized the investigation and vitiated the conclusions. Instead of only one unconscious, there are two. There are two levels, stories, houses, realms of the unconscious. And it makes a world of difference to which one a phenomenon belongs, or to which it is assigned, in psychological practice. The subconscious is unconscious, because it holds all that has once been in consciousness, but has been relegated to the domain of the unconscious. Its content may be good, bad or neutral. It may be the more recent acquisition of what is fine in the way of new inculcation, or it may be the surviving memory of past viciousness, or the possibility of its renewal. It may be sublime philosophical beauty, or the grossest brutality. It is happily true, no doubt, that in long course, as lofty sentiment and keener wisdom fix permanent habits of virtue in the sub-area, long dormant bestiality and gross carnalisms will atrophy off the sensitive plate of the lower mind and pass out into final oblivion. At any rate they become more and more deeply "sub" and less readily resurgent. As the poet has put it, the growth of man in righteousness and wisdom will eventually "let the ape and tiger die" out of his scope of motivation. Melchizedek, the king of righteousness, will gradually assert his rulership more completely over the entire kingdom of consciousness,

> "Till every foe is vanquished,
> And Christ is Lord indeed."

Dr. Hinkle's discerning observations as to the basic cause of neuroses, psychic disturbances and mental pathology need to be erected into pillars of true science. So far from having their causal origin merely in civil and social frustrations of sex yearnings instinctive in infancy, the disturbances are due to frustrations of a far deeper nature, inhibitions that root in profounder depths of the psychic constitution of human life than merely bodily sexual satisfaction or its thwarting. The restraints on sexual expression play their part, naturally; but this cause of inharmony is slight and superficial in comparison with the more interior clash between the god and the animal in man's sphere of consciousness. Mere sexual repressions, though they are active agents in psychoses of lighter gravity, are not the grounds of the more serious maladies of the mind. These are the outgrowth of the thwarting by the lower animal personality and its propensities, of the more vital inner efforts of the god above to adjust the habits and mechanisms of the body to *its* evolutionary aims and trends. He is destined to be the supreme ruler—the King, in the glorious language of symbolic theology—of the natural man in all respects. When this first or natural man has at last been raised in status and his dynamic forces refined and accommodated to the services of their divine transformer, then he receives the evolutionary reward for his faithfulness and obedience in the form of a grand enrichment and enhancement of his own conscious powers. But until that happy stage is reached, and from the start, he is by no means an obedient and willing subject of his liege. As all the scriptures reiterate without end, he is a stiff-necked, a stubborn and a rebellious subordinate. He must be gradually converted. His natural instincts and propensities must be slowly transformed. They must be turned away from the service of rapacity and self-interest over to that of a communal fellowship with the other units of the life order. Organically he is holding the super-mind of the god in a prison, and it is only by converting his gaoler that the god-soul can liberate itself from the trammels of the flesh and assume full command within the sphere of the organic life.

The force of this "conversion" of the lower self "into the likeness of" "the glorious body" of the higher self has likewise never been seen in any adequate degree. The analogy with that great luminary which is itself the mighty symbol of the divine self is the revealing talisman. The manner in which the sun lifts up a lower coarse element such as water furnishes the interpretative hint. The light and heat of the sun can not through sheer mechanical force lift water upward. Sunlight has no arms with which to scoop up the liquid. But it does lift up the water by the agency of its power first to "convert" it from physical density to ethereal fineness and lightness in the form of vapor, in which state its gravity is overcome and convection carries it upward. A force of a "higher" range always has the power to sublimate the substance of a thing of a "lower" nature. That which can not be done with coarse matter in its denser composition can be done after the alchemy of sublimation has been performed upon it. This yields for us a chemical and physical representation of a great segment of the entire meaning of both the theological content of the scriptures and the central core of psychological study and science. The sun can cause water to rise after it has transformed it into a sublimated state. Likewise the divine soul in man can cause the lower animal nature to rise to the status and glory of the exalted human and near-divine after it has transformed it by the continuous impingement upon it of vibrations of finer nature. This is the interior meaning of all religious "conversion" ever talked about in the theologies of the world. The soul that is in man is here on the cosmic mission first to transfigure by sublimation the coarser nature of physical humanhood and then to lift it up to a level of harmonious fellowship with itself.

If a statement direct from the ranks of psychoanalysts themselves were needed to confirm the averment that disturbances arise chiefly from obstructions put in the way of the divine soul by the outer personality, it is to be found in a brief sentence from Dr. Hinkle's book, already cited (p. 435):

"For it is a fact which psycho-analysis reveals definitely and unmistakably that the actual disturbance of the individual today is involved with the problem of the soul."

She says again that the sum of man's psychological striving is his effort to "differentiate himself from *nature*." This is wholly in consonance with the gist of all ancient philosophy. But if it is his divine intent to "differentiate himself from nature," whence comes this direction, this bent, this pull to something beyond nature? From what part or element of his own constitution springs this lift to a higher selfhood? It can come only from a conscious intelligence within him that is already standing above the terrain of the animal part. A thing of a certain nature can not lift itself beyond itself by its own powers. It can be lifted to higher status only by the aid of a power already higher than itself, which reaches down from above, clasps hands with it and raises it up. Since man in his palpable physical selfhood is himself a creature of the natural order, with material body as his ostensible being, it is logically necessary that if he is to be differentiated from nature, to which he belongs by virtue of his body, the differentiation must be engineered by another part of him, not so palpable and ostensible, yet dialectically existent, namely the immortal soul within him. Then, since this work of the spiritual man in elevating carnal man to diviner kingdoms is the chief business that the total man is to accomplish in life in the world, it can be seen that interference with the program of its evolutionary errand will be a matter of central and crucial moment and concern to the whole movement, and will therefore be the cause of most serious disturbance in the smooth working of the internal economy of the life.

Jung says that it is of the greatest importance whether the libido is transferred or inverted. Nature, he writes, has first claim on man; "only long afterwards does the luxury of intellect come." He has adduced the very discerning observation that for the first thirty-five years of life the individual is a child of nature, concerned and absorbed with the acquisition of the things that give him a place of standing in the material world. In the second period of thirty-five years he shifts his interests largely from material matters over to the concerns of the mind and soul. This is oddly enough a minia-

ture copy of the life of the incarnating soul in its total evolution
in the human cycle. It is for roughly the first half of its immersion
in fleshly bodies working to establish its place firmly and stably in
its position of rulership of lower physical forces. During the latter
half of its career in the worlds it bends its efforts more largely and
freely to the growth of its own internal forces of intelligence and
spirituality. Wordsworth writes of the great and passionate interest
of his younger life in the domain of outer nature, and then of the
"years that bring the philosophic mind." The allegorical pictograph
is even carried out vividly in the Gospel drama, in which Jesus, the
type of the divine soul, runs away from his mother (nature) at
the age of twelve, symbolic of completion, and devotes himself
thenceforth to the "things of his Father" (spirit).

Here and everywhere in the analysis there is disclosed the important part played by analogy. Through the employment of this
instrument there is revealed what has so long lain in the darkness
of nescience. Part of the predisposing cause of the Dark Ages of
medieval European history was the loss, along with the refinements
of symbolism, allegory and drama, of the legitimacy of analogy
as a truth-finding methodology. The price civilization has had to
pay for this dereliction of intelligence has been far heavier than
anyone has dreamed. It closed the doors of the mind against the
most pellucid lens of possible insight into profound truth. It thus
aided the forces of darkness and obscurantism in their ghastly work
of bigotry, persecution and foul inhumanity.

Even yet we suffer through lack of it. We have been frightened
away from embracing it by the insistent cry that "analogy proves
nothing." Let the refrain be: Of course it *proves* nothing. It was
never meant to "prove" anything. It does not need to *prove* anything. Its function is not "proof" but something possibly of far
greater importance. What it is qualified to do is to sharpen vision
and quicken the mind to acuter perception. It is able to point man's
insight from the realm of the seen to that of things unseen,—concepts, cosmic processes, laws, principles, categories. Had scientists

used the law of analogy they would have been prepared to find without surprise that the atom, when discovered, would be formed over the pattern of a solar system. If they followed the implications of analogy now, they would know that death does not end the life of an inner principle or seed in human beings, but that, like the acorn or any seed of a garden plant or flower, this life-bearing nucleus will bring itself to a new period of organic existence in a rebirth in a new cycle. Analogy is the one aid to seeing provided for the dull human mind.

The strategic importance for psychoanalytic aims and practice of clarifying the sharp distinction between the two realms of unconsciousness, the sub- and the super-conscious, can not be overvalued. It will give the understanding a closer grip on the apprehension of all ethical values, since it will provide intelligence with the capability of rating psychic motivations in the category of subconscious fixations, mere addictions of habit, or in the higher category of fresh releases of insight and inspiration from the overshadowing god. It is of vital importance to know whether they are the one or the other. It will furnish the basis of a study of social and intellectual *mores* in relation to the pioneer's flash of higher insight that would dictate a change to new and freer standards. It would put in our hands the key to the science of human well-being and happiness. It is the core of all problems in the career of the individual.

Theology has been reduced to the status of an outcast, and verily it is but a corpse of its once radiant significance. Yet its doctrines, as still extant, are the empty forms of the prime truths so badly needed by humanity. The great conflict so variously and vividly dramatized in the scriptures between rebellious man and patient, long-suffering and at times wrathful god, is the open sesame that exposes to sight the complexities of the critical psychic mystery of man's being. The moral struggle within the breast of man is the pivotal hinge of all understanding in psychology. It is grounded on the real presence of the higher element, the god, in the human animal. As said, this inner guest is on the way to become the presiding genius of the organism, which is a microcosm or miniature reduplication of the macrocosmic universe. His reason, intelligence and wisdom, as the King of Righteousness, are to assume governorship over the energies that dwell in the "underworld" of the senses and the feelings, and which, lying below the level of mind, are irrational and elemental. They move on instinct and not on reason. Their range of expression constitutes that great "underworld" so ubiquitously found in all the systematic mythologies of the past, that "nether world" into which every divine hero descends, there to overcome the enemies that hold captive the soul-maiden, the psyche, and lead her as his bride out of the realm of lower darkness, of gloomy night and flitting shades. This is the rough representation of the drama in folk-lore.

In theology, the sun-hero descends into the dark realms of Hades, Hell, Sheol or Amenta, to visit "the spirits in prison" and to bring light "to those that sit in darkness," or to awaken or revive those that lie, like Lazarus, asleep in "death." For this darksome lower region is the realm of the "dead," in which Pluto, Yama, Osiris or Loki rule. The blunder of the scholastics in mislocating this Amenta, Sheol or Hades in mythology and theology as elsewhere than right here in this world of living experience is one of the crudest and costliest mistakes ever perpetrated. It has caused the untold miscarriage of the knowledge that was designed to enlighten humanity along its toilsome path of evolution.

The god-soul migrated to earth and took on a bodily incarnation for the high purpose of forwarding, under conditions most aptly ordained to achieve the result, the growth of its seed potentiality into the likeness of its parent divinity. If the general mind could once gain the ancient philosophical understanding that these human souls of ours are integral fragments of the mind-soul-spirit of God himself, seed units of divine consciousness, and that they are here on their long mission of evolution in the return cycle to the Father's mansions, earthly life would gain immeasurably in poise, equanimity and happiness. This being their errand, and their own lives being internally activated by the pressure of this consciousness by virtue of their sharing a portion of the divine mind itself, their task is to see that this work is as directly and as efficiently carried forward as may best be done. Antique documents indeed disclose that these souls, on leaving their celestial abodes to become, as Paul says, "a colony of heaven" on earth, expressly bound themselves by "broad oaths fast sealed" to descend, occupy the bodies of a race of animal-men and strictly attend to the great evolutionary business of refining their lower natures up to the point of highest human-hood, or even to touch the level of godhood just beyond. The suc-cessful performance of their mission would, as Plato's *Timaeus* sets forth, graduate them into the ranks of the gods, with the crown of immortal life as their guerdon. As has been seen, this aeonial work was to end with the weaving together of "mortal and im-mortal natures" in one new man, the glorious achievement of the atonement. "Ye shall be as gods, knowing good and evil."

Zealously, then, the divine soul incorporated in gross body stands guard, as it more fully awakens, to conserve the best interests of both itself and its animal servant, the body. When the waywardness of the personality, or its ignorance of wise procedures, or its recalci-trancy, block the way of progress along the normal path, or when sheer folly, or sloth or stupidity threaten the success of the enter-prise, the godly soul within must assert its authority or register its protest. This it does in ways of indirection and subtlety, but at any rate in a fashion to make its voice of remonstrance heard by the lower self. Some form of inharmony, some form of psychic disturb-ance, some pathological condition is engendered. This is to impress the outer conscious mind. And as Dr. Hinkle asserts, the trouble lies deeply buried in an internal impasse, which must be dissolved by probing after, discovering and removing the real core of obstruc-tion, the real nub of the psychic problem. Psychoanalysis is acting wisely in using the symptoms of disturbance as vanes of indication and diagnosis of the trouble in its deepest aspects. The soul within, watching the outer man's hit-and-miss efforts, can tolerate only so much aberration and loss of incarnational time and opportunity. It is its pledged duty to see that the external life falls measurably in line with a program that will best further the long-aim effort, or at least not too seriously jeopardize the chances of success. Psychoanalysis, Dr. Hinkle says, provides a technique by means of which the outer consciousness is aided in coming to a recognition of a deeply obscured inward deadlock, and so is helped to remove an obstruction to the development of a "greater self" within the human constitution. Psychoanalysis is built, she says, entirely upon the laying bare, or bringing to the surface, the *unconscious* motives and obstructed purposes, different from and independent of those known consciously. This proves to be exactly true. The majority of people remain ignorant of the genesis of the psychic disorders within themselves, and there was no science of diagnosis and discovery of the sources of disturbance until psychoanalysis came forward to reveal that they were engendered by the innermost true being of the individual himself, lying out of sight in the depths of the self and playing the role of the "silent watcher" and the guardian daemon. We must become "introvert" enough to probe deeply within the most obscure and hidden motivations of conduct and feeling. How apt, then, is what Dr. Hinkle says on this point! :

"For the introvert's real values lie in the unconscious, in the depths, and must be sought there and not in the world of sense."

This is to say that the supremely important, crucial and decisive motivations that seize upon and direct the self to special exertions at critical junctures in the life spring not from the vagrant and fickle desires of the personality on the surface, but rather from what Maeterlinck called the *"inconscient superieur"* and the "prospective potency" of the unconscious.

It is indeed unfulfilled need and unsatisfied yearnings deeply subterranean in the mortal constitution that give rise to neuroses, as Dr. Hinkle so convincingly states. She rightly sees that the needs and yearnings arise from remoter sources within the psyche than the outer mind's sphere of consciousness. There must therefore be postulated within man's constitution the presence of a mind or self whose intelligence reaches beyond that of the brain. There must be predicated a knower within the personality who projects his message and his wishes outward upon the attention of the conscious mind. He may do this by symbolic hints, or by precipitating a condition of unbalance and inharmony within the psychic functioning of the whole person. The task or function of that more central power resident "below the threshold" is to see that the outer personality maintains a fairly close rapport, in motive, exertion and aim, with its own superior purposes. If this is tolerably well accomplished, there is little need for overt communication between the submerged monitor and the day consciousness. The hidden god, called by the Egyptians Amen, "the god in hiding," rests content with the progress made in the outer sphere of action. But if wreckage is threatened or the outer faculties remain too long unawakened, the occasion demands his interference, and protest must be made by way of a message in symbolic language or by unhappiness generated to provoke inquiry, or new courses of action and new exertions.

Dr. Hinkle says that the need of the organism is to win a higher *integration* of its component elements. Seen from the ancient mount of knowledge of man's composite nature, the phrase serves well enough to shape out the truth of the case. Where the aim is, as in man, to "weave together mortal and immortal natures," the successful outcome partakes of the character of an integration. The practical thing accomplished is the harmonious accommodation, under the laws of a harmony of relations little different from those that govern the symphonization of musical notes through mathematically attuned vibrations, of the energies of the two natures, until their combined expression effects a concord instead of a discord. If this more lovely resultant is not achieved, there is discord within the psyche and pathological instability or unbalance in the outer person.

As long, this discerning psychoanalyst says, as the

"*higher* psychological functions of humanity remain bound in a crude, instinctive form, there will be neurotic problems to face, for the whole effort of the human being is to transcend the instinctive animal."

Here is the long unrecognized, unesteemed, ancient philosophy and theology of wise seers of antiquity coming forth to the light of modern perception after centuries of oblivion. But it can be released from the jargon of technical psychoanalytic phrasing and expressed in the form of theological dialectic. As long as the god is too crudely kept in "durance vile," in bondage under the nescience, the lethargy, the brutish grossness of the purely animal nature surging up from below, it will become restive and eventually throw the organism into discordant states by way of remonstrance. Perhaps also it might be expressed as viewed from the other side, that the coarse behavior of the sensuous animal nature of the lower man, overriding and suppressing or blocking the gentler small voice of the god, throws the relationship between the two components into a painful tension of unbalance, creating a neurosis. It is important to have Dr. Hinkle's own phrasing of this elaboration. She says in the same passage (p. 328):

"The many aberrations and neurotic weaknesses, deviation from the abstract called normal, all reveal in their very lack of fixed and rigid forms, possibilities of development and transfigurations from the un-self-conscious animal man to that highly conscious self-creative man."

This is nothing short of splendid. As disease is a manifestation of the forces of the organism struggling to regain a balance called normal health, so neurotic disturbances are upheavals of internal or submerged native forces of spirit striving to establish a harmony or balance termed normal mental sanity.

There is warrant for subjecting this reference to "the abstraction called normal" to a moment's closer scrutiny. Normality is by no means a mere abstraction, though of course it is abstractly discerned. The mental abstraction is the perception of a very real thing. It comes back again to the symbol of the "horizon" of Egyptian literature and the "cleft of the rock" in Hebrew typology, as well as the "rib" of Adam, generic man. (For the "rib" was properly a midrib, a line of cleavage run down the middle of the unified being of God, dividing it apart into its twoness of spirit and matter, male and female.) All life struggles to maintain its organic existence on a line or at a point of exact equilibration between the forces of spirit and matter. It ever stands and builds its bodies, its vehicles, precisely at the point of neutralization between centripetal and centrifugal energies, as witness all the stars in their orbits and the electrons in their path and position around the central proton. The Egyptians magnificently called the earth, on which such stabilization is achieved, "the pool of equipoise and propitiation," or balance and final atonement. The ancient astrology expressed the same idea by means of the sign of Libra, the balance. All life is eternally, while in manifestation, being tried in the balance. It can, so to say, only stand still and be localized as an existent thing when it is held firmly in the immovable status between the two equally balanced opposite poles or pulls. It stands at the neutral point of the tension. Says Emerson: "Man stands at the point midway betwixt the inner spirit and the outer matter." Only when the two energies of spirit and matter are equilibrated in one organism can the stable permanency be gained which is requisite for the eventual copulation of their opposing powers, to give birth to their "sons," the created progeny. The Christos could not be brought to birth out of the body of virgin matter (*Maria*) until that was held in *stable* relation to the power of the Holy Spirit from above. So the allegory represented the Christ as being born in a "stable." And once again a frightfully mangled allegory of supernal ancient wisdom is redeemed from modern caricature of its original majestic beauty.

So the human mind, in deepest reflection, has rightly conceived a condition of mean balance between two extremes in every manifestation of life and activity. It is Plato's splendid doctrine of the "golden mean." Life expression can be normal only when it is poised at this point of equilibration between too much and too little. Plato convincingly fixed the character of each virtue by placing it, when rightly defined, at the exact point of balance between the excess and the deficiency of the quality in question. Courage was the precise balance between foolhardy, reckless daring and rank cowardice. This must be determined in the finale by requisite knowledge of how much is too much or how little is too little. This judgment, properly exercised, yields final truth, inasmuch as these determinations are definitely those that must be made by all constantly. The "normal" in all forms of human conduct is the most consistently successful result of the best effort to establish those lines and points of precise balance between right and wrong, good and evil, true and false, which according to Plato and Socrates, are always resolvable to a merely quantitative measure of too much or too little. Man is indeed being weighed in the scales of the balance and, in Egypt's figurism, bathing in the "pool of equipoise."

CHAPTER IX

THE TWO MOTHERS OF THE CHRIST

ANOTHER most vital determination reached by psychoanalysis and well stated by Dr. Hinkle is that the crux of the psychic conflict in the human breast is the effort of something deeper in the psyche than the animal feeling "to transcend the instinctive animal." Again modern discovery has merely caught up with ancient proficiency. St. Paul and Plato, Hermes and Orpheus, the philosophers and the Illuminati, had long ago set down the terms of this problem. They all delineated the moral effort of mankind under the terms of the central situation, which set before the second Adam, the son of the woman, the product of nature's second birthing, the aeonial task of combating, overcoming, transforming and finally embracing in union the first Adam, natural man, of the earth, earthy, carnal, sensual animal man. First comes that which is natural, says St. Paul, then that which is spiritual. The natural is first on the visible scene of creation, since the second or spiritual can supervene from out the world of pure conscious potentiality into the world of actual conscious existence only through the instrumentalities provided by the preceding physical development. The body must be here before the royal guest from above can enter as its tenant and use its agencies. Or, perhaps more scientifically stated, the body must be here before the soul that is animating its growth can find the proper channel for its expression.

The victory of the soul is won, then, by its transcending the instinctive animal. "Instinct" is the form which activity takes in the animal half of man under the impulsion of the *automatism* of the subconscious. The animal lives under the dominion of the subconscious, since he is not yet man, and man, from the Sanskrit *man* "to think," is the thinker. The animal is not a thinker, except potentially and rudimentarily. The body (animal man) is run by instinct, unreasoned automatism. All the functions are governed by an automatic memory, which does not know how to deviate, or can not originate deviation. All its conscious energies or motivations lie below the level of reasoning mind.

The whole moral struggle in man is envisaged as the warfare between the two natures, the imprisoned potentiality of soul wrestling against the powers of flesh and blood to acquire dominion over them, to govern them according to reason and to tame their fierce wild energies into the service of divine law. To transmute their rapacity of selfish desire into the offices of the law of love, to swing their jostling forces into a fellowship of the elements, to make the organism a cosmos under law instead of a chaos of unintelligent blind powers, is the cyclic assignment of the second Adam, the Christ. Psychoanalysis has at last probed to the root of man's happiness and the stability—or instability—of his psychic self in his great evolutionary labor. And in doing so it finds itself standing side by side with the lost purport of the revered scriptures of the race. Men of truly divine stature gave this wisdom to the race in its childhood. They sought to embody it in the unforgettable forms of universal mnemonics. The only unforgettable mnemonics are the forms and phenomena of nature. The alphabet of the universal language of truth is composed of the symbols drawn from nature. The great Bibles are works written in the language of symbols, with allegory, fable, parable, myth, drama, number graph and astrograph the primary elaborations. The tree, the leaf, the seed, the root, the branch, the stump, the stream, the star, the sun and moon, earth, water, air, fire, aether, the cross, the circle, square, triangle, the arch, the ark, the flood, the fish, beetle, cow, cat, dragon-fly, thunder, lightning, the rainbow and a host of other forms and phenomena were the characters, the expressive words, of that forgotten language.

Pause should be made to look at just two of these, water and the fish. An enlightenment that is almost stunning in the depth of its revelation of hitherto undiscovered meaning behind such a symbology is in store for the investigating mind. The approach is through a statement in the mythicism of archaic literature that the Sun-god, the Christos-Messiah, specifically in Egypt Iusa or Horus, son of Osiris, *had two mothers,* of various names. The hint was obscure and baffling until it was recalled that the mother of life is ever the negative essence, matter (Latin, *mater*). It was but a further step then to the realization that matter—as announced to us in the first chapter of *Genesis*—is twofold in form or organization. There is the firmament above and the firmament below. There are the waters above and the waters below. (Water has already been disclosed to be the prime symbol of matter.) As water can subsist in two distinct forms, invisible vapor and visible substance as liquid or ice, so matter has evolved in two separate and distinct states. It is first, in the inchoate state, purely essence, not substance; only the potentiality of substance. It is inorganic, unatomic, invisible, the "great sea" of material potentiality, *mare,* Mary. In this state it is "the first mother," who generates in turn her daughter, organic, atomic, structuralized and visible substance, the second mother. For she becomes impregnated with the seed of spirit-mind and is destined to give birth to the Christos in man's developed body. There is first, then, the inorganic or *virgin* mother, unwedded to spirit, and the organic or wedded mother, who finally produces the godson. Born originally "of a virgin" any divine creation or "son of God" must be.

In a flash it was seen that as water typified the general all-pervading first virgin essence of matter, inorganic, the fish, as its first and universal creation of an organic structural constitution, would stand as the type of the second mother, or substantial matter. The Christ character in the allegorical depiction, then, would be the "son of the fish," or of the "fish-mother," not of the "water-mother." Imagine, then, the pertinence of the discovery that many of the goddess mothers of Sun-gods or Messiahs were actually styled "the fish-mother" of the Son of God! Atergatis and Semiramis were particularly so named. Jonah allegorism was immediately at hand to harmonize with the interpretation, as fabling the great fish that ingested, then delivered at his proper destination, the Christos. Unquestionably "Jonah" is a variant of the divine name, Jesus, which is found in some twenty-five or more forms in the Old Testament. One of these is "Joshua," as to which there is not the slightest possibility of dispute as to its identity with "Jesus." And now comes an unexpected and astonishing further corroboration. Joshua is "son of Nun," and Nun is the name of the Hebrew letter "N" and means, of all things,—"fish." Joshua (Jesus), son of the fish, or fish-mother. And the Greek world in the first three centuries of Christianity denominated the Christian Jesus as *Ichthys* (*Ichthus*), the Greek word for "fish." Augustine and Tertullian both expressly name Jesus as the great fish, and his followers as the "little fishes," (Latin, *pisciculi*). Nor is this all—or the most significant detail.

The astrologizing early mythicists allocated the birthplace of the first or natural man in the sign of Virgo, the Virgin (matter), and placed the birth of the second or spiritual man, "the man Christ," in the sign directly, or six months, opposite in the zodiac, Pisces, a water sign. The New Testament allegory uses bread and fish as the divine food that the Christ brings wherewith to feed mortal man in order to immortalize him, in the "miracle" of the feeding of the five thousand. The sign Pisces is already by name the house of the fishes, but it was also termed, by association with the opposite sign Virgo, in which the Virgin carries in her hand the great star Spica, "the head of wheat" from which the divine bread was to be made, the house of bread. And now comes the last tremendous revelation of the allegorical and non-historical character of Biblical lore. "House of bread" in Hebrew is, as any scholar knows, *Bethlehem!* There was no other place for the Christos to be born than in "Bethlehem," the zodiacal "house of bread" and of fish. And, to round out the thrilling denouement, the first chapter of *Luke* records Jesus' birth as occurring just six months after that of John the Baptist, who expressly announces himself as playing the part of the first or natural man, who must come first to "prepare the way of the Lord," the spiritual Christ. Beyond any possibility of quibble these six months in *Luke's* narrative must be interpreted as the half year on the zodiacal chart and as understandable only thus, and in no sense historically. This is a momentous disclosure of the presence of ancient astrological typism in the very heart of the Christian Gospels.

But the crown of all this revelation is still to come. One finds all these allegorical transactions already extant for thousands of years in the literature of old Egypt, and there represented as taking place in Anu, most astonishingly described in the *Book of the Dead* as being *"the place of multiplying bread."* Could anything be more thrilling in the whole field of Comparative Religion study? Jesus multiplied bread and so did Horus, his Egyptian prototype. Horus was earlier Iusa (Jesus). Horus multiplied bread at Anu. An ancient Greek or Egyptian "U" becomes "Y" when transferred to English. And so these divine transactions occurred at the Egyptian *Any,* the house of bread (and of fish, no doubt), and when the Hebrew word for "house," *beth,* is added, the result is the Gospel *Beth-any!* As the spiritual man goes down into matter in his incarnation, in the legendary and allegorical conflict between the "two brothers," the spiritual and the physical men, it is the spiritual that decreases and the physical that increases. When the nadir of descent is reached (and "Sinai" means "point of turning and returning"), and the reascent is begun, the reverse is true. It is then the first or natural man who diminishes, while the buried spiritual genius germinates and increases. And John the Baptist says: "I must decrease, and he must increase."

Likewise it was at Bethany that "Lazarus" was raised from the dead by the Gospel Son of God. As, by reincarnation, a man is re-born and resurrected to new life from the "dead" state of inertia under the lethal dominance of the instincts of the flesh and this is accomplished by the new projection of himself into body as his own son, so it is always the divine son who in all the allegories raises his father from the dead. Could anything be more staggering, then, than the discovery that "Lazarus" is an old Egyptian derivative, which with the prefixing of the Hebrew word *"El"* for "God," and the Latin masculine terminal *-us* suffixed to *Asar,* the original form of the name of Osiris, gives finally El-Asar-us, or Lazarus! So the Christ of Egypt raised from the dead his father Asar, or Osir-is. And this took place at Anu, or (Beth)any.

The identity is even carried out to the point that there are in both allegories the two women present, whose names reach similarity in the Gospel Mary and the Egyptian Meri.

Converting all this, which flows forth from the consideration of just two of the great letters of the ancient symbolic alphabet, over into its reference to psychoanalysis, it is clearly enough seen to point to the "raising" or increasing of the divine element, the unconscious in human life, from its "dead" condition in its burial or immersing in the flesh of body. The carnal nature that was strong at the beginning of the human cycle, while the spirit was overlaid and rendered "sub"-active, must now decrease, while the unconscious higher self, the savior and redeemer of its brother, must increase. The development requires the growing domination of the lower by the higher. If the lower is recalcitrant and blocks the "normal" process of the growth, there is disturbance within the household of the psyche. Impasses, stubborn obsessions, unrelenting strength of carnal desire, must be broken and dissipated, to let the soul go marching on. It is clear as can well be that the diagnosis of psychotic unbalance and instability must be charted as the complication resulting from the body's, and even the mind's, interference with the ongoing of the soul. Neurotic man is out of harmony with his own soul, is blocking the progress of the "something beyond himself" within him toward its divinely ordained goal. His condition indeed calls for reintegration. The ancients unreservedly declared that this reorientation was possible only through philosophy, which was then honored with the designation of "divine," as the philosophy that concerned itself fundamentally with the existence, functions and welfare of the divine element in the human constitution, its descent into the flesh and its redemption therefrom.

Life, for the purposes of its evolution having projected its conscious units into immersion in the watery condition of physical bodies—whence the sea as the symbol of life in flesh, and the "Red" Sea a reference to the blood—apparently must use the outer physical as its ultimate means for urging the necessity of corrections or readjustments within the sphere of its corporeal domain. That is to say, that when there is a deadlock in the psychic field, when the mind or the elementary instincts become set in rigid postures that are out of accord with the interests of true progress, the spirit within must break through or break down the imprisoning fetters by means of some irruption or upheaval in the physical or mental organism. The inharmony established by the wrong mental or physical habit will itself sooner or later work its disruptive effects upon the outer vehicle, and thus call attention to and enforce the needed adjustment. It is not at all out of line with legitimate evolutionary economy to suppose that directive life would use the physical instrument to correct the erring mental. It is the only available resort even among humans to attempt to force a change of stubborn mental attitudes by an assault on the body. There are junctures and situations in which nothing will change dogged fixations of mind except an attack upon the body. The mind can only be reached and influenced through pain or damage to the body. If obdurate opinion or determination can not be changed by mental appeal, the only resort life has is to strike at it through the physical. This alone may in such case bring the mind around to reason. Life does use this method. And it can readily be seen that this is the ultimate reason for wars. When all mental approach to difficult problems proves unavailing, physical force is the only recourse. It will be so until the race learns to be governed by its intellect and not by its desires.

Psychic instability, nerve collapse, bodily illness are then the out-

ward symbols of the soul's discontent with the lack of true growth
that should come through the concordance of the outer bodily
regime of life with the far-projected cosmic interests of the soul.
They should not be treated as abnormalities to be immediately
eradicated. It is a fine observation of Chandler Bennitt in his valuable work on psychoanalysis, *The Real Use of the Unconscious,* that
the presence of a fear complex should not be treated as a mere detri-
mental symptom to be swept away as quickly as possible or exor-
cized by mental manipulation, without regard to what it reveals.
Fear should not be abolished until its prognostic message indicating
what is at fault has been rightly interpreted. It is a sign and index
of maladjustment. The important thing is to discover the defect
and mend it, not to get rid of the symptom. Only by such a right
interpretation can it be abolished effectually.

These psychoanalytic considerations may not appear to be directly
connected with the problem of religion. Yet it can be asserted very
strongly that the whole problem of religion is resolvable into the
terms of this philosophical, theological and psychological background. For the latter stand in immediate correlation with the focal
point of all religion, which is the relation of man, or of a man, to
his God. Over this relation a thousand books penned by Christian
theologians and scholars have expended the most strenuous energies
of lucubrated dialectic in support of a thesis, believed to be the
particular gift or pronouncement of the Christian faith, that made
man's acceptance of and surrender to a Supreme Deity allocated
vaguely in cosmic heavens or seated somewhere "behind" all things,
the pivotal element in his soul's salvation. It is safe to say that this
conception of the location, nature and range of the Deity to which
man stood in this fateful relation has been the direct cause of more
mental dereliction and psychic unbalance in the history of the West
for sixteen centuries than any other agency. Misconception and unsound philosophy have presented their bill of costs to a civilization
largely motivated on their predications that is staggering in its total
of wrecked mentality, distracted individual life, eccentricity of be-

havior and wide human wretchedness unequaled in the records of mankind. That a civilization holding sway over hundreds of millions of persons for some sixteen hundred years should have entirely misdirected the focus of the psychic effort of its myriad following upon the wrong location of its guiding Deity, both surpasses belief and defies the adequate telling. In the vast aggregate of its wastage of human devotion, this must hold the palm for the most colossal miscarriage of all history. Always the mind was directed toward a God who was placed at the summit of the creation, supreme over all and of inconceivable cosmic majesty and power. He was pictured and described as the One great God of the universe. (Although it was usually contrived at the same time that he should be represented as a Person standing in close and intimate relation with each and every individual human, shrunken almost to the character and proportions of a benevolent grandfather, with his one arm around one's neck.) The God with whom man was called upon in all religion to align his life properly was no God within reach of earth, but one governing the illimitable reaches of cosmos and resident somewhere in inconceivable form and might and majesty. He was a God whose beneficent attentions and ministrations poured upon or into the human from outside, from above. It was almost blasphemy to circumscribe the human conception of him to such form as could be thought to be an integral and interior portion of the human himself. That he could be resident within the boundaries of man's own nature and operative from within outward was an idea that never came to maturity in the religious mind, albeit it did find some expression in poetry. Perennially dominant in popular thought was the notion that religion was the play of forces involved in the relationship between the mortal person and his God whose residence was somewhere at the summit of cosmic creation. Never was religion conceived to be the relation between man shallow and man profound.

Lest it be charged that this characterization of prevalent and traditional religion is a misstatement of the case, it is desirable to cite a few out of numberless passages to support the description. Here is Dr. Hopper (*The Crisis of Faith,* p. 226) saying, in reference to a statement quoted from Emil Brunner anent man's being made in God's image, that man manifests

"an existence which points back or refers to something else. . . . Man's meaning and his intrinsic worth do not reside in himself, but in the One who stands 'over against him,' in Christ, the Primal Image, in the Word of God."

Here the Deity is not removed to cosmic distances but is still kept out of the constitution of man himself, being allocated to the life of One character in history. It is expressly declared that the power activating man's salvation does not reside within himself. It is exterior. Again Dr. Hopper cites Emil Brunner in the statement that God wills to save us not by "domestic," that is, our own home or internal, power or genius, but by extraneous righteousness and wisdom, which is not, says Brunner, a power welling up from within us, not that which originates on our earth, but that which came down from heaven. Therefore, he goes on, it is our plain task to look to a righteousness quite outside ourselves and foreign to our nature. To this end it is first of all necessary in the life of true religion that "domestic righteousness" should be uprooted and external influx invited by an attitude of surrender and prayer for help from God. God indeed stands so far remote from us that if we are ever to gain his attention to our groveling appeals for mercy, it must be through (the historical) Jesus, our intercessor with the otherwise inaccessible God.

Then we have Matthew Arnold's famous phrase defining God: "a power not ourselves that makes for righteousness." And here is Dr. Hopper again saying that the true center of the self is not in itself, but lies in God. And he defines true self-knowledge as the knowledge that not in ourselves is truth to be found, but outside the self, in God. We are familiar of course with the prayer-book's weekly confessional that "in us there is no soundness nor health."

In short, the power that man is to know, as his highest culmination of certitude touching his eternal destiny, is that knowledge unto salvation is not within himself, not even as an attainment, but must be sought, solicited, entreated and beguiled unto him from divine sources outside himself, who may be persuaded to vouchsafe it to him finally irrespective of his own merits or deserts. All man's self-righteousness, even his whole offering of himself in service to Deity, is profitless; it is as "filthy rags." Man can be redeemed from his lost estate only by the free oblation of God's, or his Son's, grace in his behalf. The outcome is surrender of man to faith in the Infinite God and throwing himself on God's mercy. It is stated that man's only hope of redemption lies in and through his relation to God, who is most positively removed outside the pale of man's own constitution. A thousand citations might be adduced to the same effect.

It is invidious, but necessary, to declare that all these heaped-up asseverations as to man's dependence upon a deific power exterior to himself could not have been written but for the fatal miscarriage of the original Greek philosophic content of early Christianity. It can likewise be asserted that one breath of restored philosophic wisdom sweeps them all forever out upon the ashheap of obsolete rubbish. It is oddly true that, when rightly understood, every one of the assertions under criticism is a thing of profound truth, yet made disastrously, tragically false by a final distortion of its meaning by the wrong allocation of the abiding place of Deity for man. It is of course sublimely true that the pinnacle of man's self-knowledge is the understanding that his true saving selfhood lies in his relation to God. But calamity beyond estimate at once rushed in when ignorance swept away the knowledge that the god with whom he can alone have fellowship had been placed in immediate conjunction with his own life, embodied indeed in his own constitution. What God hath joined together let no man put asunder. But an ignorant and faithless theology did tear asunder what God and life had joined together, and centuries of theological effort have been turned into a mocking caricature of truth and sanity as a dire result. The upshot has been that an ecclesiastical power for centuries dominant over the lives and minds of western humanity has belabored its millions of deluded followers with the necessity of producing in themselves a veritable psychological self-castration. It has persuaded, indeed hypnotized them with the conviction that life had laid heavily upon them the evolutionary charge of saving themselves (from horrendous eternal fate) by means of a psychological operation *the tools and instruments of which were not all within the scope of their own endowment.* It envisaged for them their redemption from the direst of cosmic calamities through their consummating a relation with a power which was in no way amenable to their own initiative or control. It reduced them to the position of helpless, hopeless, groveling cravens. And it turned their direction of effort away from, instead of focusing it immediately upon, the power alleged to be their savior. Human culture at one stroke plunged into futility and rushed toward certain defeat the moment this twist in human understanding had been made. It seems quite past belief that it could not be seen that the thousands of books and millions of sermons dealing with the problem of man's relation to God would have had the entire crux and dilemma of their difficulty immediately resolved in clear understanding by the simple philosophical item that the God with whom man sustained such momentous relation was all the while an integral part and portion of man's own composition. So that when the problem by its accepted terms seemed to set man over against an outside power called God, the difficulty in this across-the-gulf relation could at once be clarified by the knowledge that the true situation did not set man against an external power, but only set one element of his own nature over against another equally his own. And astuter grasp of the whole truth of the matter would have added the happier knowledge that even the represented antagonism between the two elements within himself was only a dramatic mask covering the real fact of the actual mutuality and entire beneficence of the relation. The placing of God, as the power with whom man was to effect a relation of reconciliation and atonement, *outside* the human breast and brain has been the supreme cultural catastrophe of all history.

Infinite power and mind reside in the center of cosmos, surely. And this mighty infinitude of power and intelligence, in its ordering of cosmos, is perpetually affecting the life of little man. All things flow from it, and it does impinge upon the world of mankind with the touch of its myriad forces. But with that Infinitude, in Itself, and as a Whole, man has no relation, none, certainly, that can be initiated by action from his end. It is the sheerest imbecility to predicate the subsistence of such a relation between minor man and the cosmic God. God *is* present, as Emerson affirms, in all his parts in every moss and cobweb. He is present in man and in all about him. But not with God as a Whole and only with that unit fragment of God's mind and soul which has been sown as a seed in the life and being of each mortal, does man stand in close and intimate relation. Only with the infant deity within him can man have communion. If he can not recognize, cultivate and lay hold of this much of Deity transcending his own lower animal nature, all his chattering of rising to share the life of cosmic Godhood is tragic insanity. And the presumption that such a communion was possible has bred the most frightful insanity upon the earth.

CHAPTER X

IMMANUEL'S LAMP

THE sane approach to true understanding is through the realization that God has implanted in each mortal man a seed fragment of his own life. He has done his utmost to put himself within the inmost self of every creature. This he can do and has done by implanting the seed potentiality of his being in each one. More than this he could hardly do. He brake his own total body into fragments and gave one of them to each of us. This he did as the one sure way of dowering us with the capacity and capability of becoming his immortal sons. He has made himself forever accessible to us by this impartation of sonship, likeness of nature, adoption by him and final union with his own being. Closer than this he could not place us or bring us. Better than standing outside of us and listening to our beseeching, he placed an integral unit *of himself* immediately within us, so that we could never be apart from him, never detached from him.

How utterly fatuous, then, and what age-long heinous folly to instruct millions to overlook the deity immediately resident within their own native constitution, and direct piteous pleas up to heaven to draw God's eyes upon them! The whole exertion of human devotion poured upward to God and the human striving to reach God have been converted into fantastic fatuity by the ceaseless prodding of the millions at the hands of ignorant priestcraft to scorn the divinity within the human and to direct that human to look upward and outward in search of the supreme and absolute God.

The return to sanity and the rectification of all inept and withering stupidity in this connection must come through the recognition, regained from ancient knowledge, that while every assertion as to

124

the dependence of man upon God is true, vitiation of the meaning must be obviated and thrilling release of power restored, through the knowledge that the relation between the two elements is a transaction that takes place wholly in the interior of man's own life. It transpires within the arena of man's own consciousness, not being a contact between the man as a whole and another power in no way appertaining to his scope of being. Man must come again to the possession of the self-knowledge which assures him that both the human and the divine elements are within his own range of cultivation. True it must be for him that he can do nothing without the help of the divine power. The exertions of his merely human self *are* in a very real sense futile, without the saving grace of the god. In a poetic sense they are "as filthy rags." But both the natural man and the spiritual man are ingredients of *himself!* The deity that is at hand to save him *is* "domestic." It is not extraneous. That it is has been the fatal falsehood and sad miscarriage of Christian doctrinism. It has been no less than devastating, calamitous.

Psychoanalysis, arm in arm with ancient philosophy, comes forward now to correct the falsehood and place man's redeemer once again within the close reach of the mortal himself. It comes to make God directly accessible to man again. And it shows how man may reach him without the abject and stultifying "surrender" of his humanhood, as the price of buying "grace" from on high. How far afield from truth and sanity must be that religion which preaches that God would be at pains through an evolutionary effort covering millions of years with billions of his creatures to build up such an agency of ongoing as the human consciousness and its human powers, and then demand that for further advance at the very time when that consciousness and those powers are gaining strength they should be surrendered back to him or thrown away as useless! If, however, it is made clear that in the turn of the cycle of growth, in the changing relation between the two elements of himself, evolution demands that the human side of him be subordinated to a place of subserviency to the divine part of him, then understanding can prevail and sanity and intelligence can direct the movement. The theology of "surrender" can then be held in true balance and not felt as a tearing of the self apart. It will indeed be seen in its true light as a more stable integration of the self.

The theological writers have used the word "man" or its pronoun "he" without regard to Paul's high-pitched shout at us: "Know ye not your own selves, how that Jesus Christ is within you?" Likewise they have ignored many other scriptural statements that tacitly or avowedly scream the same mighty truth at us. Always the insistent exhortation delivered by priestcraft to countless laity was and is that man should obliterate his humanity *in its entirety*, that he should repudiate the whole of his nature, both his meanest and his own best, and, rejecting himself as a lost creature, turn completely away from himself and toward God. And this God was unfailingly pointed to as lying outside of, above, beyond him in infinite transcendence. Even when writers speak of the necessity of man's self-transcendence, they merely imply the transcending of himself as a whole through the agency of God's influences exerted upon him from outside, and not initiated (unless by frantic plea) by man himself. They never mean that man himself should by his own exertions transcend himself, or that higher man should transcend lower man, all within the area of his own capabilities. It is even asserted that God's agencies on man's behalf begin where man's resources end. Even with Plato's categorical assurance in the *Timaeus* (which was for centuries until the coming of Aristotle's works the main light of Christian scholastic exegesis and theology) that God had implanted in each human the seeds of his own imperishable divinity and indeed given his instructions to those conscious units of his own being ere they were dispatched to earth to be the souls in mortal bodies, Christian understanding never clearly grasped the implications of this anthropological datum so as to spread the absolutely crucial intelligence that it was only the mortal part of the dual creature, man, which was to be put off in proportion as the immortal part was engrafted upon the stem of life.

It is a sad comment necessarily made on Christian theological ineptitude that while uttering the very words of the sublimest truth, it still totally missed the ultimate and vital truth of the language. Never in all history has the shell of the truth been preserved and the kernel so completely lost as in Christian doctrinism! Here is Augustine, filled with the sturdy wisdom which he had gained in Manichaeism and while sitting at the feet of Plotinus, writing the lofty truth (*De Civ. Dei,* XIV, iv):

"From the soul and from the body, which are the parts of a man, we arrive at the totality which is man: accordingly, the life of the soul is not one thing, and that of the body another: but both are one and the same, i.e., the life of man as man."

With the reservation that of course Augustine does not mean to wipe out all difference in nature, function and attributes between soul and body in his assertion of their identity, here is a Christian statement of the grand truth.

Let us put after it, for comparison, the passage written in reference to Augustine's statement, from the pen of a modern writer making an unusually strong apologetic for the Christian system. It is from Dr. Hopper's *The Crisis of Faith,* p. 224:

"This definition regards man as a unit, as a person, as a complex whole—of body, soul and spirit. It is constant in the Christian view of man. But it is formal and structural, and its significance does not acquire its full import until this unit, man, is given a positive orientation towards God, the world and his fellowman such as we find in the Biblical view of man as an image of God."

Here is truth, as far as words go, but still the total antithesis of truth in ultimate mental rendering of the meaning. To be sure, the significant import of the threefold constitution of man does not come to view until the proper "orientation" of the elements toward each other is effected. This is considered by the writer of the passage a point of absolutely vital and final determination. Yet it adds

not a whit to what is already implicit and even naïvely seen in the
sheer statement of the tripartite composition. If man has three parts
the simplest intellection must assume that the interrelation of the
three is the central thing to be known about them. This is almost
childish in its rudimentary character. But, missing this naïve discernment, the writer goes on to display his failure of comprehension of the whole grand import of it all by asserting that the relationship between the three component elements in man comes to
no significance of value until another relationship, introduced abstractly from outside and superimposed upon the already total
nature of threefold man, is postulated as the central fact of ultimate
and saving import! This is to charge that the equipment which
life has evolved in man and put into his hands for achieving his
evolution is not adequate for the purpose. Life equips man with
the means and instrumentalities for his progress towards life's designed ends and confronts him with the necessity of forging ahead,
with dire punishment the consequence of his failure. Life holds
man responsible for failure in the use of the equipment provided.
Yet, declares the voice of Christian theological lucubration, man's
most sincere and successful endeavor, even his complete fulfillment
of his effort with the tools provided, is failure and defeat. His entire
discharge of the evolutionary task set before him is still nothing
either to his credit or to his victory. He is a miserable beggar still,
and if not rescued, without the least suggestion of his merit or
demerit, he is lost. To such unconscionable miscarriage of sense
and logic is Christian theologism driven by its failure to localize
deity within the pale of man's equipment.

This is not to deny for a moment that there does subsist a relation
between threefold man as a unit of being and the Power manifesting outside his life in the world about him. Every conscious unit
of life or being bears a relation to all other units and to the body,
mind, soul or spirit of the Whole. And *this* relationship is not
"domestic," but is "extraneous," as Emil Brunner claimed. But man
has no known means of exchanging ideas or maintaining psychic,

that is, mental or spiritual, communication, as between one consciousness and another, with the God-mind that is the central creative power behind the whole cosmos, regarded as external to himself and treated as a unit consciousness. This supreme mind-power is indeed "described" by every great philosopher in world thought as the Unknowable. It is the Infinite. So utterly inaccessible is it to man's puny mentation that even his attempt to conceive of it is pronounced futile. How infinitely more futile his effort to communicate with it, as an organic personalized intelligence, on the basis of any ability to speak to it or to apprehend its language or thought! That man can "talk with God" in any such sense, or that *this* God personalized himself to "talk" to Moses (regarded as *a* man, and not man generic or collective) of old, in any sense conceivable to the human mind, is quite a monstrous absurdity. Sane human thinking has never accepted it. Rightful conception of what Biblical allegory *means* is made possible only when ancient philosophical constructions are apprehended and in their light it is truly seen that the god (or seed projection of God) with whom man *can* communicate is that unit fragment of the divine mind or consciousness which has been placed within the constitution of the individual man in its universal distribution among all humans. God placed this unit germ of himself immediately within the nature of man, for the very purpose that his own total consciousness need *not* pay attention to the infinite myriad needs of the countless creature lives. The idea that—as expressed in Christian literature throughout the centuries in numberless instances—an individual human can engage the whole attention of *God* on his cosmic throne, considered as the grand unit Total of organic consciousness, is surely the "all-time low" in mental imbecility. There are no words fitly to characterize its folly and doltishness. It is the supreme "dunciad" of history.

Nevertheless it is still sublimely true that God has provided a way by which a portion of his consciousness is in attendance upon the immediate needs of every creature. Only it must be conceived and understood with philosophical rationality and not simpleton folly. It must be understood in the way in which it is true and not in the supposititious method of its impossibility. God is an ever-present associate and help in trouble for every one of his creatures, by virtue of the fact that he has already taken the measure of placing a unit portion of himself, with the whole of his being potentially latent in it, within the very organism of the creature. He has sent his "sons" forth to carry out his work in creation. They are of his identic nature, one with him, and are in him as he is in them. They are consubstantial with him. Sonship is theirs through the sheer fact of their being seed emanations or generations from his own body. They are indeed his own life, projected out from unity into multiplicity. As the Greeks so clearly expressed it, God *distributes* his divine life among all his creatures, since a creature is such only because a unit of divine life has generated him.

The ancient sages, knowing this, held it to be blasphemy against God (or the god) for man to "worship" *any* power outside himself. Christianity has wrecked this magnificent perspective and has stultified an enormous percentage of the sincerest effort of the Occident for sixteen hundred years, by directing man's conscious aspiration for "God" outside the field of his own area of control. The havoc and wreckage from this misdirection of serious endeavor in western world history is past calculation.

To deny the immanent presence of God's own life and mind within the core of man's being is flatly to reject the basic teaching of every religion that has inspired the soul of humanity through all time. It would be to make meaningless the very name of Immanuel, God with us, God dwelling in us. It would reduce to nonsensical babble the half of all religious philosophy, the principle of God as immanent deity, and further it would fly in the face of a positive statement of those scriptures on which the whole structure of Christian systematism rests,—the Bible. For in the *Book of*

Ecclesiastes it is unequivocally declared that the soul is from God. At death, says the Speaker, "the body returns to dust and the soul to God who gave it."

As a disastrous consequence of Christian misconception of the lucid ancient meaning of the doctrine of the immanence of God, there has been unduly prevalent in all Christian history a chronic hesitancy to commit the governance of man's life and the issues of his "salvation" wholly into his own hands. The strength and persistence of this attitude furnishes all needed proof of a calamitous miscarriage of precious truth. For it bespeaks only too loudly that the term "man" connoted not man containing God, but man devoid of God. If man of himself could do nothing to effect his salvation, this very predication could be made only on the assumption that his nature included no part of God's presence in him. There has been a fear of letting man stand and wage his evolutionary battle alone. Always the road to a safe retreat was kept open, so that in case of dire need he could fall back upon and receive help from God, the great power transcending him. The half-timid reminders that God is ever present in his entire creation were minimized, if not positively negated, by the ever-resurgent asseveration that of himself man can do nothing. God in the end must elect to save him, and "grace" is a voluntary free gift from God. Man can neither earn it nor demand it. He can only beg for it. All of which blandly and blindly ignores the hub truth of the whole situation, that God has already placed all of his power that the personality of man can hold directly within his organism and all that man needs to do is to awake to the fact of its presence there and to learn how to utilize it to highest practical advantage.

The glaring fatuity of the traditional Christian position is seen in the consideration that from the premises of the problem, the given terms of the situation from the outset, it is a chimera of igno- rance to assume that man *can* stand alone, actually cut off from divine influence. It is now and ever has been impossible for him to stand apart from and bereft of God's presence. For one half of him *is* God. As he can not dispossess himself of one half of his organic selfhood, and can not dismantle the structure of his being, he simply can not stand without God. For God is not only in him from the beginning, but half of himself is God. To stand outside of God one would have to destroy oneself. And so he never needs to go outside himself to find God. Every religion above coarse animism and fetishism has in perpetual chorus exhorted humanity in its search for God to cease looking outward and to probe ever more deeply within. This is so true that all too much of religion has run into exaggerated introversion, where it has grown moldy and sickly. The argument here is categorical and not debatable. The testimony is uncontestable and its meaning unequivocal.

This gross distortion of Christian theology which took the conception of its millions of devotees as to the accessibility of divinity from its true location within the soul of humanity and placed it afar in cosmic heavens, has been a predisposing cause, no less than colossal in effect, of untold suffering in Western life. It has indeed been one of the chief ingredients in the fear complexes besetting Western cast of mind, and has under our very eyes led myriads down into mental unbalance and neurotic derangement. Abnormal religiosity is credited statistically with sending more inmates to mental sanatoria than even sex abnormality.

Dr. Hopper concludes an unctuous passage asseverating man's final dependence upon God—conceived as outside himself, since anthropomorphized and personalized in the Christ of the Gospels, a historical person—with the sentence (*The Crisis of Faith,* p. 226):

"Outside of Christ there is no humanism, properly speaking, but only a perverse humanity."

Humanism, he argues, can not be the true basis of philosophy, because in the ultimate man must look above, beyond, outside himself, for the only real ground of his redemption. Yet this is said seriously, in spite of the fact that this author has written elsewhere a sentence that negates and falsifies the one just quoted—if it is true (p. 235):

"The self is a synthesis of the finite and the infinite."

The latter is a true and well-knit declaration. And it throws every word of the first statement into untruth.

Humanism is in the end the only basis for a rational and correctly grounded philosophy open to man's acceptance and operation. If *all* the elements of his problem are not within his conscious control —if a single one, and that the most vital of all, is not within his prerogative, but lies outside and beyond his reach in a distant God, then man is nothing but a marionette with the wires of his activities pulled by a *deus ex machina,* and his own effort *does,* truly and horrifyingly, not avail him a whit. But this is unthinkable. The human mind *must* believe that its own human effort counts. Humanity would be engulfed in perpetual despair and life would be a persistent mocking irony, cruel and pitiless, if the mind *could* believe that effort counted for nothing. To deprive human life of the sense of its counting for ultimate good or evil in every act, since there is the ingrained consciousness of moral responsibility in every act, would be to rob life of the fundamental dignity appertaining to it. For without accountability for our acts there could be no groundwork for dignity. The entire ethics of great revered religious systems would be a laughing travesty if human effort did not avail. For every such system exhorts to righteousness and outlines the penalties flowing from unrighteousness.

But the humanism that should replace a dependence upon transcendental deity must be one that does not leave God out of the human constitution. The crime of orthodox religionism is in *tearing* God out of the human organism; the crime of equally blind humanism is in *leaving* God out of it. The first puts deity in the wrong place; the second omits it altogether. There can be no humanism, but only half-humanism, or more definitely animalism, if God is left entirely out of the situation. More than the animal-human must be recognized in the definition of man. The divine-human must be admitted. Taking Dr. Hopper's and Augustine's own words, that man is a synthesis of the finite and the infinite, the animal and the god, meeting on the plane of the human, then true humanism becomes the proper name for the philosophy that unites all the essential elements of the total problem. So that man need not go out of doors to achieve his proper and salutary alignment with the ascending scales of reality.

It can so readily be seen how the whole structure of the ethico-spiritual problem has been contorted into an endless tangle of semi-true and semi-false presentations by the mere failure to know and concisely distinguish the two sides of the duality in man's make-up. It has arisen because theologians continued to place God outside of man, despite all the many categorical assertions in the sacred scriptures of the world that he was an element within the area of man's own conscious being. To aver that man is a hopelessly lost creature, enmired irredeemably in the sin of his own fallen nature, and that he must go out and seek God upon whom to anchor securely the hope of his salvation, is precisely like hypnotizing a person and telling him he must go find his hat, which he has forgotten is on his head all the while.

The Hindus have an allegory of the gods in the beginning of human creation. God had agreed to grant his immortal life and divine nature to man, but in order that man should learn to value these great gifts at their true worth, the question arose, how the supernal gift should be communicated to him and where located, so as to be accessible, yet not too easily. One of the celestial hierarchy suggested that it be placed on the highest mountain top, where man would have to exert himself strenuously and climb high to obtain it. Another ventured to name the depths of the sea, where great ingenuity would be required to discover it. Finally God himself settled the discussion: "We will put it in the very last place he will ever think of looking for it—in the hidden depths of his own being."

Of all religions Christianity has been the most ludicrously self-duped. It sends back an echo of lying mockery to Paul's ringing shibboleth, "Christ in you, the hope of glory." Christianity is far more harlequin than Diogenes looking with a lantern to find an honest man. It is going about looking for the lantern which it is already carrying.

Jesus said peremptorily, Ye shall have no need of the sun to shine by day, nor the moon by night, for—ye have light in yourselves! "Let your light shine." Bring it out from under the bushel of inhibitions and obscurations imposed on it by the carnal nature and set it on the hilltop of your own being. Ye *are* the light of the world; but how great and fatal the surface blindness that fails to recognize the light in its shining!

Perennial obtuseness has marked the effusions of pious theologism because in advancing predications concerning the relation of man to God, the word "man" was used in a sense which from the start abstracted the divine half of the synthesis of god-man from the total man. This left man standing as mere animal, which of course needs to look upward to God for evolutionary help. But man is not mere animal. Let Plato reassure us: "Through body it is an animal; through intellect it is a god." What can be the meaning of the many scriptural passages which say that the sons of God came down to earth to share our mortal nature, if not that they are incorporated with us in the same organism? Had the true synthetic conception of man, as embracing (the germ of) deity in his own composite entification been held intact, the entire course of Occidental history, which has been a holocaust of frightfulness under Christian guidance—indeed under Christian compulsion—would have been charted over happier pathways.

A revered scripture asks: "Who by searching can find out God?" Yet a sacred tome of the Hindus with equal pertinence places God closer to us than our very flesh: "Closer is he than breathing, nearer than hands and feet." Laplace said that he had pointed the most powerful telescope into all parts of the heavens and no trace of God could be found. Rather should he have pointed the instrument in the opposite direction, not to the outer objective world but to the inner subjective one. The reason Laplace did not find God with the telescope was that he looked for God under a wrong description. Of course he did not find the anthropomorphic Personage he pretended to be seeking. Yet he was seeing God all the time, seeing his outward body, or seeing him as Emerson says we see him, in every blade of grass. No less do we see him in both the worthiness and the ignobility of human thought and action. This, of course, is in the universal sense, which takes the cosmos as the personality of God and the whole as his life. More specifically, yet just as truly, God is twofold, like his reflection and miniature, man. He is mind and he is body. But it has been a universal habit of human thought to demean the body, the physical, the material side of life, while glorifying the "spiritual." In this general sense, then, the things seen and manifested are his body, as Pope put it, and the unseen order and movement are his mind at work. But if God has a body, of which solar and stellar systems and galaxies are the cells and organs, it is, according to human modes of conception, no less proper to say this is God than to exclude it from the definition and description of him and to say that only his soul is he. When we see a man coming down the street, we say, There is the man, or That is the man. We do not make an arbitrary distinction between his physical and his conscious self, accepting the one and rejecting the other. We take him as the man, body and soul. Likewise did Plato, Augustine and the wise ones of old. Not until errant modern conception takes him in the same way, as the synthesis of his two—or three—natures, including both his animality and his divinity alike and wholly within the scope of the term "man," will tragic chaos in mortal thought be diminished. When that happy amendment of bad philosophy is consummated, there will be an end to the groveling pleas from morbid and mawkish religiosity for man to surrender his inherent dignity and to deny and scorn his own powers to climb the evolutionary ladder. The corrupt Christian theology, while it has out of one side of its mouth claimed the exclusive distinction of being the religion that has proclaimed the dignity of man the individual, has out of the other corner with pitiful effectiveness crushed that very dignity by abstracting the divine leaven out of man's mixed composition and by beating down his self-sense to the abject level of the worm. This historic hypocrisy and duplicity of Christianity lacks little of being the most hurtful disservice rendered to the race by any religion. When corrected, no longer will it be the sickly fashion to preach to man that he must be saved by God, externally. Instead he will be told that the man of him will be saved by the god of him, and the face of humanity will at once be irradiated with the benignant glow of a new understanding. His mind will be redeemed from its jangling discord with truth to a grateful and renewing harmony with it.

When to this readjustment in his conceptual life there is added the discernment in psychology that man's conscious is the living moment between his stored past and his potential future, that it is open at all times to the ingress of motivations from both sides, then also will sane comprehension come to birth and a new range of intelligent government of psychic states will be brought under conscious control. At last there will be evolved out of the depths of good human intelligence the more specific technique of the god's control of the animal in the human breast. People will be freed more and more from the devastating sweep of massive emotionalism misdirected by bad philosophies, and will more soberly, yet more happily, place the hand of philosophical wisdom at the helm of their life direction. They will know that deep within them dwells the unconscious, with its greater wisdom available for their guidance, if they learn the better to lure it down into the conscious.

CHAPTER XI

THE BATTLE ON THE HORIZON

THERE is a strange corollary that runs with the recognition of the dual segmentation or composition of man's nature. Psychoanalysis has brought out some aspects of it. The duality manifests in a rather remarkable series of correspondences between the phenomena on both sides.

It can start from Paul's declaration that the natural precedes the spiritual. "First that which is natural, then that which is spiritual," says the Apostle. As must obviously be the case, the body of God must be formed and in function before his spirit can manifest its life in any given area of creation. Spirit must be instrumentalized or implemented if it is to create and animate concrete worlds. It must first form its instrument with and through which to work.

The clear intimations from these reconstructions of ancient wisdom following its fatal mutilation at the hands of medieval benightedness constitute a new mandate for all true religion. The clarified knowledge provides the *magna carta* for a religion redeemed from psychic charlatanism and sanctified hypocrisy, from bigotry, nescience and insincere motivations, to become again, as of old, the moral and spiritual beacon of mankind. The new-found correlation or kinship between the modern discovery of the unconscious and ancient philosophical and psychological principia invests religion once again with dignity and with a sanctity that springs from recognition of the deeper intrinsic values now perceived to lie within the psychic area. The ultimate criterion of sanctity is always that of utility or beneficence for the whole advance of an evolving entity toward its destined goal. Things are not sanctified merely by being held in traditional and often artificial awesomeness.

They become sacred by being found contributory to values rated high in the economy of most enduring good.

Foremost of all among the beneficial agencies which the combined new and old psychic sciences now place afresh at the service of mankind is the understanding of the vital technique by which religion must work pointedly and not diffusely toward its high ends. The nub of a religious striving that will be efficient to the highest degree is now indicated as centered in the relation between the conscious and the superconscious. This is the chief point and nodal focus at which the effort toward a spiritual uplift of the individual must be directed. For here is the locale of the great aeonial Battle of Armageddon, which the Egyptians so astutely allegorized as being fought at the meeting-point between the subconscious and the superconscious, the "horizon" line between them. Progress and well-being will henceforth be measurable by the amount of the potential quality of the superconscious or divine nature which can be brought down "out of heaven" by the conscious, incorporated in its daily program of self-directed activity and made a permanent possession by transference through habit to the custody of the subconscious. If man does not wish to remain bound in the automatic unconscious of his animal mentality, he must bestir himself to throw off old habitudes and elevate the tenor of his life by bringing down more luminous and more dynamic potential from the god-ego dwelling in the area of higher frequencies of vibrational consciousness awaiting the perfecting of his receptive capacity.

The Old Testament *Psalms* and *Proverbs* and the New Testament books alike strike hard at the human vices of sloth and lukewarmness. The exigencies of the soul's incarnational situation and the terms of the covenant entered into with the higher deity before descending alike demand the ego's close attention to the evolutionary mission he came here to discharge. The old books continue to insist that the thing is urgent, that opportunity passes with time and that there are tides in the affairs of evolution that can not be missed without heavy penalty. Disregard of opportunity will entail serious consequence. One is enjoined to be "diligent in business, fervent in spirit" in serving the Lord of higher consciousness. The business of the inner mind is paramount in the enterprise. The great human ordinance of the Sabbath was instituted to the end that one entire day in every seven should be devoted to the interests of the presiding genius of the organism, following six days given to the secular matters pertaining to the physical life. A new light indeed might creep over the face of humanity if this one day was truly consecrated, not to morbid sentimentalism and groveling pietism but to philosophical enlightenment and the combined ministration of intelligence and beauty. For "without vision the people perish," proclaimed the prophet, the truth-speaker of old. The pathway to more radiant and more abundant life runs in one direction and along one fairly narrow track. It runs atop the ridge of open consciousness lying between the subconscious and the superconscious. Only on that path has man accessibility to the god. The only true and right felicity for the mortal lies in opening as widely as may be the highway between his mortal self and the deity who has, in a dramatic sense, condescended to come and take up residence in the upper reaches of his demesne. The only or at least final criterion of culture is the degree to which the conscious mind can lay itself open in ever more expanded receptivity to the vibrations of the superconscious. These are always pitched, so to say, in the octave immediately above its ordinary or habitual range. Whatever technique will be found to govern the development of this enhanced capacity or this high art will be the most "practical" skill and employ the greatest genius in all the area of life. It will embody the principles of the science of true culture. For it will empower its practitioner to place himself directly in touch with the flowing currents of both meaning and value, under the influence of the most dynamic release of vital quality that life can give to man. It is in truth man's communion with God.

It must never be forgotten, however, that the god himself is climbing the ladder of evolution, the same as is the human and the animal. The poverty of modern knowledge in the field of anthropology consists mainly in the total want of understanding that man is not a simple unit of organization, but is in reality a composite creature, compounded of flesh, feeling, thought and spiritual will, each necessarily subsisting within the organism by virtue of a body of material fineness or coarseness exactly constituted to express its vibration of life. The highest grade of this hierarchy of being is of course the leader and the king. And he is far ahead of his companion travelers. He stands in the higher grade in the school of evolution. Where he stands his younger associates will stand later on. What is important for intelligence is that the god requires the experience of incarnation in order to actualize his as yet undeveloped potential of reality in the concrete. This is almost a lost canon of understanding, yet it is strategically close to the nub of all practical wisdom. The god is subject to the law of being which makes polarization of the two nodes of reality, spirit and matter, the operative modus of evolving life. As Plotinus has told us more clearly than anyone else, the soul comes into earthly body in order to develop her latent capacities into actual faculties. He says: "It is not enough for the soul merely to exist; she must show what she is capable of begetting." She remains, he adds, "ignorant of what she possesses" until she is made aware of her potential riches through her deployment of them in answer to the exigencies and contingencies met in a life of actual awareness in a physical body on a planet. That which is real, but as yet unmanifest in the creatural consciousness, must be *actualized*, to follow Plotinus again, in a life of open consciousness. And for this possibility and this service she is dependent upon her union, for cycle after cycle, with the negative energies of a physical body.

We find Dr. Hopper (*The Crisis of Faith*, p. 257) saying that which is a crucial nub of understanding:

"Men of wisdom ever since [Socrates] have held that true self-knowledge is the clue to fulness of life."

And he adds (p. 259):

"Everything depends on man's understanding of himself as he relates himself to the Absolute. He must know himself both inwardly and out-wardly against the perspective of the ultimate meaning of things. He must know himself not merely as one object among other objects, but as an immediate subject of experience occupying inwardly the precarious point of infinite commitment."

Here is indeed great truth expressed, worth deep reflection. The statement that man only comes to know himself as he relates him-self to the Absolute, the core of real being, and that he must know himself against the background of the ultimate meaning of things, is downright truth. But the immediate practical implication of this insight has never been seen or acted upon. If man can not guide his course intelligently unless he knows, broadly, his *ultimate* goal, which knowledge alone can invest his every step with its true meaning, then the deduction is sound, that philosophy is the most important study his mind can engage in. This was the insistence of the wise men of old who named philosophy as the kingly or divine science. It has never been decisively apprehended that the rightness of the present stride can not be determined if the long perspective of man's path and the distant vision of the ultimate goal, or, as Aristotle called it, the *entelechy*, is not known. To walk —and to have to walk—now, with no knowledge of whither the walking is to take one, or what is the proper direction of the walk-ing, is the hazardous predicament of man when he is without philosophy. And the psychoanalysts tell us from clinical experience, that people who have no positive philosophy go mad. A world without positive philosophy has gone mad, again and again. It is not to the credit of Christianity that in the third century it killed philosophy and substituted faith. Renaissance came when the shift was made from faith back to (ancient) philosophy. The implica-tions of this turn in history have never been canvassed. It is a costly dereliction.

That the race might have in its childhood the requisite knowledge to guide its historic conduct aright toward a known distant goal, religion was fashioned to embrace philosophy, and that in turn embraced anthropology and cosmology. These were accounted necessary to enable man to orient himself aright in his evolutionary environment. It told him where he stood, whence he had so far come, whither he was progressing, what was his set task and what his own equipment to perform it. It told him he was the human, standing on the horizon line between the heaven of spiritual immortality and the earth of physical mortality. It told him his present consciousness was a blend of incipient divine mind with the mind of the subconscious animal. "An animal's mind shall be given unto him," says Daniel to the king, and the king always typified the divine in man. Lecky observes in his famous *History of European Morals* that in ancient days "philosophy had become to the educated most literally a religion." The later decay of religion was brought on and marked by the decadence of philosophy and the substitution of pietistic unction.

It is a point of great significance which is brought out in Dr. Hopper's sentence last quoted, that man must know himself as the subject of experience occupying "the precarious point of infinite commitment." Brilliant light would be released again for the human mind if it could recover the principle of truth known to the ancient Egyptians that the only point at which potential power or quality becomes *actual*—where the static electricity of life and mind is transformed into kinetic or power current—is at the meeting point between the positive node of conscious spirit and the negative anode of unconscious matter. In this life, described by the Egyptians as "the lake of equipoise," and in symbolism known as the zodiacal house of Libra the Balance, life is brought from latency or unconsciousness out upon the plane of open consciousness, or the actual.

Intelligence should long since have caught the esoteric hint from the prefix "con" in *con*sciousness. It means "with" or "together."

Consciousness comes only when the two segments or ends of being are linked together in tensional relation and opposite pull. Reality burgeons forth into actuality at the mid-point of neutralization. As the scriptures have so forcefully shouted at us, life must be weighed in the balance, in the scales of the judgment, that from the test its true being may come forth and be known to and by itself. Life can scarcely engender consciousness if it does not split asunder into the dual polarity. For to know itself it must objectify itself to itself, and for this purpose it must stand itself as matter aside from and over against itself as spirit. There can be no consciousness unless there is something for it to be conscious of. Consciousness can not exist in the vacuum of sheer Absoluteness.

The Egyptians denominated the god in evolution "Lord of the Balance." With conscious power developed he stands in control of the equilibration between the soul of life and the physical embodiment and strives to maintain the equipoise between the two entities. The conscious mind is therefore the ground and arena of the battle, the focal point of the energization.

Psychoanalysis has gained so much of primal wisdom as goes with the knowledge of the unconscious. Its next great forward stride must be to establish the principle of the duality in the unconscious, the subconscious and the superconscious, and the great realization that the conscious, the prime seat of all value-actualization, is the point of neutralization between the two poles of man's being. Then the science will be in position to advance to new accomplishments in practique and more competent service to the race.

It is quite worth noting what Dr. Hopper says (p. 248) relative to the threefold constitution of man:

"This distinction will be clearer if we consider that man, according to this understanding, is not a static somewhat to be comprehended formally,—as intellect, feeling, will, etc.,—but that he must be understood as a creature *in motion,* as already in course of action. He is a viator, a creature who must go a way."

It is amazing that this decidedly pivotal understanding has not been given insistent accentuation in philosophical systematism. It is equally amazing that almost nothing has been made of it even when, as here, it is mentioned. And never have the absolutely necessary corollaries of the datum been scrutinized and unfolded. A great deal of philosophical speculation has been a mere shameless dodging of the overt palpable issues presented by accurate observation of the prime data. Here it is affirmed, and with great truth, that man is a viator; he is going a way. Never has it seemed to occur to speculative philosophy that two or more questions immediately and necessarily stand knocking for answers when this is affirmed. If he is on his way, whence has he come, whither is he going, and indeed also, why is he out on the highway at all? Why is he a-journeying and what is his destination? Ancient cosmology and anthropological science rendered voluble answers to these questions. Modern philosophy shuns them. Ancient wisdom comprehended the answers; modern philosophy is poverty-stricken and lacks the resources for reply.

If man is a viator, as far as modern acumen goes, he is traveling onward, after some eighty brief summers, to individual death and extinction! By killing arcane philosophy in the early centuries, our endowments of millions of dollars for great universities have brought forth the squeaking mouse of a Bertrand Russell's "philosophy of despair." The one thing surely known to modern science is that we are traveling a hard path to—annihilation! Our solar system will cool and life—our life—become extinct. "We pass this way but once" is the perennial slogan of average worldly "philosophy" today. Its corollary, "let us eat, drink and be merry," has set the tune for common motivation to dance to. As for the *post mortem* future, religion vaguely asserts it will be eternal peace and rest. Oblivion, and no more toil, sweat, blood and tears.

Ancient sagacity knew differently. The soul was described as "the persistent traveler on the highways of eternity." The divine soul in man says in the Egyptian books that he is "stepping onward through eternity." Modern thought has no more extended vision than to depict the soul as saying, "I am Today." Egypt presents the same soul as saying, "I am Yesterday, Today and Tomorrow." "Eternity and everlastingness is my name."

The ancient world, instructed by "just men made perfect" in knowledge and wisdom, knew that man is indeed a viator through the cycles of time and the kingdoms of matter. Present vapid religion and jejune philosophy have scarcely the intellectual stamina to face the relevant questions, whence and whither. And the sorriest matter of all is the apparent belief that it makes no difference to man's mental stability whether he knows he is traveling a brief and stony path to death and oblivion, or whether he is on his way, through storm and sunshine, to an endless unfoldment of radiant life.

It is perhaps not surprising that the attitude of complacency in the face of total want of knowledge as to evolutionary paths, aims and goals should have become an expression of devout religionism in the modern day. For religion had dropped philosophy in the fatal third century and had had to fall back upon substitute formulae and mechanisms of escape and comfort. Prominent among pronouncements as to the non-philosophical character of modern religion are the two lines of Cardinal Newman's famous hymn:

> "I do not ask to see the distant scene;
> One step enough for me."

Ancient Egypt did not hold with this sentiment, but, fortified with definite knowledge of man's continuity of life, lived in the present and faced the future with a cheer and a fortitude based on something more vital than faith.

In the Mithraic system the soul of man was represented as saying at one point in the ritual: "I am the star wandering about with you and flaming up from the depths." In Egyptian the words "star" and "soul" came to an identity in the word *Seb*. In ancient depiction of truth and reality under nature symbols the soul that came to animate the animal man was presented to thought as veritably a star of divine life, light and energy descending from the heavens to inhabit a physical body. The symbol of a soul coming down to earth was the falling star, along with the imagery of the evening sun sinking into the earth or water.

The logic that supported the ancient mind in its assurance of the soul's immortality was simple and natural. The soul was a fragment of the divine life, energy and mind of God himself. As such it was as indestructible as the whole of which it was a germinal or seminal portion. As the whole visible world of manifestation was generated and sustained by the energies of cosmic mind, and mind generated it cyclically and periodically, surely mind was the eternal force behind the series of appearing and disappearing manifestations. The worlds might fade away again and again, but mind remained to create them anew. And the fragments of cosmic mind did not sally forth into cosmic adventure and undergo the stress and strain of incarnation merely to throw away all their hard and slowly won gains at the end of each sojourn in body. The ancients knew how life and mind husbanded and preserved the fruits and harvests of victories won in the battle with matter. With the closing up of the Platonic Academies in the fifth century and the utter suppression of the systems of esoteric philosophy for fifteen centuries the world of the west was left to drift along the historical road entirely without the pilotage of guiding wisdom. The horrendous record of those centuries bears testimony to the fatal consequences of despoiling human life of an enlightened philosophy.

Psychoanalysis now enters the arena of human striving after truth and knowledge and its discovery of the unconscious marks one of the great forward steps out of the murks of medieval errancy and obfuscation of mind. It supplies empirical data to corroborate what could be sensed only by enlightened philosophical vision, that *the decay of philosophy precipitates minds into conditions of neurotic instability.* This is the recovery of an item of knowledge that was well established in Plato's day and is one of the few real advances toward higher culture made in the modern age. Ancient Greek thought regarded the soul in incarnation as having lost her true bearings under the illusive dominance of fleshly concerns and as wandering in a fog of ignorance, from which state she was only to be redeemed to knowledge and true intelligence by philosophy. Philosophy was held to be the true knowledge of divine things. The soul, it was affirmed, could not relate itself properly to its task in incarnation if it totally lacked the assurance of its divine origin, the nature and value of its mission to earth and the general scheme and purport of its evolutionary enterprise. Philosophy was the essential foundation of moral rectitude, of equanimity and stability of mind and of the good life in general.

It is quite important to note what Chandler Bennitt has to say in his work *The Real Use of the Unconscious.* He is discussing healing, but sets it over, as a special technique, against "understanding," or what could be called philosophy:

"Healing is not understanding. At long last it is always something less. In the living sense in which I use understanding, the most final statement of the case is not that we must be healed if we would understand, nor even that we must understand in order to be healed; it is that understanding is its own way and its own god where healing is not, and that as we increasingly understand in our entire being, whatever must still be left to the specific technique of healing will be less and less a vital matter. Meanwhile I believe that even in what are accepted therapeutic issues, it will more and more be recognized that the individual cannot cooperate in the healing medical realities where their application contravenes his still more fundamental sense of things."

What Mr. Bennitt here denominates understanding and again refers to as a "still more fundamental sense of things" is equivalent to what the ancient sages termed philosophy. His evaluation of it as a more basic and essential element in the psyche than any temporary or specific influence employed in healing is a discernment matching the ancients' knowledge of its place deep in the core of human being. This observation of Bennitt's should stand as a rebuke and corrective for much modern spiritual-cult preachment and practique. Eccentric religionism has given a tremendous vogue to the notion that physical healing is the indisputable proof of the rightness of the cult philosophy in whose name the healing is performed. Not only is this not so, according to this psychoanalyst, but the vital truth is that the healing is always less important than the philosophy. The thing of intrinsic value is always the understanding in its deepmost issues. It is the eventual determinant of the individual's health or his need of healing. Understanding is ultimately the ruling factor in the individual's life, and healing is only an effort to rectify disturbance when understanding has not held a true grip on the life.

It is evident, on this analysis, that there lies buried deep in the organism a sense and apperception of values in incarnational life that transcends by far the welfare of the body and its illness or health. Again it must be granted that such values must be connected with a part of man that does not perish with the body. These values do not rise and fall in any immediate or direct parallelism with the rise and fall of the condition of the body. They are obviously not fully enhanced by the body's healthiest state nor deflated by its worst condition. Bennitt ventures to assert that they verily transcend the issues of life and death alike.

"Our life object is not merely not to die, nor even to live long and healthily. It is to attain the ultimate realness . . . our daily aim is further and more deeply to integrate our existence . . . as we go. It is with these finalities and these practicalities that I am concerned."

And he adds:

"Greatly as any individual in trouble may desire to be well, he will do this only for something further. I automatically assume that any patient has a sense of his business in life as something beyond health. This business includes his deepest total connection with reality."

No healing can come, he states further, through any specific medical or psychological technique, when the individual's evolutionary status is such that frustrations and troubles can be handled "only by the realities of advance in a living understanding, and not merely by those of ill health and cure." And such guidance from the inner *daimon,* he says, "can be given only by an individual who is himself deeply in touch with meaning." Meaning is indeed the touchstone of the whole matter. The mind that can not discern the forms of meaning into which the events of life and the cosmos fall is little better than a piece of flotsam on the moving wave. It is heading for imminent wreckage. Indeed Bennitt expresses a climactic maxim when he says that "truth must make not only sense, but significance; it must be not only clear, but meaningful."

All this is cardinal truth, and well spoken. Bennitt is on the right track; modern psychology at last is on the right track. The new science of semantics is an important formulation. *Meaning,* even transcending significance, is the keynote of the modern mental movement. There are issues that lie deeper than even health and success in the worldly sense, that are not, necessarily, met and satisfied with a healthy body and a long life. These must be the concern of some other portion of man than his external self, for health and long life would pretty completely fulfill the main needs of bodily man. By inference they must appertain vitally to the history of the ego-soul. And this is the unconscious. The ego has his own interests. He is wrestling doubtless with the exigencies and crises, the halts, impasses, deadlocks, obstructions, frustrations that mark his progress on the upward road. As his life is subterranean to that of the body he tenants, the symptoms which these contingencies bring to manifestation in some form of disturbance in the life may not be obvious or clear to the outer mind. Hence the need of a special technique that probes beneath the surface phenomena to locate the more esoteric and occult origin of inharmony. This technique is the special discovery and implement of psychoanalysis.

If the new approach of modern psychology to spiritual esotericism through the discovery of the unconscious is not beaten down and obscured and again lost by the oppression of crude mechanistic philosophies so rampant in the age, this period of history will be catalogued by later analysts as marking the dawn of the recovery of ancient truth after sixteen centuries of benightedness. For now again, as in ancient times when wisdom reigned, the part of the divine soul in human life, in its health and in its ills, is recognized and healing practice embraces a technique which penetrates to the inner seat of the soul instead of treating merely the outward superficial symptoms. The body is in Greek *soma* and the soul is *psyche*. Psychosomatic medicine or practice is still in swaddling clothes. Perhaps it is yet a long way to the place where in the treatment of human maladies psychology based on the soul will be the most effective curative agency and philosophy the perennial preventive medicine.

CHAPTER XII

THE CHILD IS FATHER OF THE MAN

IT has long been a maxim of both biology and philosophy that each individual recapitulates in the early or initial stages of its growth the entire previous phylogenetic history of the species to which it belongs and indeed that of all zoölogical evolution. This is to say that each new individual in the stream of evolving life quickly retraces in its birth and early growth the biological history of the race from monocell up to the complex and differentiated forms at the point it itself occupies. The childhood of the individual then republishes the long-past childhood of the race. The human foetus clearly exhibits the stages of unicell, multicell, worm, reptile, bird, vertebrate, mammal and all intermediate forms up to the human as at present constituted. It would have been thought that the knowledge of a principle of evolution so pregnant with intimation as this should have yielded more patent discovery and application than it seems to have done.

That it has come forward as a principle of elucidation and understanding in the field of psychoanalysis, however, is one of the robust attestations of the great basic rightness and fruitfulness of this modern development in psychology. In full view of the profounder aspects of the human psyche revealed by this new science it will not come as a surprise that psychoanalytic research has discovered almost the principal keys and solutions of the complexities of mental problems in the previously disdained terrain of childhood. The chief clues to the unbalance and irrationality manifesting in adult life are generally to be traced back to inhibitions and frustrations in childhood. The experiences undergone even in infancy are seen to set the stage for abnormalities that come to the surface in later life. The child conditions the man. Childhood comes first and through the intense sensitiveness of its consciousness to impressions and its durable retention of memories it in reality gives birth to the adult man. Men and women are but grown children. The substance of mind can be said to be in childhood quite plastic, hardening and crystallizing, however, as childhood passes. The impressions made upon it in its tenderer condition at the start become solidified for permanency and fix the life habits over the pattern of the first molds. He who can bend the twig has shaped the tree. He who conditions the child has formed the man.

In the course of time it was destined that psychological investigation should seek the causes of mental abnormality back in the individual's childhood. The evidences of this connection were abundant and would not forever miss discovery. The finding was delayed only by the inveterate recalcitrancy of the modern mind to the wisdom of the past. Principles announced in the tomes of archaic mastership would all along have furnished modern research with the fundamenta of discovery and a true psychological science. For every fresh revelation coming from present-day study in the field of psychology is but a re-affirmation of data known of old.

Such a splendid work as Jung's *The Psychology of the Unconscious* is largely an elucidation of the symbols and dramatizations found occurring in the dreams of his patients, and all approached and systematized through a comparative analysis of them with the stories and formulations of ancient mythology! The world has not yet appreciated the significance of this correlation. That a psychoanalyst should have to resort to the allegedly fanciful if not fantastic constructions of such products of racial child-mindedness as mythology and folk-lore for keys and formulae by which to reach a comprehension of the dreams of a modern young woman, has not been measured in its true dimensions of significance. And that the same psychologist has been able to announce that he has, in lifelong study, found the same set of symbols promenading in the dreams of his modern patients as he has found in the whole field of ancient religious symbolism, in the Bibles and folk-lore of the nations to remote antiquity, is again a fact which has not found its true evaluation. The obfuscations of medieval benightedness still dim our vision and make us slow to recognize great truth even when we stand in its very doorway.

We stand, then, face to face with these great determinations: the basic conditioning factors in the individual's psychological life are established largely in childhood and, for purposes of later rectification, must be re-located and dealt with through adult correction of infantile fixations; the propensities and instincts dominating the child mind, and thus clinching their hold on the whole of the life period of the individual, are both analogous and directly kindred to the instincts and proclivities of the race as a whole in *its* infancy, and are dramatized in consciousness by the same symbols now as then; and lastly that the whole battle in consciousness for all individuals is epitomized in the finale by the formulary that it is the eternal struggle between the reason, knowledge, intelligence and wisdom of the divine counterpart in man, that comes to open consciousness in *adult* life, on the one side, and the instinctive, natural, irrational, infantile forces of physical life, that dominate in the *childhood* period, on the other. Both in the individual and in the race as a whole, the great Battle of Armageddon goes on between the powers of adulthood and those of childhood. In the terms of Greek or Platonic philosophy it is the conflict of the higher *dianoia*, or thorough knowing, the genius of divine intelligence in man, with the irrational instincts of the purely animal nature, which man shares by virtue of his body. The forces that build the body must have play first; the powers of mind come later to unfoldment, to be the king and ruler of those natural energies, to employ them for its purposes rationally determined.

The childhood of the race, as of the individual, develops the natural man, whom Paul says comes first; the adult period brings the mind to function, so that the forces of nature may come under the direction of intelligence and be made the agencies of the creation of a cosmos out of an elementary chaos. Life must first deploy the forces that build the universe physically and then evolve the mind to direct them in the accomplishment of its purposed ends. Mind itself must have its genesis in physical nature. It is brought to birth in the womb of matter. Just as solar energy is neither light, heat nor kinetic power while in its pure state, but only develops these manifestations of its nature when brought into contact with a material body, so pure spirit, pure ideality, is not mind until it is harnessed, so to say, with the elemental energies found potential in the atomic matter of physical organisms. Mind can not come to function in pure abstraction, of its own sheer being. It must be the product of the forces generated in an organism. In short it must be instrumentalized in and by a brain. Life first builds its physical body, since only through the implementation of such a structure can it bring its powers of consciousness to concrete realization to and for itself. And the forces it uses to build the structure fall below the level of mind and are irrational. They are denominated in all ancient systems the elementary powers. St. Paul so clearly says that the race was under the governance of these "elementals of the earth" and "elementals of the air," or "the elements of the world," before it developed the rulership of the higher mind. And most pertinently for the interests of our exegesis he states that this "bondage to them that by nature are no gods" prevailed in the period of our evolution "when we were yet children." Then it was, he says, that "Christ died for us." True indeed, since the "death" of the Christos or divine mind principle came with its first entry into the life of body. And until that entry, in the far developed stage of biological evolution, in the old age of Mother Nature, animal man could have no knowledge of divine mind. To the truth of this analysis the three or more allegories of *aged* women bearing the Messianic Son of God in the scriptures bear most striking testimony. The natural man can not know the things of the spirit, declares the Apostle. And he adds that when we were yet children we did not know God. Surely this was so, for the god had not yet risen to function in the animal organism.

How amazingly the author of the *Epistles* set forth the basic principles that are only now being brought to light by the more enlightened approach of modern psychology! He not only marked out the anthropological grounds of the psychic conflict in the nature of man, but with the utmost perspicacity delineated the many varied aspects of the struggle. In what trenchant terms does he represent the fierce combat between the soul and the flesh! When he would do good, he says, he perceives *in his members* a law which wars against the law of the mind. This conflict is the source of his wretchedness. He refers to the flesh as "the body of this death." To be carnally minded is sin and "death." The interests of the spirit are in opposition to those of the flesh, which he says mean death.

Psychoanalysis has now discovered that for the maintenance of normal sanity and for the more complete integration of the individual's life the higher intelligence of adulthood must "frustrate" the animal instincts of childhood. Here in the proverbial nutshell is the summary manifesto of the science of psychoanalysis. "Disturbance" is not abnormal, is not psychopathic, because it is the function of developing mind to *"disturb,"* even to *"frustrate,"* the instinctive automatism of the animal nature springing quickly to life in the recapitulatory process in early childhood. This pitting of the two natures against each other in the life of mankind is the ground of the whole moral problem of the race. The issues of evolution depend upon the course of the battle, the ebb and flow of the tides of mental and spiritual force. Ascetic religionism decreed that the animal in man was to be crushed, smothered, extirpated. But this was false theory and ruinous practice. The animal is not to be crushed. He is to be domesticated, so that his wild energies may be turned to the use and advantage of mind, the king. And through his association with man the thinker his genus is in the course of the cycle to be elevated to the level now held by the human, while man advances further to godhood. The gods resident in the inner-

most recesses of human nature are divinizing man as man in turn
is domesticating and humanizing the animal. In each case the end
result is the neutralizing of conflict between the evolving faculties
of consciousness and the blind instinctual forces of physical energy.
It is mind seeking to harness the wild forces of elementary chaos.

Turning back to study the mind of childhood, psychoanalysis
should not have been surprised to discover that its phenomena were
a miniature replica of those of earliest humanity. Says Jung (*Psychology of the Unconscious,* p. 28):

"Consequently it would be true as well that the state of infantile
thinking in the child's psychic life, as well as in dreams, is nothing but
a re-echo of the prehistoric and the ancient."

Here is one of the main supporting pillars in the temple of
psychoanalysis. To re-examine the infantile mind of humanity in
its early period it was but necessary to look at the infantile mind
in the child. The two sets of phenomena would be found analogous
and kindred. Both bespoke the play of the irrational and instinctive
forces. In neither had mind come to assert rulership. Both were
under the governance of Mother Nature. They had not graduated
from her tutelage to enroll in the school of Father Spirit. As twelve
was the number of spiritual perfecting, the Gospel allegory has it
that Jesus deserted his mother at that age and sought "the things
of his Father." The intimation that these higher interests were
concerned with the mind is conveyed in the allegory by the particular that he was found in the temple in profound disputations
with the learned doctors. Nature herself carries out the force of the
analogue in the fact that at the age of twelve, or at puberty, the
child passes from childhood into manhood and begins the active
development of the mind. And again psychoanalysis finds its basic
principles exemplified and vindicated in both nature and the scriptures.

The tracing of parallelism in the two sides of the analogue revealed the most significant correspondences. The infantile mind of early humanity, lacking mature reason and piercing intelligence, devised an elaborate series of allegedly fantastic representations to account for and explain the reality of the world about it. This process gave rise to the wondrous volume of ancient myths, the cycles of epic legends, the hero-tales and folk-lore among all nations. The universal prevalence of such productions is in itself a phenomenon of extraordinary character. It represented, not, as is mistakenly supposed, the effort of infantile mentality to explain the mysterious reality in whose bosom its life was cast, but the discerning inventiveness of mature mind to explain the mystery *to* the child humanity in terms suited to its then limited capacity to understand. The child mind would hardly be able to devise the elaborated and involved complexities of the Grecian or Egyptian myths. Children now do not invent Mother Goose and the fairy tales. These are given them by the elders, being assumed to be in a form suitable for apprehension by the immature mind. As a matter of fact the myths are most astutely constructed to convey the profoundest of moral and cosmic truths. Infantile mind could *not* have hit upon such marvelous and precise dramatizations of verity. The marvel of their typal accuracy and pictorial fidelity to truth has never yet been fully seen by students. They obviously were the creations of a genius for consummate dramatization unparalleled in human history. But as the representation was designed *for* the child mind of early mankind, it was cast in forms that would be appreciable and meaningful to the infantile stage of the race's mental development.

The analogue of the child's rearing in early life under the care and tuition of the mother is another of the numberless instances wherein nature presents in the small a living ideograph of universal truth or truth in the large. There is no mythology in which the mother is not the typal representative of the great Mother, Nature. Nature mothers us and mind or spirit fathers us. Nature develops and provides for us the physical mechanism of life; spirit comes to birth through it and seats consciousness on the throne as ruler.

The mother-forces dominate the child; the spirit or father-forces rule the adult. The ancient representations of the mother and child yield a new and profounder significance when viewed in this light. Both mother and child typify physical nature, operating before the advent of mind. They speak of nature and her progeny, the physical world. They tell of the production and preparation of physical life to become the vehicle of mind, the king. They go before him to prepare his way and to make his paths straight.

But when he comes he must supersede their irrational governance with the reign of reason. Their habitual and instinctive activities must be bent to subserving the offices of intelligence and conscious design. Their wild and impetuous sweep in given directions must be curbed and eventually turned into channels of service for the achievement of goals set by the divine knower within. Their blind elemental forces must be harnessed to the chariot of cosmic Purpose.

The attempt and effort of conscious mind in evolving man to administer this "conversion" of elemental instincts into helpful servants sets the scene and supplies the motive for the great moral conflict in the breast of humanity. It is the father powers against the native forces of the mother and the child. As Jung has so well shown, the instincts of what the Greeks called *physis,* or nature, predominate in the first thirty-five years of a human life, but give place in the second similar period to those of the mind, philosophy and intellectuality. The first period builds the body and establishes its sustenance, comfort and well-being. The second advances from those concerns to the matters of life and consciousness, to the effort to gain knowledge and understanding.

A second and more particular item of the parallelism between the racial and the individual childhood periods is well adduced by Jung, citing a passage from the scholar Abraham (*Dreams and Myths*) as follows:

"Thus the myth is a *sustained, still remaining* fragment from the infantile soul-life of the people, and the dream is the myth of the individual."

The assumption that the myth is an infantile creation because it was extant in the early life of the nations (if only three or four thousand years back of the present can be considered an "early" period in the history of humanity) is gratuitous and conjectural and has arisen only because of the decay of philosophic enlightenment in the dark ages. A better understanding is formulated in the statement that the myths were designed and constructed by the loftiest genius for dramatization of truth and were adapted to yield instruction and enlightenment *for both the infancy and the adulthood* of the race and of the individual. Their truths were ageless and their application universally relevant. They were designed to be remembered, if not understood, by childhood, and to be understood by all in their maturity. They were given to the race at an early stage, because they were intended to stand as guiding light for the whole race throughout the evolutionary journey. But it is impossible that they could have been the creation or the product of the child-mind.

They were put forth in the race's childhood because the mind of childhood is receptive to impressions stamped upon it and will hold vital truth, even if only the shell of the truth or meaning is perceived, until the maturing mind can probe into the kernel and discern the living essence of truth therein. It has not been perceived that the prime purpose behind the promulgation of the myths was their preservation in racial memory. They were taught in the childhood of the race, and repeated in the childhood of the individual in each generation, that first of all they might be perpetuated. They were constructed in a fashion that rendered them automatically easy to remember. They were set to poetic meter and rhythm, so that they held their place in memory like music. And even the scriptures were constructed on the pattern of number formations, based chiefly on the number seven. This has come to light in the discovery of the almost universal prevalence of the chiasmus structure in the Christian Bible and the omnipresent run of multiples of seven in the numerical values of numberless phrases, verses and other groupings in the Greek and Hebrew translations of the scriptures.

What is impressed upon the child mind is hardly ever lost, perhaps never really. Therefore the ancient impartation of knowledge in allegorical and symbolic and dramatic forms was made with the motive of transmission and remembrance, so that adulthood in every generation might not be wanting the ever-significant structures of truth to redeem to esoteric meaning. And, perhaps of most challenging import is the great understanding, lost for so long, that nature carries in her phenomena the eternal pictorialization of living truth. For human understanding the one final and irrefutable language of truth is the symbolism of nature. For nature *is* truth and verity in the concrete. Its every form is a hieroglyph of reality, staring us in the face. A living creature, with all its habits and characteristics and traits, is an epiphany of ubiquitous law and universal modus. The life of a vegetable is an epitome of all life. For there are varying levels and degrees at which life manifests, rated as higher and lower, and the manifestation at any of the levels is typal of the one universal procedure.

Hence the masters of ancient knowledge put forth their sagas of profoundest cosmic truth almost entirely in the language of nature symbolism. "Go to the ant, thou sluggard; consider her ways and be wise," might be cited as the key slogan of the teaching of antiquity. The writings of the sages send the thought of the reader again and again to the bee, the snake, the bird, the cat, dog, lion, crocodile, ape, dragon-fly, locust, grasshopper, the tree, the bush, flower, grass, leaf, root, mountain, river, lake, brook, sea, water, earth, air, fire, cave, island, hill, meadow, swamp, rainbow, thunder, lightning, sun, moon, star, constellation, summer, winter, month and year. Wheat for bread, the grape for wine, and the bee for honey stand as the three great symbols of the divine soul in the mortal body.

The life of the child and of early humanity alike stand far closer to nature than that of the individual or the collective adult. The child is born in the lap of Mother Nature and he is bathed within and without by the stream of her ubiquitous forces. Her influences shape his physical body and the automatic functioning of her powers carries him along toward maturity. All this being so, it is the decree of fitness and necessity that any cultural heritage formulated for his immediate and continuing behoof should be framed and expressed in the language of nature symbols. For these are the things whose constant objectivity in his life dowers them with pedagogical power and enlightening significance. Their known phenomena hold the mirror up to truth, for they are that truth themselves in the concrete. Through and behind the visible world of actuality there broods the other world of invisible reality. The visible thing is the only lens through which the figures and shapes of that deeper reality can be brought to focus for the human mind. The philosophic aphorism that the things of the outer world are cast in the image of "those things which are above" is the statement of man's only means of rising to an apprehension of spiritual realities. When seen, they are revealed to be not foreign and exotic creations, but bear the familiar stamp of the known things in the world here below. The seen world is man's only clue to the realities of the unseen world.

The obvious effort and aim of the archaic literary constructions then was to embody the principles of truth in a language and in narrative that would hold the mind close to nature and her forms and phenomena. This was the language, not *of* childhood, but *for* childhood. But it is equally the language for adulthood, for even now, in an age of the world considered adult, the same language of symbol and myth still beats back the efforts of the united acumen of world scholarship to grasp the esoteric meaning. And it is still claimed that these masterly devices to purvey the most recondite truth and wisdom were the spontaneous creations of the race's "child-mind."

The sages availed themselves of the known capabilities of the mind in the childhood of the world and the childhood of each successive generation to achieve the primary aim of preserving their writings in memory. Both the race and the individual possess in their childhood a virtually unforgetting memory. For both function in the realm of the subconscious. The child, the animal and child-humanity all alike live consciously at the level of the subconscious. Their actions are directed by instinct and automatism. Mind has not come to play in either of them as yet. Hence the phenomena of conscious life in all of them display similarity and are to be measured by the same standard. Their various manifestations are kindred and analogous. Their activities are motivated by the autonomic nervous system, their memory is automatic and practically unfailing and impressions are made everlasting by repetition. The human child of course stands above the animal, but he nevertheless passes through the *animal stage* of evolution and still bears the animal nature with him in his physical body.

It is now possible to summarize what this unfoldment has dialectically been leading to. The myths, symbols and dramas embodying the mighty ancient wisdom had to be given to child humanity in a form to be eternally remembered. They had to be given *in* the race's childhood and *to* the race in its childhood because humanity was still in its animal stage and both the animal and the child have automatic powers of memory. And they had to be framed in a language and under imagery based on naturographs, because natural phenomena constitute the only universal lexicon or alphabet of unerring truth. They constitute the only language universally comprehensible, and, what is still more, the only language capable of yielding to each level of intellectual capacity and development the truth which that stage is able to grasp. It teaches simple truth to the simple and profound truth to the sagacious. In brief summary, truth had to be organized and indelibly stamped upon the subconscious mind of the race so that it would live automatically, and be perpetuated for the use of the conscious intelligence when at a later stage that genius burst into flower in the denouement of organic evolution.

What Jung and Abraham and other students say about the myths of early humanity matching the myth-making power of the subconscious today (or *vice versa*), and the dreams of the under-mind continuing to cast up the wrack of the ancient language of myth and symbol has pertinent bearing upon the entire subject of mind-analysis. The repetition of the ancient symbols in modern dreams is interpreted to be the method adopted by the subconscious—which is the recorded memory of the race's and the individual's past—for the most part to protest against the willful suppression by the present conscious mind of the instinctive native propensities and calls of the natural or animal man for their expression. It is in brief the form of the first or natural-animal man's protest against the repression of its instinctual life by the incipient rise of the second or spiritual man's mind to dominion over the whole life of the organism. As such it is inevitable, natural and good. The concern of the individual is to manage it with the least degree of tragic conflict and severe disturbance. It is not abnormal that disturbance should come. The tragedy is that it should come under such conditions of unintelligence and unbalance that wreckage should so often occur.

It is well to note a dialectical point in the form of Abraham's presentation of the identical function and status of the myth of the early race and the dream of childhood. It has been an assertion of this essay that the myth was not produced or created *by* the child mind of early humanity. If now the myth and the dream symbol or dream myth are of parallel order and status, then the parallelism should hold in respect to their origin or production. It can not be said that the dream of the child mind in individual childhood is a conscious creation of the child's genius. It is in reality simply given *to* the child. It is more of the nature of a projection into the child's mind by a superior intelligence. It is now recognized as the projection from the unconscious. The child mind did not consciously and designedly produce it. It came down "from above," or out from within. If there is instruction, then, in the law of correspondences, as most certainly there is, the conclusion is that neither was the myth in early history a conscious creation of the child mind of infant humanity.

In the light of all this it is of interest to hear Jung in a further elaboration of the idea dealt with here (*Psychology of the Unconscious*, p. 29):

"The conclusion results almost from itself, that the age which created the myths thought childishly—that is to say, phantastically, as in our age is still done to a very great extent (associatively or analogically) in dreams. The beginnings of myth formations (in the child), the taking of phantasies for realities, which is partly in accord with the historical, may easily be discovered among children."

It is probably a bit difficult to allocate a precise or scientific meaning to Jung's use of the words "childishly" and "phantastically" here and elsewhere. Always the first word and generally the second carries with it the connotation of a mental picture that either misses or weirdly caricatures reality. Phantasy is commonly taken to be the creation of illusion. Its formations do not match truth or reality. Sometimes a slightly more generous allowance on the side of reliability is made for phantasy when speaking of the phantasies of the poet as depictions of the actual. But generally the word carries the imputation of fallacy. Phantasies are fictions of the mind made in an effort to explain or interpret reality, but missing its faithful portraiture. They are imaginative failures and falsities.

Jung confirms this broad definition of the meaning of phantasy when he says that the mind of childhood is addicted to "the taking of phantasies for realities." Its imaginings about the world and life are not true pictures. This can be readily granted without debate, inasmuch as it is conceded that the mind of the child is not fortified with the data of experience and the developed powers of the intellect to interpret things aright, or at least according to the norms of adult mentation. But when the eminent psychologist goes on to say that, because the child makes erroneous guesses about reality and conceives with the error of infantile incapacity, likewise the mythmakers of antiquity "thought childishly—that is to say phantastically, as . . . in dreams," when they constructed the great myths, it is obvious that he is guilty of a *non sequitur*. He convicts himself of bad logic on two counts, both, oddly enough, brought against this conclusion by himself! For, in the first place he himself devotes some hundreds of pages in *The Psychology of the Unconscious* alone, and more in other works, to an elucidation of psychoanalytic rationale and interpretation entirely on the basis of constructions supplied by the ancient myths, which thus are found to be accurate and reliable norms of truth and reality. And, secondly, his own work, as well as the whole burden of psychoanalytic science, has validated the authenticity of the dream, when properly analyzed, as a faithful picture or dramatization of reality. If, in the ordinary derogatory sense of the terms, it is affirmed that the myth and the dream are childish and phantastic constructions, then Jung's entire splendid contribution to psychological science must be written off as similarly childish and phantastic, for it is based solidly on the *truth-telling character of both the dream and the myth*. The dream is the production of an unconscious faculty now recognized to exercise the most recondite intelligence, not to say incredible genius in the art of semantic dramatization. Likewise the myths of ancient formulation are seen by psychoanalysts themselves to be marvelously astute creations to represent the profoundest conceptions and motions of the human spirit, which they do with astounding precision and clarity. If both are "childish and phantastic," then childish phantasy must be elevated to the rank of the supreme faculty of the human psyche.

Phantasy may reign in the conscious life of the child, when its imaginations conceived to picture reality widely miss the mark of truth. But the dream is not the conscious production of the child, neither is the myth the production of child humanity, that is, humanity functioning at the child level. The dream is given *to* the child and the myth was given *to* humanity in its childhood. Until the study is oriented in line with this understanding it will not yield true insight or clarification.

Civilized society is shocked from time to time by the exhibition in certain quarters of the crudest forms of gross animalism or brutality. Jung says that these always remain germinally in the unconscious and can surge to the surface when conventional restraints are temporarily relaxed. Some of them are so gross and bestial in their manifestation that Jung is led to say that "today we feel for such a thing nothing but the deepest abhorrence, and never would admit it still slumbered in our souls." But it is well to note his statement that we go through the period corresponding to the animal evolution in our childhood, when by analogy at least we are classified as little savages. He says (p. 35):

"Yet all this does not affect the fact that we in childhood go through a period in which the impulses toward these archaic inclinations appear again and again, and that through all our life we possess, side by side with the newly recruited, directed and adapted thought, a phantastic thought which corresponds to the thought of the centuries of antiquity and barbarism. Just as our bodies still keep the reminders of old functions and conditions in many old-fashioned organs, so our minds, too, which apparently have outgrown these archaic tendencies, nevertheless bear the marks of the evolution passed through and the very ancient re-echoes, at least dreamily, in phantasies."

In childhood we each quickly recapitulate the age of animal barbarity and thereafter keep it, as it were, buried in the basement of consciousness, covered over as well as we are able to contrive it, with the traditional masks and façades of "civilization." Wars, crime waves and occasional reversions to the elemental and the primitive at times lift the lid of conventional restraint sufficiently to allow an upsurge of the native animal forces.

One of the discernments brought out by Jung in connection with mythology deserves a word of comment. He observes tersely that the masses never free themselves from mythology. This is hardly more than a trite notation, since the masses are those who remain bound in the commonplace conventional and traditional, the accepted standards of conduct and thought. The myths have played their part, perhaps away back in time, in setting the established mores. Thus the life and influence of the myths are perpetuated down the ages. In so far, however, as the myths did originally portray, no matter with what subtle deftness, the realities of man's history, it is inevitable that they should linger as normative influences over the consciousness of the masses, even though, as is always the case, the kernel of their real meaning has been lost, and only their desiccated husks survive. In this sense it is the fate of the vast majority of mankind to be perpetually influenced if not ruled by conceptual phantoms! The saving consideration in the situation, however, is the fact that in large part the phantoms are the wraiths of truth formerly apprehended, but since lost, and that so long as there is even the subtlest suggestion of true and vital meaning in the traditional forms of thought and behavior, the dominance of the mores will not work outright catastrophe. Even the phantoms of truth have saving grace.

It is admittedly a journey somewhat afield from the main thesis, but nevertheless of much importance to note what Jung has wisely observed as to the relation of the myth to history. Speaking of the "mythical tradition" he says that

"it does not set forth any account of old events, but rather acts in such a way that it always reveals a thought common to humanity and once more rejuvenated. Thus for example, the lives and deeds of the founders of old religions are the purest condensations of typical contemporaneous myths, behind which the individual figure entirely disappears."

The very husks and shells of the myths, still prevalent in universal tradition, are capable, as Jung intimates here, of "rejuvenation." And this is the hope of humanity. It is always possible that intelligence may return in sufficient force to revitalize the myths with their original dynamic potency. This is the need of the world of culture today. The obstacle that so stubbornly blocks the way to this renaissance is the incredible fact that large sections of what was created as mythology have been crassly and stupidly mistaken for veridical history itself! Ages of mental hallucination and ideological folly could have been obviated if the myths had not been obtruded into the terrain of objective history. Possibly nine-tenths of the material embodied in the Christian scriptures has been taken for ancient Jewish history, when in truth the book is almost entirely a collection of aboriginal mythical constructions. So obvious is this to competent students who have conscientiously surveyed the field of ancient religion that Kalthoff has written the following doubtless well-considered paragraph (*Entstehung des Christentums*):

"The sources from which we derive our information concerning the origin of Christianity are such that in the present state of historical research no historian would undertake the task of writing the biography of an historical Jesus."

And he strengthens this with another asseveration (*Ibid.*, p. 10):

"To see behind these stories the life of a real historical personage would not occur to any man if it were not for the influence of rationalistic theology."

The Messiahs, Sun-gods, Saviors, Christs and Jesus figures, of whom there were scores in the religions of early times, it is to be inferred, were not historical persons in the flesh, but the typal characters designed to portray man's ever-coming divinity. They were mythical figures and not men in history. Kalthoff goes on to say that the divine element in Christ was always considered an *inner* attribute and possessed or manifested by the Christ figure in common with humanity, which is to evolve the same divinity in its own life. He adduces the fact that everywhere the Christ figure is shown exhibiting "superhuman traits; nowhere is he that which critical theology wished to make him, simply a natural man, *an historical individual.*" Well had it been for western civilization if it had been known that the alleged lives and deeds of the founders of old religions, as well as the "historical careers" of a score or more of Messiahs and Sun-gods and Christs, were, as Jung says, "condensations of typical contemporaneous myths, behind which the individual figure entirely disappears." When myth was converted into "history" the Dark Ages began.

The great need of a distinctive differentiation between the two forms of the unconscious, the subconscious and the superconscious, is vividly emphasized when we compare certain of Jung's statements with one another. We have seen the psychologist saying that all the memory-record of our past in the animal stage of evolution, with all its inhuman bestial manifestations that he admits are so revolting that we hesitate to believe we carry the memory of them in the depths of our being, is buried in our consciousness and may surge upward from the unconscious. Yet with this characterization given to the content of the unconscious, Jung is found writing that

"comparison with the sun teaches us over and over again that the gods are libido. It is that part of us which is immortal, since it represents that bond through which we feel that in the race we are never extinguished. It is life from the life of mankind. Its springs, which well up from the depths of the unconscious, come, as does our life in general, from the root of the whole of humanity, since we are indeed only a twig broken off from the mother and transplanted."

And again he is affirming that

"since the divine in us is libido, we must not wonder that we have taken along with us in our theology ancient representations from the olden times. . . ."

Everywhere in psychoanalysis the unconscious is the seat of the libido. The libido is that inner governor who, from behind the throne of consciousness, dominates the life and speaks to the personality in the devious and often obscure language of dreams and symbols. A hundred times the libido is described as the voice and consciousness of the past, of the youthful history of the race in its individual recapitulation, the surging force of the native elemental mind of the race, speaking generally against the suppression of its drive for recognition and free play by the restraints of civilization.

Assuredly it can be seen that the libido is here described in the terms and characters of two things that are at the very opposite poles of rating in spiritual or cultural values. It is at one and the same time the memory of our animal past, with all its horrific and revolting murder-lust and brutality, slumbering in the depths of the unconscious and capable of resurrection therefrom, and also equally the immortal part of us, the "divine in us," the very god-nature nursed germinally within us. This is to ignore or erase all difference in grade and status and nobility between the god and the animal in our constitution and to make the unconscious the dwelling place of the divine genius as well as the lair of the beast. Surely it can be seen that it is the voice of the animal which speaks to us out of the past that we have lived through and compressed into the subconscious, and that it is the voice of the god which speaks to us out of the as yet unborn future whose terrain in the superconscious we are little by little adventuring into. To heed the voice of the animal is to sink back in retrogression into the repellent past; to hearken unto the voice of the god is to step forward into more inviting prospects, and to follow rosier pathways through the meads and uplands of evolution. The terrain of these two regions of consciousness in the human nature is precisely what was meant by the ancient Egyptians in their allegorical division of their country into "the two lands," or "Upper and Lower Egypt," the location and histories of which have perplexed even such a noted Egyptologist as the late William H. Breasted and others. The student of Egyptian history will note that time after time one Pharaoh after another is obliged to fight a war from his capital in Upper Egypt with the kingdom of Lower Egypt, conquer it afresh and unite it again "under the double sovereignty of the crowns of Upper and Lower Egypt." Over and over again a kingdom divided against itself in two warring parts has to be unified. It has never dawned upon the savants that this is beyond reasonable probability as history, and points to the trick of allegory. For it is an exact repicturing of what takes place in the human constitution, where the two kingdoms, that of the animal and that of the god, are long hostile to each other and must be reconciled and brought to an atonement, by the stronger agency of the divine as it wins victory over the "lower Egypt" of the human realm. Even Paul tells us that a wall of partition between us will be broken down, enabling the two natures to merge in harmony into a new creature, "so making peace."

In this connection it is appropriate to present what Jung has to say as to how the truth embalmed in the myths is to be apprehended. After remarking, most discerningly, that it is more or less imperatively demanded that the psychoanalyst should "broaden the analysis of the individual problems by a comparative study of historical material relating to them,"—and Jung himself has done this most exhaustively—he goes on to say that

"It is a well-known fact that one of the principles of analytic psychology is that the dream images are to be understood symbolically; that is to say that they are not to be taken literally, just as they are represented in sleep, but that behind them a hidden meaning has to be surmised. It is this idea of a dream symbolism which has challenged not only criticism, but, in addition to that, the strongest opposition."

What is true here of the dream symbolism is true also of the mythic symbolism. Jung repeats it—and underscores it—"*it is not literally true, but is true psychologically.*" It is easy to understand and pardon a symbologist's contemptuous fling at uncomprehending scientists and scholastics in his further comment:

"In this distinction lies the reason why the old fogies of science have from time to time thrown away an inherited piece of ancient truth; because it was not literally but psychologically true. For such discrimination this type of person has at no time had any comprehension."

Indeed Jung goes so far as to assert that

"Dreams are symbolic in order that they can not be understood; in order that the wish, which is the source of the dream, may remain unknown."

This pretty well matches the statement of the Jesus figure in the Gospels that truth was given to them that are without in parables, lest, hearing, they might understand and be converted, and seeing, they might believe. This is to imply that the subconscious presents its symbolic messages furtively, wishing to remain unidentified in connection with its wish, unwilling to be known as sponsoring such a wish. From the very fact that such a furtive motive would not be easily ascribable to the god, who likewise presents his wishes in the higher interests of the personal life, and would have no reason to dodge recognition, it would be inferable that symbolism in dreams is a usage of the subconscious or animal memory alone. This, however, is not the case, since the very highest messages are likewise clothed in the most complex and recondite forms of symbolism. The god and not the animal is the consummate craftsman in the formulation of the symbolic dream. Must it be said that modern psychological science has shown itself totally incapable of recognizing any difference between the two voices of the god and the beast in human consciousness?

Great stress is laid by modern psychology upon what are called "escape mechanisms" and "retreats from reality into phantasy." Religious devotionalism, addiction to idealistic philosophies, surrender to mystical experience even in poetry, music and art, are broadly characterized as houses of refuge from stark reality. But psychoanalysis itself has endorsed the ancient Egyptian and Greek division of man's psychic life into its two aspects of immortal divine mind and lower animal sensuousness, and it would be only a natural question to ask which of the two is seeking to escape from the other! Since the whole crux of the moral problem for man is the conflict between the two natures, the analysis of every phase of the struggle hinges on discovery of which nature in man is trying to

dodge its opponent. Perhaps the difficulty and the confused inter-
mixture of the two in psychoanalytic interpretation arises from
what is implied in the Egyptian symbol of the "horizon." Man
stands directly upon the "horizon" or dividing line between the
two kingdoms of consciousness, and as so poetically stated in texts
from the hieroglyphic writings, "he cultivates the crops on both
sides of the horizon," "he cultivates the two lands, he pacifies the
two lands, he *unites* the two lands." "He makes the two Rheti
goddesses, whose hearts are at enmity with each other, to be at
peace." To the soul it is said: "The horizon is covered with the
tracks of thy passing." This is to say that, as man can focus his
consciousness in the world of spiritual realities or equally in that
of carnal sensuality, he keeps continually passing back and forth,
or up and down, across the middle line of demarcation, the horizon.
Hence on the line of open consciousness, which is directly between
the two, god and animal constantly are intermingling their motivations and propensities, with the result that the clear distinction
between the two is blurred. This may perhaps be the explanation of
the failure of psychology to differentiate between the two widely
separated regions of the unconscious world, the subconscious and
the superconscious. For, as stated before, man's narrow area of consciousness is closely hemmed in between two dark regions of unconsciousness.

It is possible that in this situation lies the difficult determination
of one of the strange devices of ancient symbolic representation,
one that has too often been most weirdly and erroneously guessed
at,—the crucifixion of the Christ between two thieves. In human
incarnation and evolution the potential Christ principle does step
out upon this line of open consciousness between the two bordering
areas of unconsciousness, and it is not too great a strain on poetic
imagery to think of unconsciousness as stealing away the priceless
gift or faculty of consciousness. Likewise the conditions of stress
and strain, suffering and anguish, that necessarily go with the
struggle of the soul as it is torn between the pulls of the two con-

flicting natures, fulfill every esoteric phase of the meaning of crucifixion. In this position the soul stands precisely at the point where
divine and carnal natures cross each other, and are at cross purposes
each to other. The final meaning of the cross as symbol is simply
the incarnation. The soul is on the cross when it is linked to mortal
body. The loss of this explicit determination is one of the tragic
consequences, as well as attestations, of the debacle of esoteric wisdom in the third century.

The confusion of modern study just alluded to as due to the
failure to keep the two natures in the human breast clearly differentiated is again well illustrated in a passage from so discerning
a student as Jung (*Psychology of the Unconscious,* p. 94):

"It is shameful or exalted, just as one chooses, that the divine longing
of humanity, which is really the first thing to make it human, should
be brought into connection with an erotic phantasy. Such a comparison
jars upon the finer feelings."

And he adds that

"Nature is beautiful only by virtue of the longing and love given her
by man."

Indeed so jarring a realization has it ever been to the more enlightened thinking of mankind that soul should be brought under
the dominion of flesh and sense that early philosophical understanding and acceptance of the fact as beneficent has been almost
completely banished and religious sentiment has come to pronounce
the soul's connection with mortal body a thing of evil. Even Plotinus
is declared to have proclaimed his sense of shame at being incarnated in body at all. Centuries of Christian asceticism were activated
by the preachment of the shamefulness of the flesh. Spirit alone is
exalted; matter and body are decried. Nothing can clear this befuddlement save a return to the sagacious enlightenment that prevailed when the *Book of the Dead* was written. It was known then
that the soul could not progress to greater glory if she did not leave

heavenly mansions of dreamy blissfulness and have her powers and faculties brought out from sheer latency into actuality by taking her stand precisely on the horizon line at the focus of the tension between spirit and matter. Only there could she pass from unconsciousness to consciousness. Only there, says Plotinus himself, could she ever develop her own powers and come to know what she herself possesses.

The dynamic force of the realization that man is a god in the making so impressed Jung at one place that he writes (p. 96):

"To bear a God within one's self signifies as much as to be a God one's self."

Yes, in sentiment, but not quite yes in fact. The penalties for forgetting that man is both the god and the animal at one and the same time are not minimized by the strength of lofty sentiment. Man's divinity is as yet mainly potential; it can be realized only through the fulfillment of Aristotle's entelechy and emerge as end product of a time cycle. Its actualization is linked to time and growth, and more than that, to the outcome of a battle with the flesh. Without the battle on the horizon soul would remain forever inane, an unplanted seed.

A final word will round out the case for the claim that the failure to distinguish between the two realms of the unconscious has led to false deductions and confusion. Such a result can be seen by placing side by side two or three of Jung's statements. He has said that the divine immortal principle in us is libido and that "the gods are libido." But he also writes (*The Psychology of the Unconscious*, p. 105) that

"The phallus is the source of life and libido, the great creator and worker of miracles, and as such it received reverence everywhere."

There is no question as to the reverence in which the phallus was held in the olden time, and strange enough it symbolized not the lusts of the flesh, but the highest spiritual or divine element in man. This is all, however, on the plane of symbolism. For psychology to proclaim that the libido in man is alike the divine inspiration from the supervening world of spiritual reality and the force making for physical creation as instrumentalized through the phallus is to ignore a gap between these two that is impassable to thought. The libido has practically been broadened to make its meaning cover what might be called the whole drive of life to get itself expressed in living forms and actions of the creatures. But it seems to be forgotten that both the animal and the divine natures in man are making a drive to get each its particular segment of creative force expressed in the world of life. It hardly seems compatible with the human notions of dignity and worth to place on the same level of quality the forces that come to expression in man's life, the one through the spiritualized intellect, the other through the phallus. All life, in the monistic sense, is one, and in the absolute sense is all equally "divine." But in the area of man's perceptual world it is impossible for the mind to ignore the endless differentiations into which life splits its unit energies. It must see values as relative one to another and all to the whole. In its original uses the libido, a Latin word which when encountered in the text of Cicero's Orations against Cataline in the schools was accustomed to be translated "lust," certainly was employed to name the tremendous sweep of appetency that sought to perpetuate life through sexual function. It was at first largely restricted to the general meaning of "sex." Although its connotations have since been greatly broadened, it is hardly legitimate to extend its meaning to make it take in that other element in man's constitution which in all spiritual and ethical systems has ever been regarded as its direct opposite, indeed its evolutionary opponent and enemy! Except symbolically, it is going to be an undertaking marked for failure to ask the human mind, as it is conditioned by tradition, to affix the character and attributes of what is conceived as "divine" to the physically creative energies that find expression through the phallus.

Universal usage has allocated the play of so-called divine forces to the mind and spirit alone. In the world of relativity it is necessary to make and adhere to patent and obvious distinctions in rating and value. The libido can hardly be used to name both the godlike and the bestial natures in the human being.

Not to prolong the matter to the point of tedium, but for the importance of it all, another citation from Jung shows the same indecisive delineation of libido (*The Psychology of the Unconscious,* p. 105):

"The possibilities of comparison mean just as many possibilities for symbolic expression, and from this basis all the infinitely varied symbols, so far as they are libido images, may properly be reduced to a very simple root, that is, just to libido and its fixed primitive qualities."

This is a bit indecisive, inasmuch as it merely says that symbols, "so far as they are libido images," may be reduced to libido. But it comes close to saying at the same time that "all the infinitely varied symbols" are reducible to libido. But fully one half of ancient symbols have reference directly to the divine element in the life and not at all to the physically procreative psychology.

Dr. Hinkle has stated that "symbols dominate to an unbelievable extent man's conduct and behavior, as well as his thinking; they are the bridge over which he travels from the known to the unknown." They enable the mind, she elucidates, to conceive the shape and nature of something lying in an unknown realm, from the hint of its likeness to something already at hand in the known world. Indeed she states that this process of working over from the known things in the commonplace world to true conceptions of things of a different nature unknown to us is "the source of all cultural progress." What needs to be added, then, is simply that when we come to interpret the symbols to enhance our limited understanding, care must be taken to apply their reference discreetly within the just boundaries of their area of connotation. The longer symbols are studied, the more clearly it is seen that they constituted a language of ancient ideological communication which does not lend itself to loose poetic fancying, but carries meanings with almost mathematical succinctness. The first step toward the Dark Ages was taken when this precise knowledge of the old symbolic language began to disappear.

CHAPTER XIII

LIGHT FROM AN OLD LAMP

ONE of the achievements of this age, for which it may come to be marked in later historical view, is the restoration of symbolism to a significant role in the mechanism of culture. We have seen that the superconscious seldom delivers its messages of approval or warning to the lower mind in the known language of common speech. It speaks in the language of symbols and pictorial representations. The discovery of this fact signalizes a great and really momentous advance in technique for the deeper cultivation of the human spirit.

It is worth noting what Dr. Hinkle has to say as to the desuetude of symbolism before its present re-discovery (*The Recreating of the Individual*, p. 137):

"Until now, however, it has been chiefly a subject of academic interest belonging to a past phase of human culture and with no vital meaning for the present. Through psychoanalysis we have come to realize that this ancient process has a present value; and the mode of interpreting and utilizing the symbol, the way in which we understand it in relation to the individual, are intimately connected with his future well-being and development."

Symbols were an integral part of ancient expression because they were the one universally known, or available, and only true language of meaning transfer. Symbols were known to be the one standard means of communication of truth, because the ancients were still in possession of an important item of usable knowledge, the great fact that the seen world is the mirror of the reality of the unseen world. Understanding went into eclipse when this plank in the platform of a primal formulation of knowledge was taken out. Now it is being restored, and it is found that symbols are the substantial stepping-stones by means of which the mind can cross the gap between the objective world and the realities of higher ones. The sages of antiquity knew that if they ventured to construct the pictures of metaphysical reality over the pattern of the objects and phenomena of the known world they would never widely miss the truth.

We are face to face here with a re-discovery as important as that of the unconscious. And it is one that is a necessary supplement of the other, if the full harvest of benefit is to be reaped from knowledge of the unconscious. We shall never be able to read the communications of the inner lord of life to his outer protégé, the conscious human, without the help of this symbolism. Just as the discovery of the Rosetta Stone was essential to our regaining Egypt's lost wisdom, so our ability to translate the language of symbolism is necessary to understand the strange vernacular in which the Ancient of Days speaks down to us from his seat in the plane of consciousness just over our heads. He speaks in the language of meaning-forms and not in that of words. An object or a process from the world of nature conveys a graph of meaning that often could not be elaborated in less than a thousand words. The snake, beetle, locust, hawk and bee, the cloud, rainbow and lightning announce the principles of cosmic law with a definiteness that no words can match. Words can misrepresent the truth; nature symbols can not. They discourse upon the straight truth. They can not lead the mind into sophistry. So reliable and certain is their testimony to verity that whenever the mind wishes to confirm its insights into truth it cites the harmony of its deductions with natural fact. If a structure of exposition can be paralleled with a phenomenon in nature, it is considered to be certified. Poetry is in large part the sensing and limning of this perceived correspondence. To show that an inner construction sustains analogical identity with something in outer creation, proves that it is already accredited, being found extant in the world of real being.

A vivid line from one of Goethe's poems strikes ringing recognition of this truth of symbolism:

"To the capable the world is never dumb!"

And Schiller, while seemingly turned around to a wrong orientation to the theme, nevertheless gives out a phrase of sententious truth when he says:

"I was not yet capable of comprehending nature at first hand; I had but learned to admire her *image reflected in the understanding,* and put in order by rules." (Italics Dr. Hinkle's in quotation.)

Any one who has learned to admire nature's image reflected in the understanding has already become, as Emerson puts it, a priest interpreting the epiphany of creation. This is not an elementary step preparatory to comprehending nature at first hand, as Schiller says. It is indeed first-hand comprehension itself. For it is the interpretation of nature through translation of her forms as alphabet into ultimate meaning. This is to understand nature, for she is then seen not as sheer object, but as forms of meaning. The mind so qualified is able to look not merely *at* nature, but *through* nature to discern the archetypal forms in the divine mind. This is to read God's thoughts after him.

Misguided superficial dialectic might rise here to expostulate that since, as declared, the entire drive of religious aspiration is to transcend the natural man and the world that ensnares him, and to catch and hold the diviner superhuman, it is going against philosophy and evolution alike to ask the mind to tie itself in ever closer relation to the natural world. That, says pietistic faith, is the world to be shunned and escaped. But this is a mistake. To recommend the use of nature as an alphabet for the reading of higher truth is in no way to involve the mind in subjection to nature's own play of mindless forces. It is in no sense to enmire intelligence in her own ground of partial nescience. It is but to use her forms as mnemonics and hieroglyphics of exalted sense or as the lens of a more penetrating and magnifying insight.

Another statement from Dr. Hinkle falls in here with much pertinence (p. 441):

"The whole process of psychic development is seen to follow a kind of spiral movement in which there is a recurrent return to former states having the closest analogy to the actual physical conditions experienced. Thus in all psychic development there is a close relationship with the physical processes, *but not an identity.*"

It is well to observe, with this reminder, that analogy works through likeness, but does not claim identity.

"Through man's capacity for psychic creation he has attained a power for individual development which in its becoming follows like a shadow the actual physical processes lived through, but which possesses a reality of its own as important for human life as the actual physical processes are for all organic life. It is this reality so frequently expressing itself in the language of organic reality which must be recognized for an understanding of human needs. The light that psychoanalysis has provided has revealed a new meaning to many of the great intuitions of the past, and has shown unmistakably that they possess a validity and reality in relation to the individual life wholly unrealized by thought, but entirely realizable in the human being."

This is to say that a meaning, perhaps an actual message from the man's oversoul to his outer intelligence, comes to him in the form of an analogue with some phase of his actual experience. The supermind must speak to him in the terms of what has already had meaning for him. As already set forth, it is impossible that an abstract idea can be presented to a mind without reference to a previously known physical object or process. Even an idea must accrete whatever form, structure or organic outline it is to have from something once known. It has often been said that the mind can form no picture of a something the likeness of which it has never seen. It can formulate new pictures, but only out of a new configuration or combination of elements already imprinted in memory. The very categories of thought, as extension, quantity, number, dimension, cause, effect, quality, etc., are abstractions derived from experience with the concrete physical, which plant these concepts in the intellect. The only pathway open to the mind is through the physical, whose forms become symbols of the metaphysical.

Symbols, then, are the currency in the ideal realm. It is not too strong an assertion to say that symbols are not only the language of conception and impartation in the metaphysical realm, but that they are therefore the instruments of the soul's highest culture. It has been claimed that the mathematical symbols, pi, x and the horizontal 8 for infinity and others, have virtually made higher abstract mathematics possible. Culture hinges on grasp and communication of ideas and symbols make the interchange a near-divine art. It has been questioned whether the act of thinking could be achieved without symbols. An idea would be left formless if it could not be given suggestive shape over the pattern of fixed representation. Description could not be achieved if some known object bearing likeness to the unknown to be described could not be pointed to.

There is evidence of surprising cogency pointing to the realization that the attainment or the degree of culture in mankind bears a significant relation to the interest in symbolism. A cursory canvass of history seems to reveal a distinct and decided parallel between cultural rise and fall and the vogue and lapse of symbolic methodology. This is indeed challenging. The ancient period, during which there was extant a culture sufficiently lofty to inspire the writing of the only books that have held universal veneration throughout the centuries, obviously was steeped in symbolic practique. No more valid attestation of this is needed than the observation that these books themselves purvey symbolism as their chief method of intellectual expression, as they fairly teem with symbolism. Culture rose or prevailed hand in hand with symbolism in that era. The great upsurge of Greek culture was based on and widely utilized symbols, such as Plato's cave allegory, the myth of Er, King Minos' labyrinth, and others. The mighty wisdom of old Egypt verily reeked of symbols. The best in Hindu thought relied largely on symbolic portrayal. The Gospel character of Jesus for the most part taught in parables.

Up to the third century in Christianity, while there prevailed a strong trend to Gnosticism and Greek philosophy in the schools and doctrines of the Church, symbolism and allegorism held a very high place in exegesis, pre-eminently so in the work of the two most illuminated of the Patristics, Clement of Alexandria and his pupil, Origen. Particularly "Origen's allegories" became later a bone of contention between partisans in the Church and as a result fell under the fierce denunciation of the orthodox parties and finally were "excommunicated" by the decrees of Councils about the sixth century. Origen steadfastly maintained that beneath the letter of scriptural text, to be discerned by a more cultivated spiritual intuition, lay a deeper stratum of meaning, which was the true and vital message, supplanting the more obvious literal sense. The scriptures carried a profounder esoteric implication, concealed "under glyph and symbol," which the untutored would miss and the initiated would grasp. The milk for babes was the simple exoteric surface meaning; the meat for hardier digestion was this more deeply buried occult rendering. Philo laid great emphasis on this esoteric symbolic methodology. It is indeed a general characteristic of the body of ancient literature.

But symbolic usage largely disappeared after the fatal third century in countries under the Christian banner. For nigh unto eleven centuries little is heard of symbolism, and this period is precisely that covered by the "Dark Ages" in Occidental civilization.

Then, to put an end to the dismal night, came the Italian Renaissance of the fourteenth and fifteenth centuries. A perusal of John Addington Symonds' comprehensive volumes on the Renaissance in Italy brings to light the astonishing fact that with this great burst of enlightenment there swept in a great tide of symbolic poetization.

The intellectual instinct for symbolization indeed formed one of the chief currents of the revival itself. Says Symonds (p. 95):

"Poetry is instruction conveyed through allegory and fiction. Theology itself, he [Boccaccio] reasons, is a form of poetry; even the Holy Spirit may be called a Poet, inasmuch as he used the vehicle of symbol in the visions of the prophets and the *Revelation* of St. John."

Symonds speaks of Boccaccio's work as containing "a full exposition of the allegorical theories *with which humanism started.*" Another curious passage from Symonds may well be interpolated here, since it weighs in with a surprisingly pertinent reference to present postures in culture. He goes on (p. 96):

"The poet, according to this medieval philosophy of literature, was a sage and teacher, wrapping up his august meanings in delightful fictions. Though the common herd despised him as a liar and a falsehood-fabricator, he was, in truth, a prophet uttering his dark speech in parables. How foolish, therefore, reasons the apologist, are the enemies of poetry,—sophistical dialecticians and avaricious jurists, who have never trodden the Phoebean hill, and who scorn the springs of Helicon because they do not flow with gold! Far worse is the condition of those monks and hypocrites who accuse the divine art of immorality and grossness, instead of reading between the lines and seeking the sense conveyed to the understanding under veils of allegory."

This outcry of Boccaccio against the stolidity and unresponsiveness to the finer poetic aspects of literary culture of the fourteenth century well dramatizes the general protest of delicacy of sensibilities against crassness in all ages. It is one of the noblest yet plaintively pitiful bleatings of refinement against gross dullness. The point to be remarked here is that it came from one who performed pioneer labor in the restoration of intellectual light to a benighted Europe, and that the light which had been kindled for him and which he beamed further abroad to his age, was largely generated and carried by the torch of symbolism. The enlightenment of the Renaissance superinduced, if it was not in great measure superinduced by, the revived science of symbology.

But the Renaissance ran its course, lighting up the intellectual horizon of some generations with a mellow glow of great refinement, to be lost eventually in the sweep of the Reformation, the assertive reaction of the human spirit from centuries of stultifying blind faith, and the extraversion of interests created by the trend to modern physical science. The fine discernments and appreciations of cultured intellect requisite to capture the exalted values in symbolic usage were extinguished and disappeared. Humanitarian culture fell again to a low status, although the Renaissance had given too sweet a taste of it ever to be completely smothered out again. At any rate symbolism was once more submerged in desuetude, except in so far as it lingered in general poetry and polite literature. Even that continuation owed nearly all its inspiration to the vigorous breath that fired the Renaissance flame.

Now, once again, there is the dawning of the sun of symbolic apperception. What it heralds for humanity this time is conjectural and precarious. It all depends on the cultural capabilities of the age. The world has possessed the forms and norms of culture and lost them. With coarse, crude realism stalking the land, in music, art, drama, literature and social life, there seems little chance that a revival of symbolism can take hold and live. The requisite refinements of intellectual perceptions, the delicate nuances of human sentiment, the quietude and habits of reflection needed to catch the subtle but powerful force of natural analogies, are lacking or perilously inadequate. The set of the modern mind is too aggressively extravert to open the way for symbolism to register its values and show its light. Yet, as always before, the true culture of the world hinges upon that accomplishment. In this connection nothing is more illuminating than a fairly lengthy passage from Symonds' work. Speaking of the obstructions in the path of the fourteenth century revival, he writes (p. 67):

"The meagreness of medieval learning was, however, a less serious obstacle to culture than the habit of mind, partly engendered by Christianity, and partly idiosyncratic to the new races, which prevented stu-

dents from appreciating the true spirit of the classics. While mysticism
. . . reigned supreme, the clearly defined humanity of the Greeks and
Romans could not fail to be misapprehended."

That is, the nice discernments of symbolic meanings could not
be gained against or amid the thick atmosphere of heavy pietism
and ecclesiastical postures of all sorts.

"Poems like Virgil's *Fourth Eclogue* were prized for what the author
had not meant when he was writing them; while his real interests were
utterly neglected. Against this mental misconception, this original obliq-
uity of vision, this radical lie in the intellect, the restorers of learning
had to fight at least as energetically as against brute ignorance and dul-
ness. It was not enough to multiply books and to discover codices; they
had to teach men how to read them, to explain their inspiration, to
defend them against prejudice, to protect them from false methods of
interpretation. To purge the mind of fancy and fable, [when of course
literalized] to prove that poetry apart from its supposed prophetic meaning was delightful for its own sake, and that the history of the antique
nations . . . could be used for profit and instruction, was the first step
to be taken by these pioneers of modern culture. They had, in short,
to create a new mental sensibility by establishing the truth that pure
literature directly contributes to the dignity and happiness of human
beings. The achievement of this revolution in thought was the great
performance of the Italians of the fourteenth and fifteenth centuries."

It requires no access of perfervid unction or over-serious thinking
to be aware that this passage describes a situation the replica of
which confronts humanity at this present hour with issues grave
and fateful. It might indeed be said truly that the fate of our civilization hinges on the fineness or the bluntness of our susceptibility
to the profound intimations of symbolism. The age has given no
sign that it has cultivated the requisite sensitivity to the subtle impingement of the high values delineated by symbology. There seems
little hope that it can rise to the measure of a successful accomplishment in this field.

Henry Drummond offered to its view the generic type of such
an achievement in his *The Natural Law in the Spiritual World.*

The book was widely read, a fact which makes its eventual drop into desuetude and neglect all the more dispiriting. Had the Christian theologians possessed the open mind to evaluate the great hint of his book in due and significant measure, the postulates of religion today would be resting more firmly, not merely, as Gladstone thought, on the impregnable rock of the Holy Scriptures—esoterically interpreted,—but on that still more impregnable rock of natural analogy, than they have ever rested on sheer faith. Will the age fail once again to hold the benignant light of symbolic truth when psychoanalysis kindles the lamp anew? It is a momentous question. More centuries of war and woe will follow if the response is feeble.

There has existed for centuries an inveterate obduracy against allegorism, symbolism and dramatization of truth, as particularly found in the sacred scriptures. The sage authors of those scriptures presented majestic truth in no less majestic allegory, myth, drama and symbol; and the best that even the modern mind can do in the face of it is to snarl and sneer and snort. To continue the alliteration, to that mind it has all been a snare. There was no soundness nor health in it. It was perforce accepted and palliated as the infantile habit of "primitive" peoples. It could be tolerated in condescension. But this "certain condescension" worked to a catastrophic end in the total failure of its possessors to grasp the meaning buried in those superb relics of cryptic wisdom under allegory and symbol. The creation story, the ark and deluge saga, the going down into "Egypt," the drying up of the Red Sea (now properly translated the Reed Sea!) and the exodus of forty years' wandering, the Jonah idyll and a good thousand other major and minor items of that Bible claimed to be the highest expression of the moral and ethical grandeur of a civilization boasting its clear-seeing powers above those of all other times and peoples in history,—all these items of cardinal meaning in its own holy volume are yet a totally sealed mystery, not a syllable of their true esoteric meaning properly read or understood. It should carry some measure of rebuke to modern pride and vaunting of all-time superiority in intelligence, as well as some degree of humiliation, from the discernment that the Bible it still extolls is quite incapable of interpretation without resorting to the keys supplied—and only recently discovered—from the allegedly primitive Egyptians.

There is a modern tide of concern with so-called prophecy. The forecasts of the future made by Nostradamus, Mother Shipton and others have been brought out and given great vogue. To give any plausible conciseness to their predictions, a deal of help must be supplied by the reader's imagination. They run much on the order of ancient oracles, whose messages were vague and flexible enough to cover several possible alternatives. But there is one such utterance that challenges the attention of the most incredulous. It was that given by Count Leo Tolstoy in 1910 and published in advance of the events it predicted. It foretold the Balkan War in 1912, the first World War in 1914 starting in the Balkans, the course of developments thereafter, and contained in its penetrating vision of the near future the remarkable statement that a new religion would arise based on symbolism. It is most impressively set forth.

Likewise the savant who was regarded as the world's outstanding authority on Orphism, Prof. Vittorio D. Macchioro, of the University of Naples, in a work entitled *From Orpheus to Paul*, declared in positive terms that if religion is to survive and exercise a beneficent sway over general intelligence, it must return from dogmatic theology to symbolism. This is sound insight, since the highest metaphysical values in religion can be adequately expressed only through the language of symbols. Psychoanalysis has added its corroboration to this conclusion. The divine soul must use symbols to adumbrate its realities.

It is pretty well established that among groups or schools that in ancient days labored at the great task of spiritual culture, the Essenes in the Trans-Jordan region were the most eminent custodians of true primeval wisdom. The article on them in the *Encyclopaedia Britannica* contains the remarkable statement that "they preserved in their libraries the books of the ancients, and read them not with-

out an allegorical interpretation." The Christian historian-apologist
Eusebius makes the statement, which is surely a vital challenge to
all Christian claims, that the Gospels of the New Testament were
old books preserved by the Essenes from remote antiquity.

Psychoanalysis now opens the door to the renaissance of symbolism. This may mean as great an advance for mental science in
the domain of self-mastery for the individual as the introduction
of symbols meant for abstract mathematics. It will equip effort at
control of individual action with a technique of known scientific
procedure. And now follows a denouement in this process of investigation that comes with startling impact upon common realization. Symbolism, the newest feature of psychoanalytic discovery, is
all at once found to stand in the relation of a new intimacy with
an older aspect, indeed one that presided at the very birth of psychoanalysis itself,—sex. We have said that nature and her phenomena
stand as the outer language speaking the truth of cosmic creation,
that nature is truth manifested in the form of concrete structures.
The shape and nature of created things reveal the archetypal mind
that engendered them.

A link that helps join the two aspects of the theme being developed here may be found in Dr. Hinkle's discerning pattern of relationship between symbol and reality in her volume already freely
quoted. She writes (p. 240):

"One can gain value from experience only when it is grasped in its
double aspect as symbol and as reality; not when it is possessed merely
as a symbol, and the subjective content, expressed through the idea of
fantasy, is the only reality. Actually there are two realities, the concrete
external fact, and the inner subjective psychological factor; adaptation
and assimilation must take place with both."

This is extremely well said and timely. Every object is at once
both thing in itself and symbol of another thing less objective. And
the true "being" or "reality" of a thing is not seen until this double
refraction of meaning is discerned. As Wordsworth has brought out
so pointedly in his *Peter Bell* poem,

"A primrose by the river's brink
A yellow primrose was to him,
And it was nothing more."

Beside standing there in the meadow it carried to Peter nothing in the line of the majesty, meaning and wonder of the universal life in which it was a humble participant. But it does seem as if Dr. Hinkle has here transposed her rating of values and acclaimed by the form of her language the lesser status of the view of the thing as symbol of deeper import. She seems to imply that people ordinarily miss its value as objective reality in the implied more common grasp of its meaning as symbol. This reverses the general status of the case, for hardly any mind misses the validity of the thing as object, while very few go beyond this to the reality of the thing as symbol of subjective experience. Our whole essay is the attempt to do just that with sex, to take it far beyond its known quality as an object of sensual experience in the concrete world, and to invest it with its grander reality as symbol. There is little evidence that this task has been attempted or achieved before.

Dr. Hinkle herself stands in position to be accorded credit for taking several notable steps in that very direction. She has caught some glimpses into the long vista of truth that is opening out through the analogical approaches, tentative and timorous as they are, of psychoanalysis to the science of sex as symbol. On page 49 of her work she writes that by the technique provided by psychoanalysis

"the sexual impulse is raised to the realm of the symbol and, for humanity in whom creativeness is the never ending goal, it is a symbol of the highest significance and value."

And she continues:

"One is forced by analytic work to a realization that the representations of sexual activity are themselves used as symbols by the human mind to indicate the new goal—the creative urge toward the fulfilment of a necessary psychic development and attainment, which all the physical gratification in the world can not satisfy. Just as men use their sexual powers and achievements as a measure and symbol of their masculine strength and power on the physical plane, so *the unconscious uses the sexual symbols as the language* in which to express capacities and potentialities on the psychic plane." (Italics ours.)

The last sentence comes close to being a statement of the theme and thesis of this work. Sex is a great—a very great—objective reality in and of itself. And there the common mind of humanity has stopped in dealing with it. It has seemed so substantial and realistic a value in itself that there was not felt a need to use it as a mental stepping-stone or stairway to something of more intrinsic value lying ahead in subjective realms. *Now the task is to transcend its value as object and sensual experience and to delineate its still higher value as a symbolic language of the most exalted descriptive character.*

What Dr. Hinkle has brought out here is true and vital. The time is destined to arrive, and before too long, when the principles of analogy and the human mental capacity for analogical insight, developed to quick apperceptions in periods when symbolism was pursued and cultivated, but left to atrophy in all other periods, will be developed to an acute stage again and function like a new genius. The mind will be able to look at objects in nature's realm and see both of the realities pertaining to them, to cull both their objective and their subjective influences. It will see them as the things they are, standing there as objects of experience palpable to sense. But at the same time it will be able to see them as the Egyptians saw them, the living language of another world of reality, the world of truth, laws, ideas. It is the aim here to perform this service for the objective reality known as sex in human life. Another work will aim to do the like service for a thousand particular phenomena in the world of nature.

CHAPTER XIV

THE LANGUAGE OF LINGAM AND YONI

NOW sex is one great cardinal aspect of nature. Among nature symbols those based on sex must play as pivotal and sweeping a role in thought and philosophy as sex itself plays in life as lived. The central and almost predominant part sex plays in life is matched by the Freudian, and again more recent, assignment to it of positively crucial importance in psychoanalysis. Symbolism is the discovered modus of the operation of the superconscious; sex is the dominant strain of influence or motivation in the production of psychic manifestations. Hence sex and symbolism must be close in affinity. The thesis of this work is the interpretation of sex as symbol of cosmic truth.

Sex is the greatest word in the language of symbolism, and it can now be perceived that the intonations of that word come ringing out to the human mind with a message of meanings the most awesome and mentally illuminating in the whole history of man's questing for light on the mysteries of life and nature. Again it will be seen that the ancients knew *this* basic fact that only now is receiving some recognition in modern groping. This knowledge on their part is now certified to by their use of sex symbols, extended later to sex practices and formularies, in the religious systems of ancient nations. Their employment of this sort of symbolism, known as phallicism, has been no less than tragically misapprehended by stupid medieval and modern assumption in entire failure to grasp the true motif behind it all. The essay will endeavor to orient the modern attitude to a more competent understanding of the intrinsic sincerity, natural legitimacy and exalted significance of phallic symbolism, and to raise it again from its mean status in the

194

misconceptions of religionists to its due place of the loftiest sublimity in human consideration. The results attained by the study will come as the natural corollary of the function of sex as found at work in the field of psychological science.

Again modern mentality is confronted with the necessity, for its own better poise and balance, of recovering a lost ancient comprehension. Again it finds itself in dereliction from the more perspicacious discernment of antiquity. Again it must bestir itself to regain a lost possession of the past.

Dr. Hinkle's capable delineation of the status of sex symbolism in remote days may serve to open this excursion into the territory to be explored afresh (*The Recreating of the Individual*, p. 426). She is speaking of the Oriental faiths in the ancient period:

"These religions, unlike the Christian religion, were not antagonistic to sexuality—indeed we find its phenomena frankly flourishing along side all their worship and ritual, and incorporated with them. To these minds sexuality was not impure or unclean and there seemed no incongruity in the admixture of sexual and religious symbolism. Indeed in India sexuality itself was made an object through which control and discipline could be gained by the man."

Christian missionaries professed great horror and revulsion at finding the lingam and yoni, the male and female creative organs, and other signs and symbols of "sexuality" and "immorality" in Buddhic, Hindu and other Oriental temples of religion. Many a dollar was raised from the faithful at home to help lift the heathen idolators out of their deep mire of besotted sexual grossness by importing to them the same abhorrence of the mention of sex functionism as had come to be the heritage of New England after several centuries of adamant Puritanism. The passage quoted just now is indication that at long last the pall of a wholly unnatural evil stigma laid by the worst of philosophical distortions upon our Occidental mind for some centuries is beginning to be lifted, as the lost light of a *wholesome paganism* dawns upon our benighted mental horizon. Psychoanalysis indeed might have come earlier if sex had not been pushed down out of common normal vision under a blanket of hypothecated indecency and evil for too many centuries. There was offered little chance of the West's coming to understand the meaning of this segment of our nature as long as it was held reprehensible for anyone to study the phenomena appertaining to it and to publish the findings. Now the moral miasmatic mist is lifting, and with the first release from stigma and opprobrium come the first rich fruits in the valuable findings of psychoanalysis.

Sex is being morally neutralized, as a legitimate object of research and understanding. The nightmare of some sixteen centuries of more or less insane morbidity over it, due to the frightful perversion of ancient symbolic dramatization of cosmic truth by phallic representations, and leading to the horrendous asceticisms perpetrated in the name of "spirituality" by generations of fanatical religionists, crucifying the sex nature to "save" the immortal spirit, is at last being dispersed in the awakening of common sense to the recognition of the natural good function of the sexual instinct.

This side of the Renaissance has lingered long behind the intellectual and philosophical impulses of the fourteenth and fifteenth centuries. The Renaissance and the Reformation are neither of them completed. What an errant and ignorant Christianity threw out or extinguished in the third century has by no means all been recovered. To emphasize vividly what a wrongly oriented Christian philosophy did to an aboriginal sane view of the natural man's place in the dual economy of life, it is well to look at a concise statement made by Lecky in his famous old work, *The History of European Morals* (Vol. II, p. 291):

"The Greek conception of excellence was the full and perfect development of humanity in all its organs and functions, and without any tinge of asceticism. Some parts of human nature were recognized as higher than others; and to suffer any of the lower appetites to obscure the mind, restrain the will and engross the energies of life, was acknowledged to be disgraceful; but the systematic repression of a natural appetite was totally foreign to Greek modes of thought."

This is a challenging reminder to those in Christian circles who find it an unfailing pastime to stigmatize darkly everything pagan. There was balance, there was understanding, there was philosophical acumen holding the horizon line steadily between excess and deficiency. Lecky contrasts with this the tragic misconception of Christian moral codes, which could rise to nothing higher than the persuasion of folly that for the interests of the spirit it was necessary to kill out the element of creative impulse and all its works. And the world has ignored, excused, condoned and palliated, if not even honored, this abject subversion of reason and sanity, as the product of a holy passion for God. But Socrates and Plato labored all life long to prove that no amount of holy passion is good unless it is tempered with the knowledge that enables the human to keep his position steadily between excess and inadequacy. Holy passion is not only futile but perilous if it is misguided to the repression of a part of our nature that is designed to fulfill its function in its most perfect development.

It is well if the modern Occidental mind can be brought for a moment to remembrance of this chapter of early Christian history, as it may aid in giving a truer perspective of the road we have traveled to where we now stand. A work of great value would be a study which would bring to clear light the genesis of the human sense of shame of the reproductive functions and organs, with its ghastly brood of developments in asceticism, mutilation of the body, distortion of the mind and morbid crushing of natural happiness. In the study it would be brought to view that the usual laudation of "Christian" and the stigma thrown on "pagan" must be exactly reversed. In this comparison the laurels for sanity and wholesomeness must surely go to "pagan." It is indeed no slight ignominy that falls to the debit of Christianity in this contest. To have perverted whole segments of human psychic endeavor and natural instinct by turning them from the channels of happy exercise under God's order to the dark recesses of both morbid repression and guilty expression, must be accounted forever a heavy stain on the record of the Church of Christ.

A few startling excerpts from Lecky's work may accentuate the charge succinctly. He writes (Vol. II, p. 321):

"The relation which nature has designed for the noble purpose of repairing the ravages of death, and which, as Linnaeus has shown, extends even through the world of flowers, was invariably treated [by the Christian Fathers] as a consequence of the fall of Adam, and marriage was regarded almost exclusively in its lowest aspect . . . as an inferior state. . . . 'To cut down by the axe of Virginity the wood of Marriage,' was, in the energetic language of Jerome, the end of the saint."

To reproduce the race was a crime against Deity.

Taking the Adam-Eve allegory in its crude literal interpretation, the crabbed mind of early theologism could not get past the inevitable naïve inferences that sprang from Eve's tempting man to his fall. Woman had to carry the stigma of the first mother's weakness all through history. If the divine spirit in man was to stand against further descent into sin or supine resignation to its established thraldom, the man had to cut himself free from the woman. Women had to be cast aside as unclean, as evil, as the living form of the Tempter. And such was the lot that was thrust upon her and in which she, with equal morbidity, in large part concurred. Lecky adds (Vol. II, p. 338):

"The combined influence of the Jewish writings [as part of Christianity] and of that ascetic feeling which treated women as the chief source of temptation to man, was shown in those fierce invectives which form so conspicuous and so grotesque a portion of the writings of the Fathers, and contrast so curiously with the adulation bestowed upon particular members of the sex. Woman was represented as the door of hell, as the mother of all human ills. She should be ashamed at the very thought that she is a woman. She should live in continual penance, on account of the curses she has brought upon the world. She should be ashamed of her dress, for it is the memorial of her fall. She should be especially ashamed of her beauty, for it is the most potent instrument of the daemon. Physical beauty was indeed perpetually the theme of ecclesiastical denunciations."

To such lengths of literalism and harlequin grotesqueness had this philosophy gone all askew that "women were often forbidden by a Provincial Council in the sixth century, on account of their impurity, to receive the Eucharist into their naked hands." Against this macabre background the ancient Greeks' love of beauty and naturalness shines with wondrous luster. Let us take the space to enhance the contrast. In his second volume (p. 292) Lecky writes, with reference to the Greek epoch:

"In no other period of the world's history was the admiration of beauty in all its forms so passionate or so universal. It colored the whole moral teaching of the time and led the chief moralists to regard virtue simply as the highest kind of supersensual beauty. It appeared in all literature, where the beauty of form and style was the first of studies. It supplied at once the inspiration and the rule of all Greek art. It led the Greek wife to pray, before all other prayers, for the beauty of her children. It surrounded the most beautiful with an aureole of admiring reverence."

One sad consequence of Christian sickliness of mind may be mentioned in Lecky's words (Vol. II, p. 354):

"The domestic unhappiness arising from differences of belief was probably almost or altogether unknown in the world before the introduction of Christianity."

In one more respect the Occidental world needs to recover the high status of paganism. And once again the mind is instructed by a shocking object-lesson of appalling costliness in the destruction of human happiness, in the incredible historical consequences of such an apparently simple item as the misconstruction of an ancient theological or cosmic allegory. The rebirth of symbolism comes after its burial in ignorance for dismal centuries, with its fair promise of release to the bound mind of ages from the killing force of

moral and intellectual ineptitudes unconscionable past all belief.
It will be the only magician's wand capable of healing the diseases
of mental infatuation and the hypnotic power of superstition.

The clue to an understanding of the whole situation may be
drawn out from a piercing introspection into the implications of an
epigrammatic pronouncement of Lecky's (Vol. II, p. 3):

> "The eye of the Pagan philosopher was ever fixed on virtue, the eye
> of the Christian teacher upon sin."

If a ribald figure may be pardoned, the Pagan philosopher
sought to elevate man by lifting him from above; the Christian
theologist by kicking him up from below. Doubtless in the large
both directions of force have their due play. Yet the difference of
approach is suggestive. One aims to keep the spirit of man breathing the pure upper air of healthy life and enjoying it; the other
imprisons it in the dank malarial atmosphere of ugliness and morbidity. One contemplates an upward urge from delight in the beautiful and the natural; the other expects it from revulsion against
ugliness. One envisages righteousness and virtue and beauty, and
becomes rapt in the ecstasies of holiness. The other fights in the
shadows of remorse and wretchedness and keeps the eye of the soul
riveted on the despicable, the craven and the repulsive. The one
aims to lift up the spirit through the delights of virtue; the other
through disgust with evil.

The subjugation of the mind of general humanity under the complex of an evil attribution to sex is one of the most stupendous and
challenging phenomena in life's domain. The general mind does
not possess the necessary data of an adequate elucidation, since the
problem has its roots deep in aspects of the soul's evolutionary situation or predicament which lie beyond our ken. They may inhere
in and spring from some of the anthropological and genetic phases
of the soul's pilgrimage through the eons. Orphic books do ascribe
the soul's present status and difficulties to "ancient wrongs" and
"Moira's bounds transgressed." They ascribe its present karmic evils

to past sins, in part at least. The soul is said to have bound itself by "broad oaths fast sealed" with Deity, to discharge its high evolutionary errand on earth, but violated its oath and fell into dalliance and waywardness. It did not walk on the surface of the water of life, but sank into the depths of sense and animalism. "They indulged in their own movement; they took the wrong path . . . and swung as far away as they were able," says Plotinus.

Whatever the cause, at any rate the human race has ever stood before its own endowment of sex baffled and perplexed. Imperiously sex has dominated a major segment of all human motivation and activity, and has driven mortal man with its implacable imperative into the continued perpetuation of the race, and from one angle of view, taunted it with the consequences. Physiologically and psychologically its slave, man has philosophically been almost entirely bereft of a rationale that would enable him to mitigate its thraldom, neutralize its ravages, countercheck its impetuous tyranny, control its expression and normalize both its exercise and its social acceptance by due comprehension of its proper genre and status in the human economy. It still can be said that the race is without an adequate philosophical purview of sex.

Beyond the crude and obvious recognition of its provision for the propagation of the race and the ascription to it of a natural beneficence in this function, there is no generally agreed and fixed category of appraisal in which it should be classified. Even at times its agency in the production of new humans is not seen as a blessing. It is felt to jeopardize the prospects of happiness by ushering in new life where the chances for its more perfect development are predominantly unfavorable. It can legitimately be thought of as dooming souls to lives of mortal wretchedness. Schopenhauer has well delineated its despotic sway over mankind in the three volumes of his *The World as Will and Idea*. It is there depicted as a nameless despot, as the will of life driving its creatures on to the fulfillment of its aims. It is pictured as irrational, guided by no principle of reason, and brushing aside any such principle whenever its use by its creatures would stand to obstruct its sweep to the accomplishment of its own ends. It is painted as an insatiable hunger and thirst after life, and that not in idea or spirit, but in existence, in sense and in flesh. To gain its goal of ever more bodies to live in, it baits its lure to their generation with its irresistible honey and nectar of bliss and orgiastic ecstasy. And from deep in the profoundest well of conscious motivation—even from the hidden recesses of the unconscious, in fact—this inexorable tyrant of life channels human conduct in a direction that tends ever toward the culmination of all in a paroxysm of transport.

Its faraway reference is omnipresent, whenever male and female meet. It looks out of the eyes of the youth and maid from the moment of their first glance. It insinuates its mute but powerful appeal into every touch of the two polarized opposites, heightening the lure until both sweep into each other's embrace. Its sole "drive" is to bring spirit and matter, male and female, together for the purpose of new generation. Every act, word, look and stratagem of conduct, of those who may be its coadjutors and eventually its victims, is conditioned in reference to its fateful end of sex union and reproduction. If in life's code of values it could be assumed that the first and divinest task and end of existence for a living creature is to generate its seed and perpetuate its stream of ongoing life, then it might be legitimate to say that all general acts are subsidiary and subservient to the central consummative act of procreation, and are to be appraised as good or evil as they fall in or out of line with the movement leading toward life's renewal.

Whether to hold the tyrant as grim and beneficent, or grim and maleficent, to rate it good or berate it as evil, to regard it as enslaving or as liberating, as lovely or repulsive, blessed or accursed, has been the age-old question with which the incessant pressure of the great life impulse has confronted mankind from the dawn of reflection. So we have seen the function of sex pigeon-holed in both the highest and the lowest categories of thought and regard, as well as in every intermediate shade and grade between the two. It is at one time and in certain propitious circumstances exalted as the very flower of beauty and of good; at other times and under altered conditions, it becomes the very horror of shame and repugnance. It can be viewed in every degree of light and shadow in the gamut's interval. It can be exalted to the highest rhapsodies of Platonic or poetic purity and sanctity; a little lower down it can be sensed as good in more commonplace degree; still farther down it can be a matter of indifference, morally, aesthetically neutral; then it can be mildly repellent, conventionally taboo; and finally it can be violently distasteful and even loathsome, foul and bestial. In between it may register a thousand different nuances of tone and impressionability.

This wide variety and diversity in the modes of its subjective registry may indeed point to the inference therefrom that its assessment of good or evil character is a matter merely of the mood, background, biases, predilection and the general postures of the minds that stand in judgment on it. Indeed history sanctions this verdict. For there has never been uniformity in the social appraisal. What has seemed noble and lofty to some has appeared vicious and depraved to others. Laudation and reprobation, tolerance and resentment have often greeted the same acts. Even to the same individual a sexual determination that at one instant seemed haloed with loveliness can *ex post facto* be viewed as injudicious and turn to a canker of remorse. What absolute character or quality the thing has intrinsically of itself is often the least considered item in the mental view. Extraneous influences and not the inherent merit or demerit of the case generally govern the form of the judgment or the reaction. In the end, then, being virtually the hidden omnipresent motivation behind every situation, it takes on the infinitely varied coloring of mood, shade and value from the distinctive connection in which it occurs. So it has never been categorically judged and catalogued in specific character.

Yet certain broad general attitudes toward it have taken concrete form in the social life of different nations. Common convention in society has condemned a too free and open expression of it. Any manifestation of it outside the legitimatized forms is frowned upon and disgrace is heaped upon the offenders. It receives its highest sanctions and its virtual apotheosization in the field of romance, in the phase of courtship and mating, and in parenthood. After marriage the door is open to indulgence governed only by individual tastes and disciplines. In religion, art, literature and education its expression is varied and manifold. Many differentiations make up the general patch-quilt of its variegated vogue and role in the life of the world. On the whole it is inordinately sensitive to the vicissitudes of mood, sentiment, moral poses and personal attitudes. In the main it is maintained in strength and keenness by the imposition of restraint upon its indulgence and rendered weak and flaccid by inordinate expression.

The deepest inquiry is involved in the attempt to determine the genesis of the sense of shame that has almost universally afflicted the ordinary human attitude toward sex. Why the dialectically unsupportable posture of the human mind, exhibited in its investing with the mantle of shame and contumely the very organs and function that give us our existence, could arise and fix its clammy clutch so remorselessly and universally upon the world is a problem of the weightiest moment and needs rational solution.

To strike bottom in this recondite search it is necessary to resort to the hints and data found only in the tomes of the archaic anthropological and cosmological wisdom of the early sages. The old books give us intimations in ·data that are not too full or explicit. They tell us that, as in the *Timeaus,* "twelve legions of angels"— the true identification at last of the twelve "tribes of Israel"—were assigned the mission of coming to earth to be the souls of the highest evolved animal bodies. These souls were units of God's own spiritual selfhood, seed fragments of his own nature. One might think of them as units of his mind. They are the "Innocents" of New Testament allegorism, the designation being a reference to their never before having been "married," i.e., linked organically to physical bodies in planetary incarnation. A Hindu name given them is *Kumaras,* or "virgin youths," "celibate young men." In Egyptian nomenclature they were "the Younglings of Shu," or "the younglings in the egg." They were pure souls, units of divine consciousness, untested in the conflict with matter, and therefore sent out to be put under the test which all consciousness must meet, namely, the function of standing as the positive pole opposed to matter, the negative. This constituted the "temptation" of Holy Writ, so outrageously misconceived by ignorant literalism. It was a "temptation" only in the sense of a testing or a trying out against concrete experience the latent powers of the soul, which could come to an actualization of its still potential capabilities only by such an ordeal.

The nub of the origin of shame appertaining to the animal sex nature of man must then be located in the psychic implications of this situation. Here were units of pure mind and soul finding themselves plunged into the bodies of animals and under the necessity of procreating physically, as animals. Or the high-minded souls found themselves organically attached to bodies which procreated physically and sexually. If it is possible to project thought into something like the mental attitudes that would be generated in this evolutionary predicament, some inkling, however imperfect, may be caught of the reaction of these soul units to what must have appeared to them as a degradation of their divine status and condition. Sons of God and consubstantial with him in essence and being as they, subconsciously at any rate, knew themselves to be, they found themselves obliged to "become like us in all respects," and particularly to reproduce in the fashion of animals.

The possible realization of the force of this contrast is not so remote to us as at first view it might appear, since these two elements are still present in our nature, or indeed constitute what we ourselves are. One needs only to recall Plato's definition of man: "Through body it is an animal; through intellect it is a God"—to sense the possible mental attitude of the god in us toward his animal counterpart in us. The emerging self-consciousness of the ego-soul became aware of its attachment to the gross instincts of the animal-soul. The animal functions had for a long time been performed by the animal unconscious, as they still are. But little by little the expanding consciousness of the infant god could look down upon these manifestations of the instinctive life of the body and reflect in some sort philosophically upon them. Surely, sooner or later, as the nobility of the innate divine nature asserted itself, the reaction of the god to the sexual expressions of his own organism would take the form of disgust and revulsion. Something suggesting what we can only call "cosmic shame" of his having to perform like the animal would be generated in the mind of the higher self. Plotinus, as has been noticed, expressed it in a manner almost as drastic as that of the Christian Fathers, in his confession of shame at having a body at all. Some modern spiritual cult systems come to nearly the same attitude. Some even ban sexual expression entirely for their members. The essence of this predicament is in truth back of the many scriptural statements as to the Christ's having demeaned, degraded himself by taking on our nature. "He despised not the virgin's [that is, matter's] womb." Before the rational faculty in the developing ego-consciousness could dialectically work out the "naturalness" and beneficence of the cosmic arrangement that tied or imprisoned soul in bodies, this instinctive revulsion of the god at sight of the body's performance of the creative acts must have taken deep lodgment in the ego-mind.

So came the sense of shame of sex. This is obviously how the genuinely most sacred function in all life on its physical side fell under the onus and stigma of universal infamy and turpitude. Plato, Hermes, Orpheus, Zoroaster, the *Zend-Avesta,* the *Bunda-hish,* the *Zohar,* the *Vedas* and *Genesis* disclose in cryptic form the story of the birth and growth of sexual shame. It goes to the very roots of the human constitution. It came as the result of the original compounding in one organism of the two diverse elements of deity and animality, and their enforced "marriage." *The god conceived a feeling of shame at being subjected to the carnal mode of procreation incident to his incarnation in animal body.*

It is a bit of ancient evolutionary allegorism that has, like the rest, escaped understanding by modern intelligence, that the "sons of God," when sent to earth, were variously cautioned "not to marry the women of that place." They were enjoined to see that they made "no alliances with the natives of that country." These odd injunctions leave something to be desired in the way of explicitness. Nevertheless they can have reference only to two possibilities inherent in the case. They can point to an avoidance of precisely what did happen, namely, the asserted miscegenation of the early races of men with the females of the higher animal species, which bred the several ape types. Or they can be taken allegorically as being an allusion to the necessity of the soul's not losing itself in entire identity with the life of the body. The soul was to tenant the body, build up gradually its rulership over it, hold it in reasonable and salutary subjection, transform its nature and eventually merge its forces with it, or "marry" it. The injunction not to marry the women of that country could therefore be taken as a caution to the souls about to incarnate to help them hold true to the fulfillment of their oath or convenant, which bound them not to lose themselves in the animal nature, to successfully "walk on the water" of the sea of life—water being the exact typal symbol of the animal nature, the body being seven-eighths water—and not to sink into the depths of carnal sensuality. It is by no means a stretch of mental chicanery to make the term "women" mean the physical body of mankind. For the feminine was ever the symbol-type of the physical side, matter or body. The man in humanity marries the woman in humanity when soul and body unite and eventually merge their positive and negative potencies in a new creation. The entire structure of the moral teaching in Old and New Testaments, particularly in St. Paul's searching analyses of the Christly virtues and the carnal vices, rises to ever clearer and more forceful comprehension if read in the light of these lost ancient presentments of the anthropological formation of mankind.

Soul was masculine as generative of plan and action, and body was feminine as performing the function of motherhood for all life and growth. Body was ever represented as "the wife and sister" of spirit, not to say also its "mother." And the story in *Genesis* is instructive for our theme in that it sets forth that when the separation of unisexuality in primeval life into the duality of male and female had been consummated in the garden, then "the eyes of both of them were opened," and they saw that they were naked, and they were ashamed. This is the allegorical depiction of the awakened sense of their position when plunged into incarnation at the level of the beast. It was the soul's reaction to the realization of its descent from the heaven of spirit to the gross realism of life in body.

A phrase used by the Greek philosophers well brings out the recognition of their status. They perceived that they "had fallen into generation." It brought them "under the law," as St. Paul puts it, of sin and death. They had plunged into what the sages of early days denominated "the death of the soul." For such in fact was that diminished potential of life and consciousness entailed for the god-unit when it entered into its union with body. "Death, to the soul," says an exponent of Greek philosophy, "was to descend into matter and to be entirely subjected to it." This is indeed the "bondage in Egypt," "that slave pen," as the Moffatt translation of the Bible renders the phrase in the Old Testament. As souls in bondage to the flesh, we are the sons of Hagar, the bondwoman. When we awaken our divinity and engraft it on the body of the physical, we become sons of Sarai, the freewoman, and thereby enjoy the "liberty of the sons of God."

Down in the "underworld" of sense and matter, buried in flesh and goaded to enjoy the lusts thereof, the god retains enough of the unquenchable fire of divine spirit to be aware, if at first dimly, of his celestial dignity and high estate. At times the sense of loss of his former home and realization of the degradation of his life in the sensuous mire of animal reproduction flash through into his apprehension and generate the shame of his "fall" into matter. Buried thus in the depths of the "nether world" of mythology, hiding in the unconscious of man's life, the soul conceives the feeling that its tenancy of body is a thing of evil designing, low and base. The body is "of the earth, earthy," and the soul feels the dishonor of attachment to it. Plotinus advances the theory that the soul recognizes that its immersion in body arises from some defect in itself, of which it should be ashamed. If it had lived up to its possible greater perfection, it would not have needed the physical experience. This, however, is gratuitous. The soul may be ashamed of its imperfection, but only in the sense in which a seed or sapling should be ashamed of not being a perfect grown tree. It is on the road to being such; it is, as Hopper reminds us, a viator. When the Christos has arisen to his full stature and has asserted his lordship over the entire man, he becomes the high priest after the order of Melchizedek, the King of Righteousness, and he presides at the marriage of the two long-warring but finally reconciled orders of life in one new creative union. And when soul at last drops the "body of shame" of the perishable flesh, and clothes itself anew in that glory-body of empyreal light which is from above, then truly it has put on the wedding garment of the redeemed.

In the *Pistis Sophia,* the Gospel of the Gnostic Christians, Salome asks the Christ when his kingdom shall come on earth. He replies: "When you shall have trampled underfoot the garment of shame; when that which is without shall be as that which is within; when there shall be neither male nor female, but the male with the female shall be as one." This is in full harmony with the postulates of the ancient teaching, that at the end of the aeon the creative life which had divided into male and female poles of energy, returns to androgyneity or undifferentiation for the period of unmanifestation.

This sense of shame wells up from the unconscious, from the

Amen, the "god in hiding." "For a little while" he is made lower than the angels, to be crowned with glory and honor that even angels have not won. But from his temporarily submerged place he speaks out in warning and admonition, or praise and commendation, to the conscious self in the language of symbol. The voice of the unconscious, in its department of the superconscious, is the voice of Deity, not absolute and infinite, but Deity undergoing its own evolution, and as compared with the lower animal self, practically omniscient and infallible. As Heraclitus has written, "Man's genius is a deity." Here in man's temple of body it is a deity tied to the inhibitions of an organism of flesh and sense. While his mind is set to the task of redeeming the animality of the body to humanhood, he feels at times the meanness of his lowly estate and the shame of his nakedness is strong.

It still remains anomalous, logically, that the mind of the race should hold in contempt the functional mechanism of its own physical perpetuation. The strange quirk of this predicament is that sex is held in both extreme categories of the lowest and the highest moral appraisal at one and the same time. It is pretty generally regarded as low and base, while it is at the other end evaluated in terms of the highest sanctity. Its position is therefore relative to mood and viewpoint, or the peculiar cast of philosophy determining the judgment. Motherhood, for instance, is both celebrated with all the halo of romance, sentiment and beauty, as in poetry of lyric character, and also made the butt of scurrilous ribaldry. It is rated according to the dictates of time, circumstance and subjective standards of conception.

Jung outlines a thesis to account for the almost universal low rating of sex functionalism which has the merit of a psychological *raison d'être* at least. He ventures the idea that the race, or the human mind, in order to fend itself from the daily impingement of this insistent force, or to escape its imperious domination, has besmirched it with infamy, pretending to see in it something vile and unclean, something unspeakable and unholy. But, says Jung, instead of enabling man to destroy the power of sexuality in this way, the struggle to defame it has only warped and distorted, injured and mutilated its expression. For not without destruction of the individual can such a fundamental instinct be thwarted, he adds. Life itself has needs and imperiously demands expression of them through the living instrumentalities provided by nature. All nature answers to this freely and simply except man, and his failure to recognize himself as an instrument through which living energy is coursing, and the demands of which must be obeyed, is the prime cause of much of his misery. Despite his possession of intellect and self-consciousness he can not without disaster to himself refuse the task of fulfilling his own needs. His great task is the adaptation of himself to reality and the recognition of himself as a channel through which a stream of living energy is flowing outward to the fulfillment of divinely designed objectives. His blocking them in any way is perilous.

To crush out the sensuous libido overtly is a sin against life. Jung goes so far as to pronounce it "a sort of self-murder." The deliberate renunciation of the chance to express the strong demands of nature "must stifle in himself the wish for it," and this is suicidal. The human will, actuated by social compulsions, drives it inward, when its need is to come forth into expression. This is to "introvert libido," in Jung's phrase, and disastrous consequences follow, we are assured.

"Whoever introverts libido,—that is to say, whoever takes it away from a real object without putting in its place a real compensation—is overtaken by the inevitable results of introversion. The libido which is turned inward into the subject awakens again from among the sleeping remembrances one which contains the path upon which earlier libido once had come to the real object." (*Psychology of the Unconscious,* p. 98.)

This is a fine discernment of psychology. For this introversion clearly is seen to force the ego back into subjective fantasy among the images of its childhood and early racial past, the evolutionary fruits of which have already been gathered, when what it craves is new experiences to further its advance into ever-expanding life. The suppression holds the spirit bound in old forms, when it cries aloud for freedom to test new ones. The only salvation from disaster in the introversion is, as Jung notices, the substitution of a "real compensation" for the repressed desire. Such would come in the form of a higher realization on the part of the ego that the thwarting of sensual libido is altogether in the line of true progress and that the mere sensuous expression would no longer be advantageous. Such decisions come with the general growth of knowledge, wisdom and understanding. Animal desire must gradually be curbed and turned into paths of outlet conducive to the interests of the ruling soul. The distress and psychopathic reactions in this process are obviated when the control of libido is thus exercised from within and, so to say, has the sanction of the whole man. Abnormal psychoses result from the imposition of compulsions and restraints on nature against which the real will of the individual rebels. So we find Cicero most wisely writing (*Tusculanium Questiones*):

"Volition is a reasonable desire; but whatever is incited too violently in opposition to reason, that is a lust or an unbridled desire which is discoverable in all fools."

The intellect in man is destined to be the king and ruler of all things lower than it in the compounding of elements in the constitution of the human. The forces of libido are to come under the direction of King Mind. Mind is unfolding its archetypal plans and designs in the creation of the world and of man and libido must be enlisted in the work as servant of the higher. The soul possesses the power "whereby he is able to subdue all things unto himself," as the Bible puts it. He is able "to put all things under his feet." Libido finds its highest utility eventually in conformity with the purposes of the mind. This is beautifully said by Plotinus (*Enneads* III, 5, 9.):

"What lies enclosed in the intellect comes to development in the world-soul as logos, fills it with meaning and makes it as if intoxicated with nectar."

The mind will eventually stamp its image and the logical structure of its formulations upon the outer universe, filling the whole with the ecstatic sense of divine beauty. And in this work the mind bends the forces of libido to its purposes. In the end libido itself finds its own apotheosization in becoming the servant of mind.

The old Bay Psalm Book recites that

> In Adam's fall
> We sinnèd all.

And Adam's fall was, and still is, held to be the descent of the angelic spirits into the realm of the flesh and their participation in fleshly modes of procreation. Upon human sex has been unloaded the entire obloquy of the "original sin." The grievous sin of Adam and Eve was their indulgence in sexual union. Their lives were "pure" before the fatal commingling. The carnal copulation opened their eyes to their state of sin and shame. Taken allegorically there is philosophical meaning behind these representations. But, the allegorical sense wholly lost, and ignorance clutching at superficial understanding, the creation legend in its weird falsifications has stained the mind of humanity for two thousand years with the taint of half-insane turpitude that blackens mentally the conception of every child of the race. For deep in the background of every human consciousness there still lingers this dark psychological cloud whose miasmatic moisture was generated by the mental poisoning of every generation in its childhood, that every child born of the natural method of sexual union is "conceived in sin." In sickening revulsion from the imputations of this theology, it is not too censurable, perhaps, except on the grounds of its mental stupidity, that modern spiritual cults have in many cases held before their women members the real possibility of their giving birth to children by a wholly spiritual process. The fault does not lie with nature, the methods and processes of which are designed by God. It is to be located in the human folly that can be bred of ignorance. As has been pointed out in so many other items of doctrine that came down from ancient sources, here again is to be noted the wreckage of sanity that has come again and again in human thinking as the result of failure to understand archaic methods of representing sublime truth by allegory and symbol. Perhaps in all history nothing has been so costly to one half of humanity as this miscarriage of ancient symbology.

CHAPTER XV

PHALLICISM TRANSFIGURED

AGAINST the fickle and fluctuating approach to the appraisal of sex made by modern sentiment and feeble philosophical conception, it is possible, as the result of symbolic methodology, to set forth a view that will enable the mind to lay the foundations for erecting a more stabilized and settled judgment on the mooted question. By the aid of analogical processes it will be possible to anchor the mind to a cosmic significance in sex that will serve to fix vacillating opinion and attitudes in a more permanent frame. If it can be shown that sex is at root the constitutional law of existent being and if its functions can be seen as the representation of the modus of all creation, an amended view of its character and beneficence will be gained. This will be of incalculable value to thinking mankind. This view is to be gained through the avenue of approach which sees in sex not the end value of itself in itself, but sees it as the symbol of values in the supersensible world and in cosmic creation which lie beyond its own sphere of function and experience.

Sex hints at the existence of criteria of appraisal of its utility and character which lie beyond common ken, but toward which, by analogy, the phenomena of sex themselves point, and which the mind, thus aided, may lay hold of if it be astute enough. In brief, however much sex may mean as immediate experience, its own weightier significance can better be seen in the light of what it indicates *as symbol*. The light that comes into the focus when the telescope of symbolic vision is directed upon sex as symbol is unimaginably illuminating.

Our work is dedicated to the proposition that sex, used as symbol, stands as perhaps the most luminous guide to the human mind on all the central problems of life and thought. Had the early analogical instinct of discerning mind not been killed out, it might have been known all along that if life is governed by universal law, the known method of life propagation in the vegetable's, the animal's and man's world would be an index of all cosmic creation. And if early tomes of exalted wisdom had not been relegated to the status of infantile or primitive speculation, the terms and elements of the entire problem of existence could have been kept inundated with a flood of meaning, for the more explicit enlightenment of the human faculty.

Theology, as has been seen, was anciently acclaimed as the "King of Sciences." It had won its exalted position in antiquity by virtue of its immediate contribution of light to man's understanding of the meaning of life and the universe. Its principles met and solved the chief problems of philosophy by dint of the fact that, as conceived and formulated, it maintained a relation of the closest intimacy with the world of nature, as well as to man's constitution and life as these were linked with nature. No more than now was theology a mere nature cult, a worship of the growth and death of vegetation, an agricultural ritual, as is so tediously claimed by modern students and writers in the wake of a reading of *The Golden Bough,* or other collections of ancient and "primitive" religious usages. We have read of the worship of Ceres, the goddess of "grain," and of the "corn myth," and other religions of planting and harvesting, of the autumn death of the god with the seed sown and his resurrection in the spring with the germination and upgrowth of that which was "dead." And not in two thousand years has there been one scholar's brain clever enough to tell us that these formulated myths of the dying and germinating seed were not the vaporings of a primitive nature-worship, but that *they were the natural analogue of cosmic and spiritual principles which govern all creation.* It is time that modern ignorance be rebuked and the blunt declaration be made that the ancients never worshiped nature—except as Wordsworth or any poet of beauty worshiped nature.

But they did something with nature that the modern is not yet intelligent enough to do: they used her forms and phenomena as a faithful and enlightening transcript and reflection of supersensual truth. Ancient religion was kept in basic relation to nature, through the force of the ancient knowledge that *nature was the one infallible index for the mind's apprehension of the truth in metaphysical realms.*

Theology was never held bound in nature's domain, but it certainly could be said to start from it. Resting on this sound base, it could fly aloft to the highest realms of spiritual cognition and could maintain its grip on reality therein by grace of its keeping its eye always closely fixed on the incontrovertible veritude that life had exhibited to man's constant gaze in the world of natural fact. The mind's view of nature would hold its vision steady to truth when it ascended into the worlds of thought and intuition. It could pick up the laws and principles which it had abstracted from its observation of life in its manifest forms and apply them with certitude to the discernment of the structure of the metaphysical universe. Ancient intelligence had grasped the truth that God had inscribed his *archai,* or fundamental laws of being, in and upon the visible works of his hands. The firmament showed his handiwork and the world was no less full of his truth than of his glory. Early intelligence was keyed to an ability to catch the voice of the "tongues in trees," to hear the "sermons in stones," to read the "books in running brooks," and to discern the mind of "God in everything."

But the link that connected the mind of God with his works in human conception was cut by the wave of ignorance that engulfed Christianity in and after the third century, so that theology has suffered the loss of its original sanctions in intelligence, and has since stood bereft of its intelligibility. It has now become an outcast even from the seats of its own professors. It is today decried and neglected. It is held to be practically irrelevant to the problems and the struggle of life in the world. This is because it has been reduced to irrationality and meaninglessness. Without its guiding star religion has become largely a psychological extravaganza, a mélange and a mirage of faith, intuition and wishful thinking falsely denominated prayer. The things of the unseen world are doubtless more wonderful than those of the seen, as St. Paul exhorts us to believe. But what has been too quickly forgotten is that *the visible world is the only lens of vision through which man may focus his view upon the unseen realities.* A wise adjuration from the Talmud admonishes us with one of the most pertinent philosophical maxims ever pronounced. It runs to the effect that if we would strive to know the invisible world, we must open wide our eyes on the visible! For there the mind can perceive the analogues, the types, the reflections of the truth in the invisible worlds.

At some point in the historical course man lost the ancient analogical faculty. He lost the daring of mind which had enabled him to leap over the great gap between observed physical phenomena and the structure of the laws that produced them. He lost the genius of insight whereby he had been able to see one truth in two worlds, the obvious world of existent form and the inferred world of structure and meaning to which the outer form stood as clue and key. He had fallen from the philosophical level to the Peter Bell status. He saw nothing beyond the things under his eye. His ignorance and blindness cut him off from transferring the form of known objects over to their meaning-forms in the noumenal world. Nature could not speak her message to his dull mind.

The modern eye has gazed continuously upon the movements of sun and moon, for instance, in relation to the earth, and has utterly missed the astonishing play of a most thrilling love drama enacted between the two luminaries each month, which was designed to yield man instruction upon the analogous romance going on between the male "sun" and female "moon" within the sphere of his own nature. This one feature of natural phenomena indeed stood to the ancient mind as the central light on the entire problem envisaged in religion, the relation of the man to his god. Analogical genius is in the end the key to man's finest culture. The ancients possessed it. In the fatal incidence of darkness the faculty has been dulled and lost. The ability to trace correspondences between the visible and invisible aspects of truth is the great skill that leads to philosophical sagacity. Correspondence opens the eye of the mind to discernments that otherwise would remain unseen.

The effort will be made to present the parallelism between the department of nature known as sex and the higher cosmic *archai* with such completeness that there can be no missing the perception of identity between the two worlds of phenomena and noumena. The interpretations deduced will go to prove that the two worlds do stand in parallel relation to each other, or that one reflects the other. The essay draws upon material that has never been absent from human gaze. It aims to transport the phenomena from this world to the land of ideas. It purposes to turn things and processes over into significance. It strives to have them seen conceptually. It aims to make perception the mother of conception.

It will be found that the ancient seers of truth built their systems of interpretation and philosophical conception upon this working principle of analogy. They formulated the structure of elucidative understanding upon what they saw in the world of living nature. And, seeing that the modus and pattern of creation in the physical world was a type and reflection of creation in the whole cosmos, they introduced *phallicism* into the sacred literature *as the great central symbol at the heart of all meaning.*

Little could they have dreamed that their representation would ever engender a ghastly misconception, or that an age would ever supervene so sunk in intellectual languor that it would mistake the symbol for the thing intended to be symbolized. In phallicism they resorted to the phenomena and functionism of human-animal pro-creation to typify the modus of creation in the large and in the universal. Their procedure was directed by sheer intellectual inti-mations and the loftiest of moral considerations. It had no lesser motive than to aid the feeble powers of the human mind to grasp the forms of higher realities through the instrumentality of a vivid picture of something known which bore likenesses to the thing unknown.

Sex was chosen as the most lucid mental lens through which the laws of cosmic creation could be discerned in vivid outline upon the screen of human thought. This was done because the primal fathers of humanity were conversant with a fact that has not been seen or stated in hundreds of years, namely, that creation in the total, in the cosmos, *is as genuinely an act of sex* as is creation in the life of the creature. All evolution, all cosmic process, is one all-embracing act of creation. And it is in the highest sense of the words a sexual creation. Every chapter of the manifestation is a *Genesis*. Indeed it was seen of old that all life did was to regenerate itself anew. The foundation doctrine of ancient theology is "the eternal renewal." Life in the total acts to perpetuate itself exactly as does life in the single unit. Life attends to one thing before all others: it dowers every one of its creatures with the mechanism and the inexorable instinct to reproduce itself. It has made the generation of seed the all-engrossing prime object of every living being.

Creation does not mean the mere beginning of becoming, but covers the whole process. Life is ever in process of creation, for all life is a never-ending becoming. To be sure, it is not all one constant progression in a straight line and even pace, but is an intermittent advance, proceeding in ever repeated cycles. The movement has its intervals. Each cycle has its genesis, its birth, its upbuilding, its growth, its zenith of manifestation, and its decline, decay and death as the embodiment wears down. Each round of the wheel has its beginning and its end. But just as surely as a human life advances steadily over a long series of minor cycles, and carries the seed or ark of consciousness and identity of nature from the end of one revolution to the beginning of another, so does the imperishable principle of conscious life achieve unbroken continuity by spanning the intervals between the manifest periods to maintain its becoming through all. The cosmic enterprise is a continuous creation. And it is sexual.

Where, then, in the natural scene would the analogizing genius of the ancient diviners look to find the image and reflection of the giant cosmic creative act? Where else indeed but in the natural creative or procreative processes open to view in the life of the microcosmic unit, man? In his own sphere man is creator, progenitor, father. Within his own organism and under the direction of his own will and intelligence he can imitate the Supreme Cosmocrator and renew life. Indeed in the speech of the Demiurgus to the hosts of souls about to descend into incarnation, found in Plato's *Timaeus,* these angelic spirits were instructed to imitate at their level the procreative function of the Great Father at the summit of being. "That mortal natures therefore may subsist and that the universe may be truly all, convert yourselves according to your nature to the fabrication of animals, imitating the power which I employed in your creation."

Man was one of the creatures mentioned in *Genesis,* "producing seed after its kind," creating progeny in his own image. By the invincible imperative of life's own genius man was led to exercise this generative function, as were all the orders of life below him in the scale. The penalty for total failure to exercise the prerogative was set at nothing short of his own total extinction. Reward for the natural and ordinate exercise of it was the happy consciousness of the perpetuation and expansion of life itself, the most opulent richness and aggrandizement of being in every direction. Whether consciously sensed or not, instinct carried the persuasion that if creation on the part of Supreme Deity was the prime act of being, then creation on man's part, and up to the summit of his capacity, must be for him the crowning achievement on the physical side, for the perpetuation of organic existence, and on the mental side, for the plan and order of such existence. If man is made in the image of God, reasoned the early mind pursuing wisdom, it must be that the marvelous mechanism and the psychic energies engaged in man's kind of procreation furnish the creature mind with a copy in miniature of the grand universal creative ordinance. The human creative methodology must be a type-form of the highest creative procedure, or of all creation. God's creative manual must be like man's, *but at an inexpressibly higher level,* both of character and of magnitude. The feeble human mind is powerless indeed to conceive the difference in grade, degree, quality and purity, so to speak, between the two modes, the cosmic and the human-animal. But in spite of that difference the mind must not falter in its effort to see the higher as conforming to the pattern of the lower. For so Hermes Trismegistus instructed us. Life's one central law is that the energy of being generates and animates all things by the one omnipresent impulsion of creative force and that therefore all creatures partake of the nature of the one life. All things are the manifest expression of the one creative impulse, and therefore their existence displays the operation of laws that are homogeneous throughout. The universe is ruled by one law, which is never less than identical in all its manifestations and productions, but which at the same time permits the development of endless modification and infinite variation in the concrete deposit on the physical periphery of creation. Life proceeds from a core of similitude and self-identity in unity and runs out in numberless streams of diversity and multiformity.

Looking, then at the lower manifestation of creative process open to view in his own life, man the creature, at his grade of intelligence, would be able to discern in it the features of creation as a whole. And the seership of antiquity did by this method discern the clues by which intelligence was able to formulate an integrated structure of all creative work. These clues have always lain exposed to mental sight. They are just the particular features of the animal-human creative function taken as a language of meaning on a higher plane of conception. In his generative capacity man was no less the analogue of divinity—Christian philosophy and conditioned sensibilities to the contrary notwithstanding—than he was acclaimed to be in the mental, spiritual or intuitional aspects of his selfhood. He must be so, or the affirmation of his creation in the likeness of God would be true in a partial degree only. It would not be wholly true. It would be a maimed and mutilated truth. If God has soul, or is soul, and manifests it in body and in his works, man must carry the resemblance through the whole of his nature. And his nature is dual, soul and body. So the functional life of his physical portion must stand as a clue and guide to comprehension of God's vital economy. The present work rests on the truth of this dialectical proposition.

It may be considered a rash venture, an unmitigated presumption, to attempt to envisage God's creative mind through the mirror of man's procreative functionism. But it is the only approach available to thinking, and besides it is the one indicated as true and legitimate by the authority of the books of wisdom accredited and venerated by the intelligence of the race over the ages. A gain of considerable proportions for all future culture must be the reward of such an inquiry, if it be only the uncovering of the lost significance of the mangled subject of phallicism in those tomes of antiquity. It will be something of undoubted benefit if a clarification of the motive sanctioning the employment of this phase of symbology can be achieved. For it has hung like a cloud of infamy upon the sensibilities of the world for too many centuries. Through the loss of understanding of the high motive back of the usage, and the ascription of other than the purest of interests and intents on the part of sages employing it in the composition of their books, the theme of phallicism has dwelt for long ages under the shadow of an evil imputation. Most schools of religious thought held sex symbolism to be a symptom of degeneracy in religion, whether in theory or in practice. It has come to be rated as, at its worst, outright worship of sex. It has not been seen in the light and character of typism purely. It has been taken to be sex worship, and that on the physical fleshly side, not sex as philosophically understood—the phenomena of universal polarization of spirit and matter, "male" and "female."

Even when not taken in its bald crudity as veneration of the actual sex forces, it has been supposed to be concerned with attempts to generate lofty spiritual raptures by certain forms of sexual expression, as in the alleged practices of Hindu Tantrika "sex-magic," or other sorts of sex sublimation and transmutation of sex power into spiritual force.

It has been alleged that by sexual energizations of one kind or another high psychic faculty may be awakened. Some social communities and colonies are declared to have practiced formal rites of a sexual nature with certain advantageous results. Whether natural and salutary or the contrary, these manifestations have been directly operative in the province of sex and have been assumed to be aspects of phallicism in religion.

Perhaps, being almost wholly expressions of human or animal physiological functions, they can be said to have little more claim to be classed under religion than has eating or breathing. They are dragged into religion from far out on the periphery. They belong more properly to physiology, to sociology or the remote fringes of psychology. Only by that tendency which disposes people of serious tenor to spread religion out to make it embrace every act on any plane of life interest, might it be subsumed under the department of religion. If this is what is intelligently presumed to be meant by the phrase "phallic worship in religion," there can not be too quickly or too sharply drawn a vital distinction between the two things, "phallic worship" and "phallicism."

The first is the worship or cult of sex as an end, directly or indirectly, in itself, or as means to an end in the field of sex. The object of the worship is sex, as man knows it, physically. The second, phallicism, on the contrary, is not a worship of sex as in any way an object in itself. The direction proceeds away from sex on its physical level and ascends to the loftiest regions of abstract conception. The mind merely uses the facts of sex as a starting point or as a concrete adjunct to mental formulations, to help it arrive at a conception of life in its supernal economy. In fact, although it starts from the physical view of sex, or what sex presents to thought, it in a moment almost loses sight of that in the vistas of understanding that the mind is led into by the intimations of analogy. Or if the original objectivity is retained, it is soon invested with a glow of significance and a quality of purity never sensed before.

The vast difference between sex worship and phallic religion is that whole gulf between engrossment in sex for what it yields physically and interest in its phenomena entirely as symbol of something far transcending its bodily expression. Sex worship begins with sex and—stops there. Religious phallicism also begins with sex, and only then on its mental side, but proceeds from it to the loftiest regions of conceptual ideation. No more does phallicism mean sex worship than did the Egyptian use of animal symbolism denote animal worship. Phallicism uses sex as symbol of high truth; the Egyptians used the characteristic life traits of animals in the same lofty way.

This study is concerned with sex only for the sake of its utility as symbol. The need for clarity and the purposes of exact analogization will demand at times the frankest statements of sex functionism. The one single intent is to lay out the lower pattern clearly enough that the perception of the identity of the higher with it may not be missed. Our concern with physical sex is in this way purely academic. Much will be gained for the view of sex from all angles if a frank presentment of its features will serve to establish with a new certainty the sublimest elements of spiritual religion. Our treatment of the theme is as entirely disinterested as is the treatment of the nude in art.

We have seen that the very condition of God's becoming conscious of himself—an *a priori* postulate of his creating at all— inhered in the logical necessity of his breaking his primal unity apart into self and not-self, spirit and matter, positive consciousness and negative unconsciousness. God therefore threw himself apart

into a duality, which is intimated by the division of life into male
and female in the *Genesis* allegory. Understanding of this bifurcation of the One into the Twoness is the first fundament of all
philosophical systematism. It is the largest single datum facing the
mind and standing as the basic premise for thought. It is the
cardinal item in the mind's attempt to rationalize the universe of
life.

Stolid minds are incapable of true wonder and go dumb before
the everyday actualities. But a mind of philosophical capability
never ceases to marvel at the existent phenomenon of bi-sexuality
in the human race. "Male and female created he them" never loses
its power to stir the cultured mind. The fact may become so commonplace as never to excite thoughtful consideration at all. The
constant presence of the fact itself wears thin the mind's power to
respond with fresh novelty to its implications. Merged also in practically unconscious mentation is the recognition that it is the division of life into duo-sexuality that keeps the world and evolution
a-going, that it is the impelling fact back of an immense segment
of all life's activities, that it generates the heat, so to say, that drives
the wheels of progress and fires the aspirations of men, and that
it is at the root of nearly everything in the cycle of living interests.
Art, poetry, the drama, religion in part and now psychology draw
their vital breath from the ramifications of the sex endowment. A
schoolboy essay could enlarge upon the theme that all romanticism
in life arises out of the involvements of the sexual division. It produces the family unit of social and governmental civilization. It
suffuses the entire period of youth of both sexes with the glow and
halo of its seductive influence, so that nearly all the energies of the
adolescent epoch are absorbed in the effort to keep the personality
stabilized. The gradual discovery in one vivid realization after another by the growing boy and girl of the mutuality of the sex
instinct and its mechanism, enjoining upon all mortals the virtual
mandate of throwing themselves into the arms of the "opposite sex"

for the procreation of the race, as well also for the normal development of the individual life, is a constant, even if largely suppressed inward experience of massive weight and power. The sheer fact of sex differentiation never lets go its constraining grip on mind, imagination and behavior all life long.

The first and later verses of *Genesis* find categorical confirmation every time the biologist gazes into his microscope and catches a tiny cell in the act of multiplying by fission. It receives corroboration also in the tree-buds, the seeds, the white and yellow of the egg and the myriad exhibitions of dual sexuality in all nature.

The universe is stabilized at the neutral point of the pull or tension between the two forces. Matter is of equal importance with spirit, since its force must equilibrate that of the latter if there is to be a neutral point. At this neutral point where stabilization is secured all consciousness and all values demonstrated through it are brought to birth.

Man is thus confronted with this most important of all data of knowledge for his life on this planet. His race is bi-sexual and he must realize that all essential values must be brought out through his willful exertions for good or ill expressed at the point of the operative interplay between the positive and negative aspects of every situation. In all religious and philosophical enterprises the power for good direction of effort inherent in this knowledge has been lost through the submergence of the systems that purveyed ancient wisdom. Human counsels have for centuries lacked the true basic grounds for wise decision. On the other side, by the oddest quirk of ignorance, the persuasion has everywhere gained currency that spirit is all-precious and matter is despicable. Untold perversion of all essential values has followed in the train of this misconception, with calamitous repercussions in human sufferings past all accounting.

One consequence alone has involved measureless wretchedness,—the carrying out of the alleged superiority of spirit over matter in the imposition upon women, matter's symbol, of a position of in-feriority throughout history. The unmerited contumely heaped upon matter philosophically has worked over by unconscious in-ference and been wreaked upon woman, the material symbol. Not only the flesh of the body, which warred against the life of the spirit, but as well the allegorical personalization of the physical side, woman, received the brunt of the ignominy of being regarded as the force hostile to the spirit's flowering. Never has this false view of allegory and dramatization been so flagrantly exhibited in its glaring erroneousness as in this miscarriage of meaning due to the mind's failure to hold the elements of the problem in sane per-spective. That the weight and stigma of evil imputation should have worked over from the philosophical typing and heaped its virulence upon the innocent head of woman in history reveals the sad de-ficiency in the human mind's grasp of real meanings. If matter is evil, then by direct and cogent inference, woman too is evil, as she is the symbol of motherhood, and matter is the universal mother of life. Matter in fact means mother.

We have already seen, however, that all this miscalculation, with its dire consequences for womanhood in history, grew out of the misconstruction of the concept of "evil," in the foundations of philo-sophical thought. The mere fact that matter had to be dramatized as standing in nodal *opposition* to spirit, for the wholly beneficent purpose of eliciting spirit's inchoate potentialities, became transposed over into a supposed *hostility* to the soul. The result of the mis-conception was that a measureless tide of human confusion and unhappiness swept over the reaches of Western history. It is time that philosophy regain its sanity and that the sublime knowledge be broadcast once more, that spirit and matter separate out of their primordial unity, and that the worlds come into existence on the might of the force that plays between the two in tensional relation to each other. Again at the end of the aeon they cease their "en-mity" and merge again into each other's being, and the worlds dissolve. Even when they separate for mutual interplay they do not lose their grip on each other. They simply slip into the opposite ends of the field and exert their reciprocal influence on the whole area between. Life in non-manifestation is one; in manifestation it is one-in-two, spirit and matter. And the intercommunion of the two begets all existence.

CHAPTER XVI

LOVE AND HATE

THE world of studentship has never followed with seriousness or constancy the mighty implications of the ascription of masculine gender to spirit and of feminine to matter. With the expectation of finding that an examination of the relationship between male and female will yield an enlightening *theoria* of universal creation, the challenge to inquiry now is to face the data frontally and not only with an open mind, but with an eye keenly fixed to see what is there. Even then it is necessary to use the clues and threads of discernment that have been provided us by ancient insight. It is found, then, that there will be no mistake in undeviatingly reading spirit or spiritual reference for the male symbol or personation, and matter or the physical for the female emblemism. The fact that this usage will prove its unfailing pertinence and dependability, in all cases with astonishing precision, will come as itself a revelation of no minor moment to those not conversant with the almost mathematical faithfulness and reliability of these forms of ancient symbolic method.

The place to begin the examination is at the point of the breaking apart of the unity into the duality. As to this, it must constantly be borne in mind that in spite of an act of bifurcation of itself, Deity does not destroy its eternal oneness. It has not become two, even though it has cleft its being into two aspects. It has not become itself and something else not itself. This is logically impossible. It has converted itself into a duality. It has not become two, in any sense exterior to itself. It has evolved a twoness within itself. God can not, dialectically, project anything outside himself, since he is all there is. All things are and remain inside the being of the Supreme. God can no more become two than man is two, from the mere fact of his having, or rather being, both a spirit and a body. God—and man like him—is a unit, although he is a compound of dual energies. The conflict and tension between positive and negative polarities is ever necessary to bring the life of God forth to view in concrete worlds. So life has to set up this stress and pressure within itself. How could Being lay hold of and so move substance to form its creation if it could not oppose one arm of itself, so to say, against another arm, so as to be able to get a grip on the material to be moved into place for the creation? Figuratively speaking, how could it create if it could not oppose thumb to fingers, left hand to right, lever against fulcrum, conscious design or will against objects, mind against matter? Tensional opposition of the two pulls of a polarized duality is as inevitable as the fact that a coin must have two sides. There could be no existence, no things, if there was no front and back, up and down, in and out, to and fro, movement and inertia. Duality, presaging the subsistence of a strain between the two portions, is an inexorable postulate of conscious being, and sprang into appearance as soon as life emerged from the unseen into the visible stage and took organic form.

The interaction begins the moment the two sides are established as distinct units in the being of the whole. It takes the form of the only thinkable action that two things can exert toward or upon each other,—a mutual tugging and pulling. They are set in relation to each other in much the same way as are two balls of lead tied to opposite ends of a string and whirled around on a central pivot, with the significant difference, however, that the "string" is not a "dead" connection, but a living stream of dynamic forces that are determined by the powers exerted, positively from the one end and negatively from the other. The pushing and pulling become the great natural laws of attraction and repulsion. They are the first and cosmic form of the meaning of the Battle of Armageddon. As the twoness in tensile opposition is the necessary condition of the stability of anything, the law is that two opposite poles attract each other and two similar poles repel each other. This must be so, if anything is to cohere and remain itself. If the two opposite poles repelled each other, the atom and the universe would collapse. Rather it could not have come into existence in the first instance. Positive and negative poles must fly into each other's arms, embrace and multiply, if there are to be worlds.

We have here the ground of one of the most relevant of ancient philosophical pronouncements, Empedocles' declaration that the world was engendered and activated throughout by the two forces of Love and Hate. Love is seen as the attraction and Hate the repulsion. And by this naming and characterization it is possible for the limited intellect of man to understand dialectically why the prime essential nature of God is denominated Love. As he is the unit being of all being, the constant motive of all his expression is the universal attraction of the two portions of his own Self for each other.

The two nodes of his wholeness can do nothing else but "love" each other. At the same time the two similar poles in the countless units of his multiplied manifestation can and must likewise "hate" each other. Love is the law of God's being—when he has thrown himself into the dual expression—since the two elements then are constrained by the unabating attraction toward each other. So then Love becomes the fulfilling of the law, for no other activity of life transcends or nullifies this first law of mutual attraction within the framework of the universe. It is operative in every unit of life, in every fragment, in every organic system from the atom to the super-galaxies. God can not help loving—and hating—once he has sundered his totality into spirit and matter.

Then spirit must "love" matter, and matter spirit! Soul must love body and body soul! Man, intellectual and spiritual, must love the world of matter. The voice and hands of pious unintelligent religionism may fly up in horror at the philosophical determinations that spring immediately into view in the wake of the obvious dialectic. And well they may, for, properly understood and held in a balanced rationale, the true envisagement of the elements of the problem enforces a view of these things that does indeed undo and reverse the poor twisted attitudes of orthodox befuddlement. The first dawn of welcome sanity to break upon the dark night of centuries of pitiable error is this cock's crow of the resurrected voice of philosophy proclaiming once again that spirit does love matter.

A happy release of the human spirit from unnatural constraint under false mental postures will ensue for common consciousness when it can be freely postulated in thought that the soul does love the body, and that man, spiritual, does love the world with sufficient strength that he comes into body to enjoy its delights and meet its tensions. The strength of the blind pall that has afflicted the clearness of philosophical vision can be seen by merely reflecting upon the fact that for centuries the collective brains of the scholarly world have studied the Biblical assertion that "God so loved the world" without once discerning the relevance of the central statement there advanced. And God not only loved the world, but he loved also the flesh with a force that impelled him to throw the whole of his might, in recurrent cycles of countless years each, into the effort to expand his own being by plunging his consciousness into bodies of flesh and matter. For the physical universe is the Logos made flesh. No exterior force compelled him to become fleshed; so his act must have sprung from his own volition or desire for such an experience. These conclusions are the ineluctible products of the reasoning process working upon the premises given. As man and woman love each other, so spirit and matter love each other. In nature this "love" complies with every characterization of Plato's grand predication of balance, moderation and harmony amid all the divine elements in play. In man, where free will coupled with initial ignorance comes in to disturb the balances, disturbance and confusion have crept in. These will be corrected as intelligence awakens.

Plato in *The Phaedo* and *The Symposium* has dissertated upon this matter of the genesis and nature of love, in a dramatization that has misled shallower thought into a mistaken interpretation of his figure. To depict the cleaving asunder of God's unit being into the duality, he says that the soul of man splits apart into two, each part carrying one half of the potentiality of complete being. One part manifests in male body, the other in female, and the two separate halves, each suffering the want of completeness in itself, longingly seek their complementary halves in the world, to unite with them and thus be made whole. Obviously expounding but at the same time hiding the true esoteric meaning of his allegory, Plato clearly concealed his deeper sense under the individual and personal representation. It is surely not in the purview of Plato's philosophy to deny unitary completeness to the human ego, whether in man or woman. It is always in his system a full unit, being itself a fragment of the divine Oversoul. It can not be fractional, a mere half-unit. It is complete and perfect as a seed unit of divinity. Plato is dramatizing under the human allegory the truth that the collective being of life splits apart into the two poles and that their force of attraction for each other ceaselessly causes each to seek the other throughout the ranges of life. The individual soul-mate idea drawn from Plato's allegory is a flat misconception. If it was his real belief that the soul in a male body is only one half a former complete soul, with the other half living somewhere in a female body, what a tragedy life would present in the nearly complete failure of the two halves to discover each other! Nature would not be party to a scheme which in her operative order registered close to ninety-nine percent failure. Plato's imagery is, as is the sportive punster play on the meaning of words in *The Cratylus,* neither amusing diversion nor literal seriousness, but high-pitched allegorical and dramatic truth, playful on the surface, but grandly meaningful in the cryptic intent.

Plato almost indubitably drew this form of portrayal from a line in the Egyptian scripts which says that "the soul makes the journey through *Amenta* in the two halves of sex." Many reports are to the effect that he visited and studied in Egypt. It is conceded in general that Greece derived the substance and genius of her great philosophies from Egypt. The possibility of reading anything measurably close to the true meaning of this passage has been killed in the first place by the utter failure of Western scholarship to locate the Egyptian *Amenta* in the proper world. The meaning has been thrust clear out of its true world and over into another realm where it can have no pertinence, through the stupid translation of *Amenta* as the region of spiritual consciousness *after death*. It must be asserted as a discovery of an age-old error and a datum of the most momentous significance in all antique research, that *Amenta* is the life on earth, or earth itself, and not any heavenly abode. *Amenta* is the home of the living mortal, not the realm of the shades of the dead. And this is said in the face of the datum of comparative religion that it was expressly denominated the land of the dead.

The seeming contradiction is resolved into agreement when it is known, what all studious zeal has never yet uncovered, that the ancient philosophers and "theologists" by a trope of occult significance designated the souls living on earth as "the dead." To them the life in mortal body brought "death" to the soul. "Who knows," cries Socrates to Cebes in the *Gorgias,* "whether to live is not to die, and to die is not to live? For I have heard from one of the wise that we are now dead and that the body is our sepulcher." And Paul says that "the command that meant life proved death" to him. In the wake of Egyptian formulations of truth Greek philosophy very distinctly regarded the soul while on earth in fleshly body as suffering a death, from which, to be sure, it would be reborn in its periodic resurrection "from the dead."

The Egyptian statement, therefore, concisely affirms that the soul makes its pilgrimage through the cycle of bodily existences "in the two halves of sex." Yet all the ancient philosophy stands on the positive assertion that the soul is one and indivisible. It is that in a human which makes him the *individ*-ual. Therefore the division must refer to the incorporation of unitary souls in male and female bodies. Half the souls are in male, half in female embodiment. As the Greeks say, "souls are divided about bodies." That is, souls are distributed out amongst bodies. For again they say that it is the function of gods to "distribute divinity." Jesus, in taking a loaf and dividing it, distributed the fragments in the Eucharist, and thereby dramatized the same idea.

Sex appertains to the vehicle of outward embodiment, not to the soul itself. There are not male and female souls. The soul is in large part still detached from complete immersion in the flesh of the body. It projects only a tentacle of itself down into body. It is the opposite qualities of positive and negative in the mind, the emotions and the physical senses of the corporeal appurtenance that are drawn by the law of polarity toward each other across the boundaries of sex. Only in this world and only then in the realm of bodily affections and proclivities is sex manifest. In the heaven of higher consciousness where soul resides in its native habitat there is neither marriage nor giving in marriage, for the soul is without sex. It is androgyne, the type of the original male-female unity in embryo, not yet male *and* female.

Those marvelously preserved repositories of hoary truth also tell us that at the inception of the human race, in the initial stages of the soul's incorporation in bodies that grew ever less tenuous and finally fully fleshed, the race itself was hermaphroditic in its generative mechanism, and that only after thousands of years did it effect the full segregation of sex in two bodies of opposite polarization. A few verses in *Genesis* are a shorthand brief of this long process.

The sane purport of Plato's subtle indirection is that the soul of humanity collectively, the world-soul of Plotinus and the oversoul of Emerson, goes through its *Amenta* of experience in this world about equally split between male and female bodies, and that each half longs for union with the other under the law of attraction of opposite natures. But there is another yearning of the soul which is not specifically activated by the law of sex. It transcends sex. It is just the longing of one unit of soul consciousness for another unit. Sex does not affect it, engender it or minister to it. It is that higher divine attraction which urges the lonely unit to seek union with the whole group. It is the longing of the part to be united with the integrity of the whole. The part, the fragment, is driven by the divine impulsion to seek reunion, after each separation, with the whole. It is cut off from this communion while in the flesh by the walls of the body. It can communicate with kindred souls only across a gulf. If, however, soul in male setting can find this congenial response from soul in female body, both Platonic and romantic love can have play. That union is doubly blessed. With common humanity it is the physical attraction of opposite sexuality centering in body that is the main bond of attachment. Generally this is quite quickly reduced in force, so that there is then the possibility that the higher Platonic mental and spiritual affinities can come more fully into expression. Sex attraction still constitutes the strong dynamic in romantic love.

It is difficult to depict the overwhelming power of this romantic attraction in the psychic realm of mortals. It manifests as a positive hunger on the part of one for the other. It is a veritable chemicalization within the blood, and surges through the nervous system and suffuses the brain. It is a ferment and unrest, an urge that impels toward embracing, or merging oneself with, the opposite pole. One can know its carking and corroding virulence only if one has experienced it—as who has not? Vicariously we can see its potencies reflected in the behavior of animals in seasons of mating.

Total repression, thwarting and denial of fulfillment almost disrupts the vital economy of the organism. Animals show suffering and abnormalities in health. Humans sometimes pine away. To such a wreckage of her powerful drive for happy expression nature attaches almost fatal penalties. If, through unsound and unbalanced religious ideologies or fervors, the soul too stoutly restricts the body's order of animal normality (for the body is an animal, as Plato says), it has its own resources and its own ways of striking back at the unwise master. Its own suffering or derangement entailed by the too rigid denial of its due expression reacts to the detriment of the soul, whose servant it is.

There is a fell quality to the mating urge that gives it the force of a natural and unimpeachable authority, which appears for a time to sweep away every obstacle and override the obstructing power of every consideration, whether of advantage or injury. It carries a virtual cosmic sanction with it. Romeo and Juliet, Abélard and Héloïse, Dante and Beatrice, Hero and Leander, if not just honest John and plain Jane, feel that the world must stand aside and make way for the course of this true love. Flesh almost trembles and is consumed under the pulse and throb of the insatiable longing. It is nature's, life's, God's imperial order to the two individuals to unite their opposite forces and thus achieve its burning desire for multiplication of being and expansion of consciousness. It is its immitigable mandate thrilling out through every tide of blood and nerve impulse, that it may have more abundant life in the whole of its body. As Schopenhauer so elaborately and forcefully depicted, it is the will and idea of the world enacting its program. To insure beyond all possibility of failure that its evolutionary development should have an unbroken continuance, it impregnated its creatures with an enormous profusion and overplus of virile tendency. So dynamic is the voltage of this charge that it wholly disqualifies the rational element in most cases and drives blindly toward its goal, unhindered by any rational deterrent. It hypnotizes or paralyzes the reason, so that no consideration from that side may block it. It puts to sleep every sentinel that might be standing guard to challenge its right to advance. And it haloes its objective and emblazons its pathway to it with the most radiant aura of exaltation, and the most exquisite redolence of delight that life provides out of its armory of enchantments.

Life has laid upon all its creatures this royal charge, which none may dodge with impunity. This is the law of sex in its physical area.

But, because philosophy has been decried and contemned, man has been too oblivious of that other manifestation of sex within the boundaries of his own personality between two other lovers, namely his soul and its body. This is beautifully portrayed, in addition to the many fine Biblical allegories of it, by the great Greek myth of Eros and Psyche. Eros is the higher spiritual soul, or Love, who descended to earth to unite with the mortal body and its animal-human soul. He hovers over her as she lies asleep, as yet un-awakened to conscious recognition and deployment of her powers. Nothing can awaken her except the impact of those higher vibrations of a supernal consciousness from above, which are superinduced by her experiences in the flesh. So Eros bends down and arouses the sleeping faculties with his kiss. "Virtue" such as passed from Jesus into the woman who touched the hem of his garment flows down from the Oversoul when the connection with the latter is established and slumbering potencies spring into conscious activity from the touch.

The prime office of religion and the entire rationale of culture is intimated in this allegory. For the central radix of both religion and culture is this power of the higher Ego in each person to awaken and transform the dormant faculties and capabilities of the lower human self. The sons of God were instructed to descend to earth, take wives from the daughters of men and raise up seed from them. It is all an allegorical representation of the union of these divine sparks, our souls, with the animal bodies, which, since they are to be the wombs of birth for the divinely fathered and humanly mothered Christ-child in every human breast, are typified as "women," the daughters, not of God, but "of men." The parenthood of the new-born sons of God is divine on the paternal side, but natural, earthy, on the side of mother-body. Heaven, as Plato hints, furnishes the seed of spiritual being for the composition of man, while earth furnishes the body, the soil or womb in which the divine seed is to be nurtured to its growth. In the Orphic hymns the soul says: "I am a child of earth and the starry skies, but my race is of heaven alone."

So the two component halves of man's life are male and female and the evolution of man is just the long romance, the wooing, winning and wedding of the two. The allegory, however, must not be permitted to strangle the reality which it adumbrates. For more and more clearly it can be seen that this is what has happened time after time in history and is the fatal feebleness of the human mind that has ever in the end defeated the spirit of culture. Allegory has been misconceived and flouted again and again and is still derided and decried in the seats of the intelligentsia of the modern world. The truth is that, while it is the ultimate bed-rock method and road to the keenest apperceptions, there exists but rarely in the individual and never in the mass the downright perspicacity requisite to apprehend its true illumination. As was the case in the Italian Renaissance, the general faculty to discern not only the beauty but the enlightening power of meaning released to the mind by symbols, was wanting and allegory failed once more. Yet it was not allegory that failed; it was popular crudity and crassness of mind that caused failure, as it always will. The world sadly needs to recover the lost faculty or genius for the interpretation of allegory and for the discovery of the wealth of meaning brought out by analogy. For the magnificent truth hidden in the ancient scriptures under glyph and symbol will not yield its purport to the world as long as the general mind remains dumb to the intimations of allegory and symbol.

Clear down to the present the scholars have sniffed at allegory. This gesture is due to their inability to honor it and live with it in sufficient warmth of companionship to catch its more subtle and recondite power of instruction. The chief requirement is that the eye of the mind should be trained to hold the allegory not as opaque but as diaphanous. The condemnation and death of allegory have come through the mind's incapacity to look through it as a lens and to descry the objects in focus in that unseen world where truth abides in its noumenal aspect. What must be seen, then, under the allegory of the two natures in man wooing and wedding each other is something that demands in the seeing a profound and subtly discerned set of values and meanings that lie altogether in a plane of cognition far above sense. The idea of marriage in the reference is but the initial push, the springboard that sends the thought off on its quest of realities that can be limned only in the highest poise and concentration of the thinking faculty. Two things, two forces, meet, intercommune and finally wed. But how is one to think of the soul wedding the psyche and creating a new birth through her? How, must first be asked, can mental and spiritual entities or radiations meet and wed?

Here is the reality to which the allegory leads the mind, and mind must be able to follow from signpost to destination if tropes and symbols are not to leave failure in their wake perpetually. The highest exercise of the great faculty of the imagination must come into play if the figure is to yield enlightenment. One must imagine, then, while keeping always in view the assumptions and principles of known natural and scientific data, that two powers like the soul and the psyche will wed each other by coming to an identity of vibratory energies, by striking a synchronization of conscious states which virtually make the two forces one instead of two. They become alike and flow together into a unity. Their currents of influence are finally reduced to a mathematical harmony in the wavelengths. This is the most plausible explanation open to brain thinking on the part of man, and while doubtless still below the plane of positive empirical knowledge as to how the subtle forces of mind operate, it soars well above the stolid immovableness of mass ideation that can think of no marriage save a personal and physical one. And just this difference measures the enormous gulf that perpetually runs its fatal chasm between the truly cultured minority and the cruder mass majority. That gulf is the most impassable obstacle to the progress of the race.

Spirit and matter, soul and body, each reducible in thought to ultimate whirls of atomic energy, are thrown by Deity into the relation of juxtaposition and vibrational impact in quite literal sense. The close relation presupposes, in its degree and kind, as actual an intercourse between the two elements as that between man and wife, if a new birth is to be engendered. Love, now conceived as between soul vibration and sense vibration, then presides at the very genesis and growth of all culture. For culture is, in essence, the increasing receptivity of the animal to the behests and influences of the higher Ego and its becoming enamored of them. Not only does sex force play between bodies of opposite polarity, but it flashes back and forth between spirit or mind, masculine, on the one side, and the feminine psyche within the same body, be it man's or woman's. The marriage spoken of allegorically in the New Testament and other scriptures is the union St. Paul glorifies as between soul and its own mortal body. Dr. Hinkle is found confirming this delineation in a very direct and indeed remarkable way. Speaking of the presence of feminine characteristics in the sensitive nature of artists, she declares (*The Recreating of the Individual*, p. 346):

"The union between these masculine and feminine entities in the psychic organization of the artist partakes of the character of the sexual act, although it is an unconscious process of the nature of which the artist is unaware. But it possesses all the physical signs of the activity of *libido sexualis,* and of the nature of his feelings he is quite aware."

It is significant that the psychoanalyst here avers that the manifestations of sexual character are sufficiently in evidence to warrant their description as sex symptoms. But this author goes even further and denominates the interplay of forces polarized as masculine and feminine as actually a "psychic coitus." She writes (p. 346):

"I have referred in previous chapters to the separation of the sexual impulse from its reproductive purpose in the human race, with the consequent overthrow of nature's limitations and its use freely in the service of pleasure instead of purpose. As a consequence of this use, in which reproduction really plays no part for the male, there has been produced a transference of *libido sexualis* from the physical to the psychical realm. Here the artist reveals its transformation into a subjective phenomenon where a *psychic coitus occurs, having for its constant aim not pleasure but purpose.*"

If the psychiatrist can speak of an intercourse between male and female components within the psychic range, at last the esoteric meaning and the amazing truth of an ancient allegory interspersed throughout all the revered scriptures receives the authentic voucher of its veracity. Only after some twenty-five hundred years are we beginning to catch up with what our wise forefathers knew.

A further corroboration of the validity of the marriage symbol on the plane of psychic energy is given by Dr. Hinkle. She applies to the higher Ego, the superconscious or evolving deity in man, the term used in Platonic literature—the *puer aeternus* (the "eternal boy," or everlasting youth, he who is ever young). She says (p. 349):

"In every case, however, the production of an art work is preceded by what can be called a *psychic coitus between the puer aeternus and the soul* within himself, and when, through some psychic interference or weakness, this idea does not take place, no art child will be produced."

She goes so far as to label this orgiastic paroxysm in the sensibilities "a symbolic incest relation" and "an autoerotic process," the capacity for which sets the artistic or creative genius apart from more stodgy mankind.

Thus the allegory of primitive truth is again tardily vindicated. Even an artist must be capable of imitating the actions of the gods in their fabled intercourse with one another and must be able to consummate a marriage culminating in intercourse between two polarized entities within his own scope of being, if he is to bring forth a child of his art. Simply this on a magnified scale, and carried on through all the later stages of the individual's evolution, is all that was connoted in and by St. Paul's allegory of the wedding between the lower psyche, the bride, and the higher self, the Christ, the Lamb of God slain on the altar of matter from the beginning of the world-aeon. Naturally the man who had not effected this marriage within himself, and therefore had no wedding garment on, was thrown out of the symbolic ceremonial. That wedding garment is verily the immortal shining body of "white raiment," being nothing less than the *augoeides,* or body of radiant solar effulgence that clothes "the glorified and the elect,"—the garment of the redeemed. What occurs in miniature in the daily life of all creative genius is but the transpiring in small cycle of the great aeonial marriage and climactic blissfulness of soul and sense in the large cycle of human evolution.

CHAPTER XVII

LOVE LOOKS BEYOND DEATH

THE forces of the psyche, the lower or animal self, lacking intelligence and reasoning power, must await the impingement upon themselves of the higher-pitched vibrations of the Erotic divinity before they can be linked to rational purposes. The Prince Charming comes down to marry the sleeping beauty, the Princess to be. He is called Charming because, as ordinary romantic love itself attests, his superior spirito-intellectual power very literally, yet figuratively too, does enchant and transform the very soul of the awakened lady. His power to wave his magic wand of beautiful allurement over her and captivate her is indeed that of a charmer. To charm is to bring under a magic spell and thenceforth to control the action of the subject. This is precisely what the spiritual soul does or is to do in its gradual gaining of ascendancy. Its exalted kingship is won by virtue of its bringing the multitudinous animal tendencies under its sway through the power mind exerts over all energies below it in rank. Paul's statement that the lower self becomes transformed into the likeness of the higher is the scriptural prototype of the fairy-tale magic as well as of the integrating power of true light and understanding in psychoanalysis today.

The psyche can not become fecund and produce the Christ-child as her son without the coming of the bridegroom who will impregnate her physical potencies with his contribution of the seed of a divine nature. Nor can he, on his side, become productively Father without union with her mothering agencies. The great mythical fables of the King of the Gods, Jupiter or Zeus, carrying off beautiful maidens on a honeymoon impulse is just the dramatic representation of the cardinal principles of the spirit-matter relation. The

Christ personages or dramatizations were always the progeny of God's mind or Logos, the Holy Spirit of the Christian theology, as male parent, descending from above, and of an earthly maiden, the virgin of the world. The sons of God are our incarnating divine souls; the women, the virgins of the allegory, are the human bodies. The bride is the matter of body, pining as she waits for the coming of her Lord.

John Addington Symonds in his lucid work already quoted, *The Renaissance in Italy,* pauses to take account of this ascription of gender to divinities, to abstract qualities and to the elements of consciousness. He ends by qualifying it as overdrawn poetic, mystical and in a word silly affectation of classical pedantry. That so generally astute a student as Symonds proves himself to have been in his fine analyses of cultural trends should fall into this blunder along with practically all the rest of the scholarly company, is dispiriting. This attribution of gender or sex to the characters in the myths and in the Olympian and other pantheons is indeed the most expressive and revealing descriptive methodology practicable. The predication of male or female nature to energies, qualities, attributes in the personae of the cosmic dramas was the most direct and plausible manner of certifying at one stroke their generative or male function or their passive female and mothering function. It is, as already stressed, the blind spot before the eye of the modern mind which prevents it from seeing the reality of sex as operative on the higher levels of mental and spiritual consciousness. This is the myopia that shuts out the positive veritude of the phenomena esoterically concealed under ancient allegory and that allows such a capable mind as Symonds' to cast his slur and slight into his judgment of the masterly dramatic genius of primordial wisdom. Time and again it is the clue of sex that opens out the tangled web of abstrusity and mystery inwrought in the great classical myths. It is not by accident or by the play of infantile simplicity of early mind, or by "primitive" fancy, that such languages as Sanskrit, Hebrew, Greek and Latin, even to German, French and Spanish, give gender

to every common noun. Symonds should have penetrated and analyzed that profound usage before he decried the sound rationality
behind the gender of the Gods and their powers. Sex in proper
physical manifestation belongs only to the flesh. But the mental
conception of sex as the eternal interaction between positive and
negative life pervades all thought. Even numbers were given sex
by the Pythagoreans. The odd numbers were masculine, the even
feminine. The number one was of no sex, the eternal androgyne.

The visible material universe is the feminine, for it is the womb
in which all birthing takes place. The body must likewise be feminine, since it is the mother of whatever spiritual entification takes
place within it. In the Greek the body was *soma,* which was identical in incarnational philosophy with the tomb, *sema.* And in English *womb* and *tomb* are, in the same way cognate. The tomb of
the body, in which the soul went to its captivity and death, was at
the same time the womb of its renewal and resurrection, as the soil
is to seed. Soil is both tomb of death and womb of new birth for
the plant.

The definition of sex here must accommodate a scope of meaning
not commonly associated with it. It is sex, but non-physical or non-
physiological. It is sex dialectically considered, yet none the less sex.
It is still the mutual reciprocity of opposites, but now on the mental
plane. It is sex in the sense in which the sun is masculine and the
moon feminine, or day masculine and night feminine, or rivers
and winds masculine and trees feminine, or right masculine and
left feminine. Such sex is determined by the nature or functionism
of a thing, whether it is self-procreative or passive and receptive to
outside influence.

It would in the ultimate demand a genius rather divine than
human, of tongue or pen, to put into words the glamorous charm
that the two poles of sex exercise upon each other. The passion
of love is in its purest and strongest form the living manifestation
of the divine nature in the human being. What lesser or different
type of magnetic pull it may exert at lower levels than the human,

or what more divinely sweet allurement it may dispense over consciousness at more exalted levels is left for the speculative imagination to conjure out. It is a presumption that each grade of life and consciousness feels and experiences it in degree and quality exactly apportioned to its status and capacity. But at whatever level or degree it is found in the gamut, its manifestation there is for the creature experiencing it the supreme impelling force in the life movement.

To give some semi-realistic view of the nature of sex attraction one is forced to resort to such terms as magnetic and electric. There will be little violence done to truth if sex is asserted to be in all forms of its exhibition exactly like a chemical reaction between elements that have affinities for each other. As two chemicals instantly unite by the law of their atomic constitution, so the two poles of being coalesce by a similar compulsion. A force almost as palpable as the pull of a magnet on iron filings emanates from the opposite sides and lays a grip on its contrary poles. As matter, which shows itself subject to the law of polarity, is found in the analysis to be of the nature of an electric force, and not solid substance at all, likewise the mutual attraction between spirit and matter must be conceived and defined in terms that describe electricity. And love between the sexes is as tangible or at least as conceivably a physical force as is electricity. It can manifest itself in things as empirical as hunger and homesickness. It can be so strong in its pressure upon the organism that its exuberant flow in free expression, or its thwarting and repression, may produce complete happiness, on the one hand, or produce death, on the other.

Indeed love is intimately bound in with the issues of life and death. This is so well seen in the procreational processes of many varieties of insects, such as bees, wasps and certain species of aphids, wherein the act of reproduction, especially on the male parental side, is immediately followed by death for the generator. Edward Carpenter has beautifully set forth the aspects of this involvement in his book, *The Drama of Love and Death.* So strong and invincible,

so unrelenting in its grip is the power of love that sometimes to die
in the overt expression of the passion is felt preferable to living
without it. Suicides motivated by thwarted love duly attest this
tragic and melancholy power. It is almost as if life said to its
children: Love and procreate—or die! For it actually does say to
some species: Love and procreate—*and* die! From which consideration it is pretty crisply to be seen by even the dim and limited
mentality of man that the death of the organism is of comparative
insignificance in the larger ongoing of the stream of life. And as
life ostensibly uses the experience undergone by its living units in
and for the work of instruction of those units, the continuous unfoldment of organic life in evolution presupposes the continuity
of the consciousness which has had the experience, since it is illogi-
cal to assume that education can accrue to beings vicariously. Logic
indicates that there must be a nucleus of consciousness which can
garner up and accumulate, assimilate and digest, the experiential
deposits of continuing existence.

By a marvelous alchemy of consciousness, as yet only dimly
limned by the human mind, yet in a way quite understandable in
the light of ordinary experience, wherein much activity, itself forgotten in detail, results in a digest of rational conception, a deposit
of wisdom, much as hundreds of tons of crude coal can be distilled
into an ounce of imperishable radium, the enduring Ego, the perigrinating young god, undergoes the myriad touches of actual life
and distills from the mass the gleaming pearls of everlasting wisdom and virtue. It must be true that the vast amounts of experience
of the Ego are "boiled down" into a small quantity of everlasting
realization and permanent wisdom. Such an understanding was the
ground philosophy of all sapient antiquity, of that genius that produced the world scriptures, immemorially revered as sacred.

Life comes into existence, affirm these venerated texts, bearing
the fruits of former existences. The soul is what it is now by virtue
of what it—and not something other than itself—has learned and
come to be. Modern biological science has not yet enlarged its view

of truth to embrace this matured science of the ancients. It relies on heredity, transmission, shunning the postulation of forces and entities that do not lie open to physical view. This is the great gap of failure that inheres in modern scientific effort to produce a philosophy that meets the questions propounded by observed phenomena. The great missing segment in the arc of knowledge is the initial principium that life endlessly oscillates between the two conditions of embodied existence (on a planet) and disembodied existence in a suspended state, and carries the gains from one cycle of expression over into the next, and aggregates them for all eternity.

In the simplest approach to dialectic it can be asked how life can carry forward its own products and resultants, if both the consciousness that engendered them and the organism in which it functioned do not continue to exist. Obviously the organism does not continue. It is scattered to dust, as *Ecclesiastes* states. The perpetuation of the nucleus of consciousness therefore is the only possible assumption on which retention of gains accruing from experience can be grounded. Intelligent religion in olden time postulated the existence in man's make-up of "spiritual" bodies, six of them in all in Egyptian philosophy, along with the physical, the more atomically sublimated one or ones of them being composed of the imperishable radiant elements of the sunlight. In these the unit of divine consciousness could subsist when the coarser material bodies disintegrated, and thus preserve its ripened fruits. Life has *some* provision for enabling the consciousness that has harvested wisdom from life to hold it in perpetuity. Otherwise the value of the labors and sufferings of every soul in every cycle would be cast to the winds, especially since modern biological science is by no means agreed as to the possibility of the transmission to offspring of acquired parental characteristics. Evolution could not be equated with experience or be seen as the result of it.

The love that has matched its values against death itself bespeaks a momentous revelation that mankind has been too slow to catch,— that the attraction and union of sex forces is the supreme means to life's prime objective, and therefore is to be rated as near the summit in the man-made categories of sanctities. The verdict of all peoples of high culture when at their most exalted pitch of refined appreciations has been to this effect.

But so high a thing becomes subject to a possible degradation correspondingly low, when handled by gross ignorance and crudity. It is contorted out of beauty by immoderation or unnatural perversion. A cultured minority alone carries the banner of sexual purity, while the immature and crass majority drags down the lovely image of sex so deeply into the mire of lower carnal propensities that it is smeared with the murk and muck of foulness. Genuine love has always had to fight its way up through this miasmatic atmosphere of alleged natural baseness to reach the heights where it can breathe the pure air and bask in the brighter sunshine of uncontaminated mental wholesomeness and sweetness. Pure religion and undefiled, high literature, elevated philosophy, beautiful poetry have ever voiced the praise and acclaimed the sanctity of love and romance. Only less clean hands have besmirched the grand passion with the imputations of moral turpitude.

The mutual attraction of the two poles of sex is the hidden theme of much mythology, and is both the burden and the gist of the ancient depiction of theological truth. We see it first in the Greek fable of Narcissus, the youth who, bending over a clear spring, saw his image reflected in the water, fell in love with it and in his ardor to woo it, fell into the pool and was drowned. Like the Prodigal Son allegory in the New Testament this is a construction that adumbrates the sublimest significance for a grasp of both Greek philosophy and racial genesis. The apologue depicts the "fall"— more properly the "descent," since it was deliberate and a normal evolutionary procedure—of the units of divine mind, the sons of God, into bodily incarnation.

But the feature of the allegorization that fairly shouts its cardinal import to our dull comprehension is Narcissus' becoming enamored of his own image in the water below him. In ancient usage water is the universal and unfailing symbol of matter and the earthly life, since the body which soul inhabits on earth is itself seven-eighths water in composition. Greek philosophy of the great Orphic-Platonic school—the source of all Greek wisdom—says in one place that "it is necessary that the soul should place a likeness of herself in matter," so as to become more conversant with herself through seeing her image reflected in the mirroring surface below. This is quite in line with the discernment already made herein, that spirit must objectify itself to itself, if it would become conscious of its own nature and being. But the moment that the sons of God project their creative forces outward and "downward" and stamp their image upon plastic substance, there is set up the attraction of polarity between spirit and matter, and the higher is filled with a love and yearning for union with the lower self. Hence he "inclines downward," as the Greeks phrase it, and by the force of the desire is drawn down to embrace matter and unite his energies with those of body. He thus becomes the soul in and of these bodies.

The "drowning" refers to the pretty complete submergence of his entire conscious life, for the initial period at least, beneath the waves and tides of animal sense and passion that flood in upon it from its close affinity with the animal body. Chapters in the *Book of the Dead* caution the soul against being "drowned" in the waters of the underworld. Many passages in the Old Testament *Psalms* have the soul crying out that the waves have come upon it and the water-floods have overwhelmed it.

It is most desirable that thought should face the implications of the allegory, which intimates the strength of the lure of matter for spirit. It is to be noted that this seduction is strong enough to draw spirit down out of its home of alleged bliss in celestial paradise into the domain and under the bondage of matter, a condition which is dramatized in all religions as the land of dreary exile, desert barrenness and lonely wandering; a place of miry clay, a swamp, a marsh, a reedy sea (the proper translation now of the "Red Sea"), a region of murky gloom and perpetual darkness; in short a dreadful dungeon or prison house, or cave, where the soul is confined as in a veritable tomb of death.

This is the allegorist's attempt to paint the power of the flesh over the soul, even when in high heaven the pull of the polarity reaches clear up from earth and entices downward from the empyrean the very sons of God to seek marriage with the daughters of the earth, namely, the fleshly bodies of the highest natural evolution. For these bodies are, collectively, the Virgin Mother, that is, organic matter never before wedded to spiritual monads, so far unfruitful and unproductive, not ever impregnated with the seeds of divine mind to become the mothers of divine birth, and so represented as "barren" in their "old age," their long cycles of evolution from primal atom up to organic body. Only "late in time" are they destined to bring forth, in the developed brain of highest man, the Christ consciousness and so become the virgin mother of the gods. This is the first great act in the cosmic flirtation, the first step in the anthropogenetic cycle of the wooing of spirit and matter, the first great romantic knight-errantry of the Prince of the Royal Lineage, Son of the Eternal King, shining in the brightness of his Father's glory, radiant son of the morning, sallying forth from the heavenly castle to marry the fairest daughter of the physical creation, and produce through that union the new heavens and new earth of the Father's eternal kingdom. Nothing less than such a majestic epic of the soul's descent is the meaning of the fable of Narcissus and others of like import.

Matching it in our Bible is a drama of the New Testament, all the singular beauty of which has faded out of sight by the historization of allegory. It is the incident of the dance before Herod, of the daughter of Herod's brother, Philip's wife, Herodias, as the result of which the divine forerunner, John the Baptist, lost his head. This beautiful bit of cosmic dramatism, like so many others, has been turned by ignorant incomprehension of its esoteric subtlety into a mere historical intrigue, as which it stands stripped bare of all its intrinsic majesty and instructiveness.

A dance, to begin with, is a movement, the motif, genius and essence of which is rhythm. It is a physical movement according to measure and interval. It is motion in structural form and figure and symmetry and balance. Hence it is a perfect representation of the movement of stellar spheres, of the sweep and circling of physical worlds in their stately order, of the swirling of electrons in the atom, of the gyrations of galaxies round the great fixed poles of central stability, where on his throne sits the King.

What, then, would be the significance of a female dancing before the King? Whole volumes of splendid enlightenment in the tomes of antiquity have been missed because interpretation has not been guided by the ground fact of ancient symbolic language, that the goddesses and the feminine characters generally typified matter, the physical side of creation. With this one clear clue the drama becomes elucidated in resplendent beauty. A woman dancing before the King! What else could it dramatize but the dance of the physical universe, the sweeping and swinging of the planets in all the grace and precision of perfect rhythm before the eyes of the Supreme Generator of it all, figuratively seated above on his throne?

Religions of old invariably used the figure of the King to typify the divine rulership of mind. Watching the rhythmic sweep of his physical creation before his entranced gaze, the King Mind is captivated, till at last he is overcome with desire to rush down and embrace that lovely form of matter and swing along through the cycles in its arms. In this we have the dramatic type of the powerful lure exercised upon the spiritual part by the material half of the creation. It is the Lorelei, the Circe, the siren call to masculine spirit. If the enchantment and witchery of maidenhood over the mind of the male is a natural, legitimate and beautiful thing, then by the same token the lure of matter for spirit—the essential condition of all generation of new life—is similarly accredited and sanctified as lovely, salutary and beneficent. There is no possibility of invalidating the force and relevance of the analogue. If the lower is not ignoble, the upper is established in a tenfold surer sacrosanctity. If there is a natural propriety and rightness in the reverence paid by knighthood gallantry to womanhood on the concrete plane of personality in all ages, then the ancient theological ascription of honor and reverence to matter as the mother of spirit is summarily vindicated.

And in the same breath the ideologies that have cast a philosophical odium and obloquy, slight and stigma of evil character upon matter as inferior and degrading, are proven erroneous and impertinent. For woman is the type of matter, the eternal Isis, the mother of life. What the vast massive human sense honors as a thing of nobility can not be made ignoble. The deference of men to womanhood belies by its very implication the philosophical derogation of matter. If there is in masculine nature an instinctive recognition of the inviolable dignity and genuine sanctity of woman and her function of motherhood, and this impulse manifests spontaneously with invariable constancy over the whole area of evolving life, assuredly the high position of the material and maternal side of the cosmic emanation must be held as vindicated. The mistaken disposition on the part of most religionism in history to berate and belittle, to brand and defame matter, to load it with theological odium, has by a series of subtle repercussions on minds so indoctrinated wrought insidious distortion in the lives of millions. For every false attitude of the mind must sooner or later develop a corresponding inharmony in the outer life. All ideal formulations eventually work out and down into a concrete expression on the physical plane. A theory, an impulse, an obsession will in the end come to overt outlet in an act, or in a bodily condition. If activity in the physical world is the long shadow of the reality of the formations in the noumenal world, projected upon the outer screen of the phenomenal world, man's natural inclination to adore woman is the incontestable seal of the queenly status of matter in the philosophical kingdom.

The whole cast of theology is basically formulated upon the incarnation and its involvements. It is built upon the pivotal thesis that spiritual beings humbled themselves under the rulership of matter and physical embodiment for the sake of carrying life ahead to new expansion of its potentialities. Here at once is the cosmic counterpart and analogue of the male's self-limitation of his freedom and the restriction of his activities in marriage. And both are a standing irrefutable dramatization of the homage of spirit before the throne of queenly matter. Angels of bright luster have indeed come down out of heaven to adore the Virgin. They have not despised, but exalted the Virgin's womb. They have not deemed it unseemly to seek newness of life through the enabling offices of matter. They have not failed to regard the lowly estate of their handmaiden, nor hesitated to come under the law of her domain.

Plato's conception that each segment of the polarity is drawn toward its opposite by the force of an instinct or hunger for fulfillment of its own lack, being itself only half of the plenary whole, is as true an account of the mutual attraction as can be given. It is an involuntary, almost subconscious sweep of urgent inclination, welling out from deep within and becoming conscious and voluntary after a time. There is a more or less clearly acknowledged desire for what each lacks and is in the possession of the other. To come into the presence of the personal living embodiment and beautiful manifestation of these desirable elements is to fall into love of them and their possessor. Their power of charm is close to overwhelming. Emerson has so well portrayed the almost luminous aura that mystical apperceptions create and fling about the person of the loved object. A radiance enshrines it, and body, voice and movement fill the adoring heart with such subtle delight that reason is thrust into abeyance and desire rules the soul. *It is the cosmic first far-off call to the two halves of a divine unity to come to the epithalamium.* It is life bidding its children live and create. It is an imperious injunction to them to complete their being. It is, as it were, the coming together of the dry wood and the flame. If the divine fire is to be rekindled on new fuel, the two must wed and conjoin their powers.

The dance of the maiden before the King has been analyzed for its esoteric meaning. The dance has consistently held a place of favor in human regard, albeit the ground rationale of that favor has hardly yet been expounded. It is perennially attractive and fascinating because it simulates in miniature the universal movement of life as activated by the mutual interplay between the two opposite forces of soul and sense. It is the most perfect dramatization possible to the human mind and body of the cosmic impulse and the universal movement it generates. The movement or the sight of it engenders psychologically the reflex awareness or feeling of that primal and pervasive impulse which thrills within the framework of the cosmos and in which all creatural life participates in degree. It tends to sweep the spectator or the participant into the tide of the creative stream itself.

Rhythm is the law of the movement of life. Its appeal to our sensibilities is due to something far deeper and more elementary than has ever been suspected. Its spell and charm over us springs from the psychological power of a rudimentary memory. From aeons of conscious experience there has become lodged within us the so-called unconscious of the race mind. Our souls, which are units of consciousness that have been for ages rolling through cycles of alternate embodiment and release, have felt the impact of the rhythmic beats of the alternating arcs of the cycles until they have become insensibly attuned to the measure. The tempo of the rhythm has inwrought itself indelibly into the texture of inmost consciousness, through the sensible repetition of the impacts. Our souls have themselves caught the contagion of the rhythm, and they immediately respond to any typal representation of the form of that rhythm by a spontaneous resurgence of the innate afflatus which it liberates. The soul has caught the habit of the swing of the measure, as of a melody, and it is ever stirred to intimations of deepest reality by the incidence of any form of the movement upon the outer sense.

The Greek philosophers asserted that life and consciousness swing alternately out from an interior center of immovability and sameness into a circle or cycle of movement toward endless difference and back again to source. And they thence assert that this grand cosmic and aeonial rhythm is symbolized and endlessly imitated by the larger and smaller cycles of outgoing and return undergone by each unit of living selfhood. All creatures in the scale of being answer to the thrill and throb of life's universal pulse. All life movement is inescapably set and timed to the one pervading and omnipresent pulsation, the beat of the heart of God. And if the consciousness of the individual unit in minor octaves in the gamut has no formal knowledge of the cosmic systematism, there are numberless smaller cycles of ebb and flow to keep it continually reminded of the eternal harmonies.

In a word, if life's larger notes in the music of the spheres are to be prolonged for our ear, so that we may catch their crescendo and diminuendo, we have an infinitude of eighths and sixteenths whose observable striking can keep us sensible of the dance. There is endless counterpoint in the hymn of advancing life. The vast cycles are composed of and interfused with multitudinous minor rounds, so that seven smaller wheels must turn seven times to turn a larger one once, and seven of *its* revolutions complete a still grander sweep. Undoubtedly this is the sense behind the crumbling of the walls of Jericho by the repetition of the priests' blasts on the ram's horn once a day for seven days and seven times on the seventh day, accompanied by their sevenfold circling of the walls on the march.

Is it asking too much of human intelligence to understand that a soul, a node of consciousness equipped to retain the subliminal memory of all its experiences in going through the numberless repetition of cycles of life and death, should retain the feeling and automatic memory thus indelibly interwoven into the context of its sensibilities, so as to be immediately responsive to the thrill of a rhythmic beat? The dance has always played its part in festival gaiety, in ritual, in religious ceremonial as well as in the time-measure of all poetry and music, and this for the all-sufficient reason that these forms not only dramatize, but themselves in miniature reproduce the actual movement of life which has ingrained into consciousness the susceptibility to rhythm. And as the run of beats or notes in each cycle moves toward a climactic denouement in the last and highest note in the octave, the continued incidence of a rhythm inevitably carries with it the intimate suggestion of a heightening pleasure moving toward a consummative stroke. The stupendous philosophical involvements of this aspect of the phenomenon will be examined in their proper connection.

CHAPTER XVIII

ROMANCE IN THE TRYSTING-TENT

THE constituent movement of life, then, is an alternate in and out, up and down, to and fro, back and forth succession repeated in one or another plan of a sevenfold scale and with almost infinite subcycles of sevens interwoven mathematically within the larger cycles. The larger wheels turn all the smaller wheels, but the smaller and the smallest preserve the type and pattern of the movements and cadences of the larger. We have in this scheme the certitude of invariable constancy of the method. All rhythms are dowered with affective influence by virtue of their being replicas of the one all-inclusive rhythm which is the primal principle of all living movement. This is the movement of conscious Mind outward from its inner courts and mansions of Infinite Being toward and into matter; to effect with its elemental energies a creative union of its ordered thought, so as to stamp the laws of cosmic order upon the sea of plastic virgin matter. As Heraclitus has put it, the two poles of being separate at the initial push of creation, they march out to their posts at the opposite ends of the polarity, and then under the force of the mutual attraction they begin to move toward each other to overcome the desolateness of their separate existence, and then stretch every nerve to close in toward thir blissful reunion.

This ever-insistent yearning for each other, be it formally conscious or unconscious, is the underlying *Drang nach Leben,* as the Germans would express it, the subconscious pressure of the eternal will to live. In man—and doubtless in less conscious forms in lower species—it is the unresting power of that energy of consciousness which came to be recognized as the "libido." It is the prime pressure of hidden motivation resident in the vast area of the "unconscious."

It is present as an immitigable blind force in the desire nature of man, lying below the level of reason, but whose inexorable behests man is driven to obey for the fulfillment of his destiny of larger life and the perpetuation of his kind.

In order to achieve its purposes beyond possibility of failure the attractive lure of positive and negative poles was made gloriously beautiful. Its seductive charm was made next to irresistible. The embodiment of each polar force approaches into the presence of the other with reverence and awe. A thousand and one colorations and nuances of the primal urge fleck the area of consciousness as circumstances and occasions condition the varied play of the life drama. The variety and contingency contribute immensely to the adventure and zest of the "game." But the constant and unfailing spring of captivating power in the lure is not so much what it brings and holds as what it continuously promises and beckons towards. Every sip at the cup's brim gives the anticipatory thrill of larger draughts to be drawn from the flowing bowl of life's golden wine. Present sweetness paints the glowing picture of a still greater ecstasy at the consummation. This recognition, when it is posited consciously to thought, is as powerful an incentive to human zeal for larger life as is the lure of the mating procedures in bird, animal or primitive man. Something deep within hints at the consummative blessedness lying ahead. The words ecstasy, transport, rapture all bespeak a transit of feeling beyond the bounds of a normal state into the throes of an overpowering paroxysm. So that nature ever leads her children on from joy to joy by holding before them a golden apple of supreme delight. The two lovers, spirit and matter, sight each other's beauty from afar and at the first approach. Each step that brings them nearer yields a more powerful thrill, which breeds a still keener longing for the climactic merging. At length the two polar energies find themselves sinking into each other's embrace and melting into each other's intimate being, as a rhapsody of divinest sweetness fills the whole expanse of consciousness.

All this "poetry" might as well describe the amorata of two human lovers as depict the philosophical relationship of spirit and matter in their abstract status. And the narrative would be equally pertinent in both cases, for the one is a reflection of the other.

The insistent pressure of the force shuffling the two polar embodiments toward each other is beyond adequate description or comprehension just because it is irrational. It is virtually hypnotic in its seizure of the active will. It is as though life foresaw the necessity of making her mandate for procreation immune from the reasoning power of the creature, which might readily find logic and cold calculation of advantage or disadvantage a substantial interference with her set purpose. The forces operating in life's behalf have always been called "elementary." They lie below the level of mind properly defined, and act independently of the will and the reason, since they appertain to the autonomic activities of the bodily part of man, from attention to which the conscious thinking faculty must be released.

The ancient scriptures molded the entire story of the mating and wedding of spirit and matter, or soul and body—which is indeed the whole gist of their message—over the analogy of the two lovers in the human domain. The body, which is the seat and stage of the great drama, was denominated the tabernacle or meeting place between the god and his chosen beloved. A vivid gleam of new comprehension is released to illuminate the mind with a flood of meanings never hitherto grasped, when a single item of improved scholarship yields a new translation for the old word "tabernacle" in the Old Testament. It has in later renderings been translated as "trysting-tent." God and man, or the divine and the human in man, meet each other at the door of the "trysting-tent," the house of the mortal body wherein soul and flesh make and keep their fateful tryst. What is a tryst? A secret meeting between lovers. That between the two lovers in the religious epic is said to be in secret because it is held down here on this obscure planet, a "far country" from the celestial hearth and home, pictured as a strange and forbidding foreign land, into which the soul undertakes a perigrination as into a long exile. All the allegories represent the soul as departing from its homeland of the celestial Eden and the cosmic metropolis into a remote and barren wilderness. This distant and inhospitable country was in one phase of depiction the dismal underworld, or nether earth, of the mythologies. It was the mysterious *Amenta* of the Egyptians; and *Amenta* means "hidden earth" or "earth of hiding." Amen was the god pictured as in hiding under a canopy. *Ta* is earth. Buried deep in the interior of the mortal body, itself "of the earth, earthy," the meeting and eventual wedding of soul and sense take place in the secret trysting-tent. There the two have their chance for acquaintance, for their attractions and repulsions, their final union, with the birth of the Christ-soul as the child of their nuptials.

This is in outline the allegory of that event, which is at the same time the miniature of all cosmic event, with which all religions deal as their cardinal subject and substance. The allegory has been thumbed and brooded over for two thousand years, and no hint of its primary significance for all human culture has issued from the whole arena of theological and philosophical reflection in that time. The entire implication has been utterly missed.

It needs to be endlessly rehearsed now that had the clear involvements and intimations of the incarnation doctrine in religion not been lost from sight, the general mind would have been spared its indoctrinated posture of affected contempt for the flesh and the soul's life of sense. The descent of the gods, or sons of God, to earthly incarnation, which is ever the central theme of the sacred books, would not have become tainted with evil connotation and damned with the epithet of "the fall of the angels." Save for the purposes of dramatic representation to accentuate the "opposition" of matter to spirit in the polarity, the descent of soul into body in no way merits the least imputation of evil. It would never have gathered that imputation had not nescience followed all too closely in the wake of pristine knowledge. That the nature of matter, into whose waiting arms the children of God's mind had to fall, was altogether good; that its uses and functions were of indispensable utility to the evolutionary deployment of spirit's own potentialities; and that a wholly beneficent character and role were to be granted it in philosophical understanding, were the clear readings of the arcana in the ancient "science of the soul," and the recondite meaning of the great ritual drama celebrated in the Mysteries of antiquity. But that munificent gift of high knowledge from the gods to early man was obscured and eventually lost under the pall of benightedness that settled upon the Western mind after the heyday of Platonism in the last centuries B.C. and the first centuries A.D. No words can competently portray the catastrophic consequences of this blighting of true vision and the obfuscation of knowledge that was vouchsafed to guide the race of men more happily on its way through the darksome labyrinth of this "underworld." Never shall be written the book that will fully picture this tragedy of nescience, this utter beclouding of the intellect of the world by the somber shadow of the legend that made the human body a thing of evil. When the health of the mind was corrupted by the notion that the flesh, the world of matter and the life of the senses were a miscarriage of divine intent, a thwarting of divine purpose and an evil abortion of divine will, the gruesome and sickly malady overspread the entire life of Western humanity.

The ascription of evil character to matter and the derogation of spirit's contact with bodies composed of it have been the core of a corrosive philosophical canker that has infected the wholesome expression of the free happy spirit of the creature man for these many centuries. It is the one most direful blot on the open tablet of the racial mind. It has sadly obstructed the god's effort at our instruction and must almost make it rue its obligation to give us its rich legacy of divine capability. The world soul, migrating from heaven to accomplish its assigned task of converting us from animals to

gods, must have viewed with amazement and grief the spectacle
of the near wreckage of its entire plan by the warping of one single
item of its teaching out of its correlations and perspective and its
misreading into bald literalness. That this one item should have
got out of hand and, sweeping into dominance over the minds of
the uncritical masses, have corrupted the true meaning of nearly
the whole of the early deposit of wisdom, must have seriously dis-
concerted the divine program based on the human possibilities in
the historic enterprise. The essential part and province of matter
had to be portrayed in the books and dramatized in the ritual. Little
could the descending gods have known that this representation,
putting matter in the *place* of opposition to spirit, but not in the
role of opponent, would fall so far awry of competent comprehension that in the course of time matter's character as the foil of spirit
would become fixed in philosophical view as a thing of positive evil.
That one half of the battery of divine potency should be stigmatized
as evil and held in opprobrious contempt in the world's mind simply
because it was the negative pole of being, was a miscarriage of
intended instruction that must have produced dismay in the councils of the spiritual hierarchy of the world.

Nor could the divine rulers of humanity have foreseen to what
inordinate lengths the fell sweep of arrant religionism would carry
out a program of eccentric and ruinous action based on the gigantic
misconception. Hardly could it have been conceived that the body,
which had been evolved through long aeons of development to be
the handmaiden of the Lord whom it housed, should ever come
to be regarded as so pestilential a menace to the interests of the
soul that its veritable suppression and mortification would be acclaimed a token of spiritual victory. The approach to God was
mistakenly assumed to run through the mutilation of all the natural
corporeal appetencies and the giving free course only to the motivations of the spirit. The resultant twisting of human life from wholesome natural joyousness to a false affectation of holiness has been

the heavy price that has had to be paid for this dismal abortion of the early effort to put the lamps of true insight into the hands of the first races.

Psychoanalysis has fallen heir to a portion of this lugubrious fixation. The falsity enters largely into the composition of the social norms, standards and acceptances that hold the free expression of the sex force under subjugation and thus cause repressions and their abnormal brood of complexes. It is one of the strongest of the chains that cause "frustrations." It thus becomes one of the main bars in the soul's prison, wherein its freedom is curtailed by the mistaken rules of the social code.

Woman, who has gathered up in her actual person enough of this stain of philosophical contempt heaped upon her cosmic counterpart, matter, to have had her life more seriously than is known darkened by the long shadow of miscarried dramatism, finds herself thrust into a subordinate and inferior position, and all through the implications subconsciously transplanted to her in person from her analogue, the virgin mother of spirit. And it can be just as truly asserted in the same breath that the shadow of this philosophical cloud can not be lifted from her path until the larger shadow of the cloud of philosophical misconception is lifted from off the name and nature of her prototype matter. When the same theological honor is paid to matter, as mother of the gods and the worlds, that is now paid to the "holy mother" in ecclesiastical circles and also to motherhood on its personal side by the masculine mind, then will woman stand in her true and honored place. Volumes of psychological research and tabulation could not present any measurably accurate estimate of the virulence of the blight which all this disparagement of the entire physical side of human life has spread out over the area of common consciousness. It has gone far over the boundary of sanity to kill man's happier life on its natural side.

In summation on this point, how can it be highly laudable in religion to accord the accolade of eternal dignity and supreme worth to the fatherhood of spirit, while the motherhood of matter is trampled in the mire of pitiful human error and contempt?

So far had this trend been carried in the early days of Christianity that when creeds and doctrines were to be formulated the religion mongers actually were impelled to throw the mother principle entirely out of the Trinity. Perceiving in the course of some centuries, however, that this lacuna deprived their religion of a potent psychological leverage to attract men into the ecclesiastical fold, as the person of the male Jesus met the psychological needs of female devotees, the monitors of the Church hastened to place the Mother of the Christ, the "Mother of God"—by this time a personalized woman of history—back in the niche of highest honor and reverence. All ancient Trinities were Father, Mother and Son. The Mother was outcast from Christian creedism, but as through a side door the historical mother was brought in to meet the needs of a masculine Oedipus complex.

The symbolism of spirit as masculine and matter as feminine must be apprehended and rationalized as symbolism purely, and not tied to any reference to men and women in their personal identities. It is as gross a folly to think that because spirit is typed by the king, a male, every man is therefore a lord of spiritual light, as it is to make the error which the world has come all too close to doing, that because matter is typified by goddesses and women figures, every woman is therefore sunk in material aims. The mind or soul in each is sexless.

Little has it been discerned that in the order and nature of the sexual creative procedure among humans there has been displayed for all the world's edification the complete and luminous hieroglyph of the cosmic creation in its grand universal scope. The tracing of this correspondence and the establishment of the validity of the analogue are the tasks of the study in its remaining section. The perception of this symbolic index and the use of its data for the lucid dramatization of eternal truths constituted the motive and utility of the ancient sacred cultus of phallicism in religion. This analysis and elucidation of phallicism as a dramatic technique of spiritual science has not as far as known been attempted hitherto. It is designed to redeem a whole large segment of vital religion from the onus and obloquy of vile character and mental disrepute cast upon it by an ignorant misjudgment of its true intent and lofty nobility. The gain for wholesome human attitudes and purity of mind to be derived from this reorientation of vision will be of measureless proportions. It will advance the whole world a long step toward the emancipation of thought from that vilification of the natural and material side of the living dualism, which has, as seen, tended to hold the feminine half of the race in a position of inferiority. The color-stain of nastiness which immoderate or unhallowed exercise of the human creative function has bred in the vulgar (the word meaning, of course, simply "general") mind has, in lack of the higher enlightenment, communicated its befouling touch to all treatment of symbolic phallicism, so that the latter has been held up through centuries of studentship as a sad miscarriage of ethical and spiritual life. It has been smudged with the tincture and taint of foulness, as the role of matter has been smeared with the mud of unworthiness and baseness.

As will be seen in the elucidation, every item and feature of the creative procedure becomes a semantic key to a large segment of the philosophical construction. These clues, all drawn straight from nature's field of marvels and all certified and substantiated by the veritude of factuality, constitute a code of criteria by which the soundness of philosophical conceptions may be summarily adjudged.

Already there has been drawn the delineation of one tremendous misprision of philosophical determination. But a whole series of even greater corrections of deeply engraven errors in common ideation will be the fruit of our examination of the more intimate aspects of the outward phenomena.

The study begins, may it be said, with the beautiful and truly

holy arcana of the honeymoon and the hymeneal ritual; it ends in
every instance in the high apotheosization of a philosophical conception into its sublime final exaltation of meaning.

The false and caricatured view of phallic religion has found body
in the idea that originally pure and lofty principles of understanding became in time traduced into a merely physical expression bereft
of all transcendental import and reference, or more simply ended
in a gross unspiritual sensualism when the earthly and physical
type-forms were misconceived as the end and not merely the beginning of the symbol's or the ritual's adumbrative suggestiveness and
moving power. The true envisagement of phallicism, on the contrary, starts from the physical, but does not linger there. It dwells
with that phase no longer than is necessary to discern in its forms
and phenomena the patterns of transcendental ideality, to which
it proceeds by the force of the mind's passionate zest to reach the
truth. To restore its proper direction in the search for verity and
to reintegrate the original fairer and more sane posture of mind in
consonance with the basic *archai* seen to be operative in the entire
sexual area will be a work of consummate value.

The allegory of "Salome," Herodias' daughter, dancing before
Herod has been seen to be the type-picture of the rhythmic movement of matter, the Virgin, in its stately circles before the king of
the cosmos, spirit-mind. The beautiful gyrations fascinate the mind
of the king and entice him to descend to earth to embrace the
dancer and swing along with her in the thrilling rounds of the
dance. The music of the spheres is the lilting melody to which
spirit dances. It is the music nature furnishes for the nuptial gaiety.
In order that spirit may feel the alternate throb and beat of the
life impulses as it swings through the cycles bound in matter's arms,
it must be tied in actual linkage to nature's formations and be
their soul. It must catch the inner conscious digest of the outer
experience. So the souls descend, insinuate their powers into bodies,
lay hold of the atomic energies and the elementary forces—denomi-

nated the seven beautiful maidens of fairy legend—and with the universal urge to rhythmic movement throbbing in its heart and thrilling through its blood, it begins its aeonial intercourse with matter.

Its first impelling drive is to push its ray of conscious intelligence as deeply into the womb of matter as it can penetrate. There is no rational formula available for understanding this impulse except the statement that it is the divine urge of one polar force acting according to its nature to merge with its opposite. Perhaps, as in lovers' first shy glances, there is the faintest thrill of anticipatory pleasure in prospect of union with its complementary part. But this descent of spirit into matter is one aspect, one arc, of its round of actual being, and must be adjudged at its due weight and significance in a study of the entire circle that rounds the view of reality.

It must be said in passing that the failure of modern study to grant just consideration to the natural analogue of this tendency in cosmic process has left science bankrupt in its effort to frame a formula that would express the complex phenomena of nature, what the Greeks called *physis*. The science of the present has done well to recognize, through the aid of Darwin's and Wallace's vanes of intimation, the great law of nature's life, that is, growth or "evolution." Aristotle perhaps defined it in more philosophical form when he named it "entelechy," by which designation he meant that life fulfills a predetermined destiny at the end of a cycle of development which carries it from seed to flower, from potential into actualized existence. In the perception of the fact of unfoldment through growth modern science has found a clear guiding principle governing the life movement *in one arc or segment of the cycle*. But even with this discernment of the method under its eye, it was left still almost philosophically blind by reason of its failure to take account of the necessary postulation of a correlative movement, by virtue of a balance with which the evolutionary impulse or current could alone be envisaged on sound dialectical bases. This unseen and unexploited principle was the law—or at any rate the fact—of *in*volution.

With all nature massing on display before our eyes the ubiquitous perennial host of palpable and ineluctable exemplifications of the principle, it seems incredible that the vaunted powers of modern intelligence, miraculous in so many of its probing insights, should have failed to reckon with an item of natural procedure so simple that its complete validation seems sufficiently established by the common understanding that what grows must first have been planted. Children at play shout, "Whatever goes up is sure to come down." In keeping with the figure, it may be said that science has foolishly been trying to understand the coming up without reckoning on the coming down. Since that which is does not come from nothing, it is obvious that whatever grows must come from its seed potentiality. Science is faithfully, religiously studying the growth in complete disregard of the previous planting of the seed. It has been trying to grasp the rationale of the phenomena manifested in the growth while steadily refusing to see that the whole nature of that which unfolds into existence is determined by the character and potentialities hidden in the seed. That which comes up must first have gone down. This the ancient sages knew. But modern frames of thought have with stubborn recalcitrancy rejected every intimation from the side of philosophy, analogy, poetry and pure reason, that points to the concept of involution antecedent to evolution. Spirit must go down into matter before it can evolve out of it.

To this obverse arc of the cycle the early philosophers gave as much consideration as they did to the evolutionary. The counterbalance of the two was necessary to render comprehension possible. Just as a ballistic expert would calculate the force of a rebound from a knowledge of the force of the preceding impact, so the potentialities of the evolution or entelechy were reckoned in reference to the scope, range and power of the forces going into physical embodiment. The homely adage of human affairs—"you only get out of a thing what you put into it"—applies here, with the slight but significant modification that life tends to get out a little more than it puts in, by reason of reaping the fruit of new and additional effort. Life multiplies itself endlessly but in repeated cycles, in each of which its investment put to usury comes back with increment.

The law of life is that one plants sheer potentiality and reaps actual power. Effort expended through the run of a cycle evolves that potentiality into concrete dynamic, expands a minute seed into a rich granary. Present thought essays to understand the oak without any reference to the previous oak that generated the acorn. It takes the cycle of growth to make explicit and actual what was only implicit and latent at the start. It is sheer ineptitude to consider the one segment of the round and not the other, or the one without symmetrical relation to the other.

A word in the Bible allegories comes out to great significance here. Its broad scope and relevance have not been seen before. It is "multiply." Abraham's seed was to *multiply* until it filled the whole earth. Jesus *multiplied* the loaves and fishes to feed a famished *multitude*. The creation is to abound and produce life ever more abundantly. God gave his righteous servants bountiful increase. Anu in Egypt was described as "the place of *multiplying* bread" thousands of years before Christianity was born. Life continually multiplies each time one seed produces multiple harvest.

But there is one condition that eternally accompanies the production of increase. That is the cyclical "death and burial" of the life unit of potentiality in the soil of the kingdom lying next below its own level, as the vegetable in the mineral, the animal in the vegetable, the human in the animal and *the divine in the human*. The seed of the life of the kingdom just above any given level must go to its "death" in the dark "underworld" of the plane below it. There it "dies" in its outer body, or suffers the disintegration of its form, which goes to the nourishment of its inner undying germ. The outer decay is only the preliminary and necessary transference of strength and vitality from the transient over to the permanent core of being. *The temporary dies to enrich the eternal.* But it is the transient that starts the eternal on each cycle of its experience in the actual. It gives it a body through which it can contact concrete worlds and gain cognizance of the higher and richer values in the scale of life.

CHAPTER XIX

THE PHOENIX LIVES AGAIN

SO spirit "dies" in matter, but dies to live again. After the brief "death" of latency it germinates and lives anew. It "dies" in the effort to involve its energies in a material organism, and must await the growth of the organism to deploy those energies again in full scope. In order to become creator of new life it must entwine its forces with the powers native in matter. In the new growth thus generated the hidden "meaning" of the involutionary process comes to light and realizes the entelechy. That which entered the ground or field of matter as potential energy emerges to view as structure of organic complexity, revealing pattern.

It is passing strange that the essence of this formulation has never been abstracted from *John's* pellucid representation of it in his verse: "Unless a kernel of wheat fall into the ground and die, it abideth alone; but if it die it bringeth forth much fruit." Life endlessly enriches and multiplies itself in its creatures, but it does so by endlessly dying. For its "deaths" are followed by "resurrections," and each revival results in multiplication of the original seed that died. That which wishes to be reborn must first "die."

Life swings eternally back and forth between the two ends of the gamut, actual organic development at the top of the cycle and amorphous latency at the bottom. It dies and is reborn and dies and lives again. It ever lives to die and ever dies to live. "He that loseth his life shall gain it." Paul dies daily unto one part of his being that he may live more fully in another. Thales wrote the intensely pertinent truth that "air lives the death of fire, water lives the death of air," and so on. Body's death is soul's more abounding life. Soul's "death" is body's more abundant existence.

"He must increase and I must decrease." Socrates caught the idea that we are "the dead" of the philosophical texts of old. The most majestic line in all Egyptian wisdom runs—the soul of man speaking: "I die and I am born again and I renew myself and I grow young each day." Says Job in the Old Testament: "I shall die in my nest and I shall renew my youth like the eagle," the fabled phoenix. A majestic verse is that in the third chapter of *Revelation,* which runs: "I am he that liveth and was dead, and behold I am alive again for evermore." For life can not *die* in any absolute meaning of the term. It lives forever, yet it ceaselessly alternates back and forth between the two stages of latency or sleep and full waking activity, which are in human parlance denominated death and life. The complementary unity of the two has been ruinously broken by the dearth of true philosophy in the modern world. "Death" is always relative to "life," and "life" equally relative to "death."

> "And life is ever Lord of death,
> And love can never lose its own."

On the basis of the allegory of the soul's descent into matter, like the sun's setting in the west, the "dead" in Egypt, meaning the incarnated, were called "the Westerners." They had "gone West" to start a new career in a free country. The soul of Osiris was said to die on the western side of heaven and be reborn on the eastern horizon.

Involution, then, is the "death" of a unit of consciousness as it descends the several steps through the scale of intensities of atomic organization of matter from "pure spirit" at the zenith to "deadest" matter at the nadir of the round. It makes its descent by converting its potencies back into sheer potentiality as it involves these in the seed. To grow again it must reverse the process. Going into matter from empyreans of vivid life is to step from active life into comparative death. Every power is lethalized by going into dormancy until it is awakened again.

Like evolution, involution is a word easily and glibly spoken, but its full significance is the greatest of life's mysteries. How life, or spirit, or at any rate a nucleus of conscious being involves itself in matter or body—how indeed an immaterial "principle" of will and intelligence can implant itself in or attach itself to a physical body, so that the latter becomes its dwelling, its agent, its servant, is the prime mystery confronting the reflective genius of mankind. Intelligence must seek an answer to the question: What does it mean when one says that spirit involves itself in matter or that a soul incarnates in a body? How can a dimensionless thing be said to be "in" matter? It almost calls for a new definition of "in." Commonly one thing is "in" another when it is enclosed more or less completely by it. This is the physical basis of its meaning. How can wisdom be "in" words, or beauty be "in" a picture or heroism "in" a deed? Simply that the things, words, picture, deed express these qualities to the mind. So the living organism shows evidences of the presence and work of mind, will, spirit.

Modern view hedges or revolts from the claim of ancient theology that the soul, an independent entity, descends from heaven and enters an infant body. This objection springs from the too literal and "wooden mechanical" conception of what the ancients postulated. The methodology may sound too crudely simple to be acceptable. What these ancient seers actually proclaimed behind a veil of outward simplicity was a recondite and complex spiritual process, that was communicated only in the arcana of the Mystery Brotherhoods. Modern scientific cast of mind clings tenaciously to the view that where function is developed in connection with a mechanism, it is the product of the mechanism, and can not be presupposed as an existent entity apart from the machine. This is all that human thought *can* make of it, if a knowledge of subtler forces in nature is not at hand to correct naive conclusions. Such finer intelligence was at hand in the ancient day, but sedulously safeguarded from the corrupting forces of obscurantism and ignorance in the councils of the initiated.

The more competent understanding of the guardians of primeval knowledge predicated the existence of the soul in the body on a basis of recondite data purveyed in the Mysteries. Soul, they said, is *not* a product of the body and its energies. It *is* an independent entity; it can subsist, in and of itself, apart from the body. Out of body it would be a soul, yet not a human soul. In body it is a human soul. It is an independent entity, but to arrive at that form of manifestation of its energies in the body of a man which wins for it the designation of "human" it must be linked to the energic powers of a human body, by affinities that are confessedly obscure to us. Yet, independent entity that it is, it does not enter the human body in any crassly physical way, but by the subtle methods of synchronism of vibrations.

In the first place it is not an entity in a crude corporeal extensional sense. It is a nucleated focus of ethereal, spiritual forces of vibrational or supra-electrical dynamism. As an atom is not a physical something at all, in the common substantial and mechanical sense, but a swirl of forces in the substrate ether, so the soul is a whorl of vivific life-force, embodying will and intelligence. Apart from bodily connection it is, as it were, static. To become kinetic and actual it must be linked with the powers of the atom released in an organic body. How is it linked to the latter?

The answer of supreme import for understanding is available in the radio and in the farmer's heated barn in the summer. How does a sonata get "in" the radio? By the provision therein of an electric charge which is able to match the wave-length and frequencies of the "soul" of the sonata that is in the air and ethers all around it. This soul of the music can not be converted from static silence to kinetic manifestation until a mechanism is provided to give synchronous channel to those sublimated waves. The soul of the music, apart from the receptive mechanism, is surely in being, as it is thrilling through the air; yet it can not be said to be in existence. It is not a piece of music actually, but only the "soul" of music. It is in being potentially, but not actually. For actual existence it awaits the presence of a mechanism co-ordinated to its vibratory nature.

The soul must be envisioned in like fashion. It is a node of spiritual energy, in being, but not existent as a human soul until a physical brain and nervous organism have been provided of requisite sensitivity to give play to its sublimated emotions. When such mechanism has been developed by organic growth and it has reached a point at which the functional capabilities of the mechanism are synchronized with the soul's own rates of vibration, the affinity causes the two to leap together, as it were, into a reciprocity of action. The machine releases the soul's energies and they in turn energize the machine.

How does the fire, which is physically non-existent (yet in being) get "into" the farmer's barn in the heat of July? "Spontaneous combustion" is the phrase for it. Here the same law is at work. The chemical conditions generated in the heated moist hay rise to an affinity with the static electricity in the air and the birth of fire is the result. These two phenomena, the radio and the burned barn, twit modern science with its failure as yet to comprehend how the soul comes into the body. Its refractory denial of the independence—not to say the existence—of the human-divine soul is as crudely stupid as would be the claim that the sonata in the air emanating from a distant station has no independent existence, and that it is only the product of your radio when you turn in the physical rapport at so many points of frequency. Its existence, that is, its presence in your room *is* the product of your radio, a function of its mechanism. But your radio set did not generate it. It merely registered it. It was generated elsewhere. The soul, too, is not a product, but only a registry of your brain mechanism. It, too, was generated elsewhere. It "hath had elsewhere its setting, and cometh from afar." It came "from heaven," asserts every scripture of the aged past. "Heaven," then, is but a station whose generating and broadcasting frequencies are something higher than those commonly capable of registry by the human brain. But the soul migrates from that higher world and comes to earth expressly for the sake of finding registry in human consciousness.

It is not a question of whether life can *be,* independent of body. It is ever in being; it ever *is.* The question that ought to be asked is whether it is *in corpore* or *in ovo.* It passes back and forth eternally from one state to the other. It steps from sheer being out into existence and again retires. When it is in existence, for which it must build a material organism, it has the appearance of being generated by the mechanism and being an epiphenomenon of the machine, its product. In fact it is merely being liberated to the outer world by the machine.

This conjunction with a body, through a synchronous rapport with the energies of the physical, constitutes the soul's involution, or descent. And the consummation of the gradual linkage of its nature with that of the body is dramatized as its marriage with the psyche. The wedding is consecrated through the handclasp of upper with lower affinities at the point where they meet on common ground.

Soul is therefore "in" matter and body because it has become one with the animating energy of body. It has become for the body its animating or life-giving principle. Thenceforth it is not only "in" the body; it becomes indeed the chief creator and molder of the body. For its formative life springs ever from within and presses outward. The body takes shape under the nature and over the pattern of the forces expanding outward from within. Soul builds and shapes the body.

In the end it must be seen that almost the exact reverse of the dictum of modern science is true,—that the body is the product of the soul, not the soul the product of the body. The real truth of course is always to be found on the "horizon" line midway between the two extreme views. The phenomenon of the visible presence of both soul and body is the resultant of the meeting and balanced interplay between the two energies of life, widely differentiated, but capable of merging. That is the great basic datum of knowledge lost since Plato's day.

It may be true to affirm that the germ of conscious life is "in" matter at all times and *ab initio*. Matter itself does contain from everlasting the seed potentiality of conscious mind. Each atom is an embryonic universe, with mind and matter already segregated in their eternal polarity. For an atom, as a unit of true being, must manifest the nature and structure of true being, which ever exhibits the polarity in interaction. But if the seed germ of soul is in matter from the start, it is there long in embryo or in latency. It must abide in dormancy until far along in evolution the sun of conscious mind beams upon it and wakens its unborn energies to conscious function.

Being in matter seminally, the egg of mind undergoes a gradual expansion of its hidden faculties into actual exercise through its response to the exigencies of its evolutionary experience. It gains a knowledge of its resources of intelligence by having to deploy them at the beck and call of the stresses and strains thrust upon it by the vicissitudes of the onward march. Evolution of mind and soul thus comes through the challenge of experience. This is involved in the "cycle of necessity" spoken of in the Greek philosophy. Enhanced capacity for conscious bliss is the soul's abundant reward for its long pilgrimages from its celestial homeland in dreary exile in far countries.

The great item of knowledge that throws into a frame of understanding the ancient systems of theology is the important fact that the consciousness which is innate in the atom, and comes gradually to more sensible awareness in the mineral, then to somewhat more vivid sense in the vegetable, and finally into fairly definite feeling of its existence in the animal, is not capable of developing beyond the stage of a vague unrealizing subconsciousness into full self-consciousness, through its own unaided powers. Its nature and status are exactly comparable to the life of seed or root in the soil in winter. In these the innate capabilities of growth are latent. Of themselves they can not move out of their dormancy. They have to await the rising of the sun of spring, under whose thrilling rays they bestir themselves to activity.

This situation is an exact analogue of the great subconscious powers of the psyche. The consciousness that has come to the point of dim subconsciousness in the animal can of itself go no farther. It can not of itself attain full self-consciousness. It must await there the coming of that sun of righteousness which will flash its beams down into the dim recesses of its being and awaken latent potentials to active expression. For those latent energies of psyche the coming of those benignant rays is the glorious appearance of their Prince Charming. For the animal it is the equally glorious advent of the lord of life who will raise its powers to those of the self-conscious human. For man, the human, it is the epiphany of the lord of divine selfhood, the Christ. In every case it is the Coming, the Advent of that power of consciousness which redeems the life fallen into matter by raising it again to the kingly estate of full creative self-consciousness. "Nature unaided fails" was one of the cardinal maxims of the great wisdom. Nature can go so far, but she can not pass the limits set to her domain. Earth can reach up to the top of the highest mountain in her kingdom, that of animal consciousness. But she can not leap from that peak into the heavens unless an arm of power reaches down from thence, catches hold of her by chains of synchronized affinities and transports her likewise into the empyrean. This is figure, but it is more. It is the precise description of the evolutionary drama being enacted perennially on the stage of mortal existence in the life of man.

The son of God has descended in the fullness of time to catch up and bear aloft on his capable wings the sleeping psyche of animal man. He comes down, like April sun, to set the captives free, to open the eyes of the blind, to release the prisoners from their dungeons, to lead them forth out of this darksome land of "Egypt" across the "Red Sea" of bodily blood through the wilderness and the desert into the Promised Land. As crude flesh and blood can not inherit that diviner estate, he must first transform them "into the likeness of his own glorious body" of ethereal sun-essence before they can become eligible for celestial glories. So they ascend with him into the mount of transfiguration and there they are changed, their faces shining like the sun and their vestures glowing white as the light.

A great release of meaning for intelligence here is that the woman, Mother Nature, left to herself, is the "barren woman." She, like Hannah, Sarah, Elizabeth and others, was childless until her old age. The Christ must come to fructify the as yet abortive creation. The fruitless unproductive wastage of the woman over twelve years was instantly stopped the moment "virtue" from the Christ had passed into her. She was then to become the mother of the Christ genius.

To achieve the awakening of dormant godhood in man the animal, life provides the means of transplanting the seed of the divine potency into the earthly body, which is ruled only by the subconscious habitudes of nature. The divine seed is transplanted to earth and buried in the inmost being of the creature. This is the outside agency that comes to nature's aid when on her own resources she can go no farther. It is the coming of the gods to help the sons of earth. As the Christmas hymn (*Hark! The Herald Angels Sing*) words it, they were

> Born to raise the sons of earth,
> Born to give them second birth.

Man, human, waits for the coming of the Lord Christ, who, as Paul says, shall change our vile body into the likeness of his glorious body and end by converting us into gods.

All this depicts the incarnation. The Egyptians, in faithful accord with their addiction to nature symbolism, portrayed it to the imagination under the term "incubation." Like any seed, the seed of divine self-consciousness that would convert animal-human into divine-human, was said to be incubated in the soil of the human garden. There it first "died," but again germinated and shot into the growth of a new cycle.

Involution, then, is the planting of the seed of Christ-mindedness in the physical body of man the first, so that as the seed germinates and the plant grows, man may be transformed into the nature of the second Adam, the Lord from heaven, and enjoy the liberty of the sons of God.

It is time now to look for the analogy of the involutionary operation of planting the seed which is to fructify the barren womb of Mother Nature and generate in her body the fetus of the Christ-child. And where is it to be found in phallic symbolism? The revelation that floods in upon the mind through this channel is nothing less than prodigious. The parallelism is so obvious as to be stunning in the force of its pertinence, if it has never been contemplated before.

In physical or human procreation the consummation of the act is the implantation of the seed of the male for its incubation in the female. Hence the male member was in all ancient symbolism the physical emblem of the soul descending into its place of meeting with the germinal potency of the female—matter. It is the sensitive arm that is projected into the interior core of the potential mother body, and is therefore the agent for the production and implantation of the seed. The phallus could not be other than the symbol of the Father's power to generate and project the seed of new life. As such it was nobly and loftily conceived. Its connotations are therefore entirely on the spiritual side. It quite fully matches the functionism of the divine soul in being the extended arm of God's power reaching deep into the heart of matter to awaken the unfertilized egg of a new birth therein to be incubated.

From this exalted significance of the erect male member comes the symbolization of generative fatherhood in such upright structures as round towers, pillars, obelisks, stone monuments and shafts, later church spires, in all religious architecture. They stood as mute spokesmen for the mighty procreative power of life, as typed by male virility. Spirit projects an arm of its living power into the waiting womb of matter and deposits its seed of future life therein. Of this great cosmic operation the phallus, erect for creative progenation, must perforce be the effective natural symbol. And such it is. It is the sower of the seed.

Creative imagination, instructed and guided by the correspondences, must strive to reach comprehensive truth from the features of the analogy under the eye. The very structure of the male organ yields further light. First is its equipment of nervous sensitivity. This is at once illuminative. It is in this regard the counterpart of the soul itself, and the soul is a fragment of God's own divine mind. God projects a seed fragment of himself into matter and that is the soul. Then the phallus is the symbol of that fragment, as being the portion that enters the female.

Physiologically these ideological parallels seem to be faithfully carried out. The exquisite capabilities of keen sensitivity bespeak the very innermost soul of life consciousness reaching out toward the polar opposite. It is as if the god in man projected an organic unit of his own sensitive soul exteriorly, so as to penetrate the negative node of life. Invidious as it may at first sight appear, it must be seen, then, that both the organ and the seminal essence it draws forth, typify the spiritual or divine creative forces.

There comes to hand on the very day this page of the manuscript was to be typed a passage from that astonishingly revealing work of Henry O'Brien, published over a hundred years ago, *The Round Towers of Ireland* (p. 101):

> "The eastern votaries, suiting the action to the idea, and that their vivid imagination might be still more enlivened by the very *form* of the *temple* in which they addressed their vows, actually constructed its architecture after the model of the *membrum virile,* which, obscenity apart, is the divinely-formed and indispensable medium selected by God himself for human propagation and sexual prolificacy."

O'Brien is one of the few who have seen with full clarity that ancient sun-worship and ancient phallic worship were identical in significance. The sun was the embodied essence of God's own emanative and creative power at the cosmic level. In man the microcosm the phallus carried this representative power, as it was the agent for the act of procreation on the generative side. Therefore all the male phallic emblems exploited particularly in religious architecture stood as representatives of both God and his stellar embodiments, the suns. Another statement from O'Brien is directly to this effect (p. 111):

> "But the Budhists, not content with this ordinary veneration, or with paying homage in *secret* to that symbol of production which all other classes of idolators equally, though privately, worshipped—I mean the Lingam—thought they could never carry their zeal sufficiently far, unless they erected it into an *idol* of more than colossal magnitude—*and those idols were the Round Towers.* Hence the name Budhism, which I thus define, viz., *that species of idolatry which worshipped Budh* (i.e., the Lingam) *as the emblem of Budh* (i.e., the Sun)—Budh signifying, indiscriminately, Sun and Lingam."

It should be explained for the sake of clearness that O'Brien puts strongly the claim that what he spells Budhism was not named after an alleged human founder, the Buddha, but was derived from the ancient Irish name for the sun, *Budh*. It is worth noting that he asserts the word means both the sun and the phallus. Scholars may rail at him for this, but there is much to support his view. It is almost certainly correct. For the sake of showing the purity of the motives activating phallic worship, another brief statement from O'Brien's remarkable work may profitably be inserted here (p. 112):

> "Such was the whole substance of this philosophical creed, which was not—as may have been imagined—a *ritual of sensuality*, but a *manual of devotion*, as simple in its exercise as it was pious in its intent—a Sabian veneration and a symbolical gratitude."

Along with the male organ regarded and venerated as symbol of generative life the seminal fluid partook of the same representative value. As to this we find Reitzenstein saying (*Die Hellenistischen Mysterienreligionen*, p. 20):

"Among the various forms with which a primitive people have represented the highest religious consecration, union with God, belongs necessarily that of the sexual union, in which man attributes to his semen the innermost nature and power of God. That which was in the first instance wholly a sensual act becomes in the most widely separated places, independently, a sacred act in which the god is represented by a human deputy or his symbol the Phallus."

Indeed analogical industry went so far as to make of the phallus an image and reflection of God himself. Correspondences are not wanting. God, so to say, lets the "life" or creative power go out of his body, go "dead," as it were, in his periods of inactivity or sleep. In turn he arises, fills his universe with the life-blood of his creative purpose and generates creative force, ejecting life-giving streams from his body. He lies down in sleep; he arises for new work. He veils and unveils his head with an outer screen of matter. He enters the world of matter, the mother. He plants his seed there. And there are further analogies which must be held for later exposition. Reitzenstein's allusion to the phallus as the "human deputy" of God is suggestive of much. The phallus performs in the human organism what the God power does for the cosmos as a whole. Its functions are analogous to those of the supreme Godhead. It is the operator in the small sphere of the same power that God wields in the large. It can be thought of in this sense as God's son, his own power in a secondary or transmitted form. Hence indeed it came to be denominated in some ancient symbolical systems as "the boy." It was the Father's creative majesty in the little edition.

CHAPTER XX

WITH UNVEILED FACE

THE next feature is strikingly suggestive of further cosmic methodology. The foreskin is found used several times in the Old Testament, obviously with cryptic connotations. In the fourth chapter of
Exodus there is given the strange incident in which Moses'· wife
Zipporah takes a sharp stone and cuts off the foreskin of her son
Gershom and casts it at Moses' feet, saying, "Surely a bloody hus-
band art thou to me!" The Lord had tried to kill Moses and the
son's foreskin is allegorized as saving the father from the Lord's
fateful purpose. Measured by the yardstick of orthodox presuppositions the "incident" is hardly amenable to any intelligible rational-
ization. One has to resort to the intimations of old Egyptian figurism to gain a clue.

The descent of the soul was always the mythological equivalent
of the "death" of the parent in the old cycle, and his resurrection
or rising again "from the dead" was prefigured in and as the birth
and growth of his son. The father died that he might live again
in and as his own son. The son's birth and glorious youth resurrected or revived the dead father. Hence there is the great scene
at Anu, where Horus, the Christ, raises from the dead his father
Osiris, a scene which is almost word for word the archetype of the
raising of Lazarus at Bethany in *John's* Gospel! Indeed the name
Lazarus is found to work back to the old name of Osiris,—Asar.
The meaning indicated, then, is that the application by the mother,
nature, of the son's symbol of virile life, the foreskin, to the feet
of the father, who is represented as under sentence or threat of
death *at God's hands,* could be seen as a variant form of the drama-

tization of the son's recreative power restoring the "dead" father to living status.

At another place in Israelite history the victorious general ordered the foreskins of the soldiers of a captured army to be heaped in a pile, with the symbolic implications left obscurely to the interpretative capacity of the reader.

Circumcision was a rite that dramatized quite realistically the cutting off of the carnal nature in the process of evolution, as the spiritual nature came to full kingship in the life of the individual.

The symbolism of the foreskin in its simple physiological status is, however, quite revealing. It is a veil of flesh that is, in intercourse, drawn back or retracted from the sensitive head of the phallus, and again drawn out to cover it. This divestiture and investiture of the most living part of the organ with each inward and outward movement is most astonishingly adumbrative of corresponding features of the cosmic creational processes. It is recounted among the allegories in the Old Testament, in *Exodus* 34, that when Moses went into the presence of the Lord on Mount Sinai, he put a veil over his face, but removed it when he came out to reveal the Lord's message to the people of Israel. It may seem a far cry from this dramatism to the veiling and unveiling of the glans of the phallus in its sacred function of generating and implanting the seed of new life in the womb of mother nature. Yet the analogy is before us and is in close keeping with the whole range of such gripping parallels. The sensitive head of the divine planter of seed is uncovered in its entry into the depths of matter and covered again as it is withdrawn. The head of the organ must surely stand for the spiritual mind of God. All poetry has limned nature and matter as being impregnated with the mind of God. God, so to say, uncovers his innermost soul as he thrusts it outward into the material universe, so that matter may have the thrilling contact with mind, and he covers it again in withdrawal. He subjects his mind to full and complete contact with matter in involution, and veils it over again in evolution.

All this detail is matched with marvelous fidelity in what the archaic wisdom discloses of the soul's own procedure as it descends into matter of body. At each step of descent from God's pure spiritual presence toward embodiment in flesh, it invested itself in a coarser vehicle, first spiritual, then ethereal, then aerial, until it finally reached the physical plane clothed in the coarse garments of substantial flesh. It put on successively a spiritual body, a psychic body and ultimately a physical one. On the return to the celestial kingdom it reversed the investiture into divestiture, first the physical garment, then the psychic and lastly the spiritual. The soul covered and uncovered its most intimate self as it involved itself in the womb of matter and later evolved itself therefrom.

If the reader catches the apparently contrary working of the two procedures compared as analogous, its incongruity will be seen to be only apparent, when it is explained that Mount Sinai is not at all the mount of celestial and divine abode, but verily this outer earth, which is the place or "mount" on which God and man alone meet for mutual influence. This rendering of the meaning of the term has been incontrovertibly established elsewhere in our writings.

There is the possibility of confusion in the handling of the symbolism here, inasmuch as it might be a question of which garments of the soul constitute its *real* clothing. The decision would rest on the outcome of the perennial debate in philosophy over "realism." Are the soul's real garments those of flesh which it dons when it incarnates, or those of spirit which it wears when in "heaven"? It covers itself with the one kind while it uncovers itself of the other kind. Esoteric philosophy asserted always the eternal durability of the spiritual bodies, in contrast with the perishable nature of the physical ones. The higher vestures would then be regarded as the most real ones. As the foreskin is a veil of flesh, and the fleshly body can be considered less real than the spiritual ones, the intimation could be that God removes all fleshly veils from his innermost nature in order to inject his highest spirit into the heart of matter. It is frequently a peculiarity of symbolic allegorism as used in the days of antiquity that the relevance works, so to say, both ways, or in both directions. That is to say that in the case under scrutiny it is possible to think of the soul, from the heavenly point of departure and of view, as *in*vesting itself with material garments as it descends toward matter, while from the material side it can just as readily be regarded as *di*vesting itself of spiritual garments. And on the return arc it can be thought of as *di*vesting itself of material clothing while it *in*vests itself in spiritual raiment. This possibility of an apparent direct reversal of meaning is present in so much of the ancient symbolic depiction of cosmic processes and is the cause of much confusion and bafflement to scholars and laity alike.

At all events the human mode of procreation, in the detail of the alternate recession and protraction of the foreskin in the process of implanting the seed of new birth, confronts intelligence with a perfect type of cosmic procedure in universal creation. So to phrase it, the god seeking his own implantation in the mother body of man, is alternately bared or unveiled to receive the full impressionable force of contact with the substance of matter as he presses to immerse his nature in her bosom, and again is covered with his protecting veil as he retires to spiritual habitat. The analogy challenges the mind and must be taken for what it intimates in the way of instruction and suggestion. It is necessary to meet the terms of the analogue fully and frankly in order to discern the astonishing faithfulness of the correspondence between creative methods at two distinct levels, human and cosmic. Spirit bares its sensitive being to touch magnetically the kindred currents of vital force in the opposite node of matter and covers itself again in withdrawing from the sacred intimacy. When spirit and matter are to meet each other for a holy communion of their energies, the veils that shield them normally are removed and their powers meet each other in naked linkage for a mutual exchange of hidden divine influences,—that life may have new birth. Only when the interior being of spirit, projected out from the generative Father of life, meets the similar interior being of matter, can there be the complete and rich com-

munion of hidden powers which draw forth from deepest wells the
creative energies of life.

From every point of view it seems that the classic myth of Ulysses
boring out the one central eye of the giant Polyphemus with the
red-hot tip of a pine trunk must be taken as phallic symbolism.
The single eye is lauded in scripture as filling the body with light.
Darkness comes with the double vision. Obviously this can not be
taken in reference to physical light and human vision at all, but
has relevance only in symbolic connotations. The red-hot tip of the
pine tree trunk would typify the male organ, and through it the sex
principle, which comes into being only with the bifurcation of life
from primal unity into polar duality. In a very direct way it can be
said that the development of sex through the split into duality puts
out the single eye of spirit. There is to be inwoven no evil imputation in the dramatism; it is just the method of expressing the
tableau of cosmic operation. The pine was one of the most common
of the trees used to symbolize "the tree of life." Life replaces the
single spiritual vision with that gained from a focus of spirit and
matter. In the Egyptian myths Horus, the Christ, is fabled as losing
his eye, as having his eye pierced by the spear of his opponent, Sut
(Satan), or having it plucked out and swallowed by Sut. (It is
always recovered or restored in the alternate swing of the cycle.)
And oddly enough, it is his eye—the singular—and not his eyes.
In this mythology his right eye represented spirit and his left matter.
And all man's vision comes as a balance between spiritual and
physical insights. The likeness of a pine trunk glowing red at the
point to the erect member is too obvious to need accentuation.

Circumcision holds still further indices of enlightenment. Like
animal sacrifice it was actually turned from a mere symbolic representation for mental illumination alone over into a physical practice!
There is not easily discoverable anywhere in the body of Jewish
sacred or ethical literature an elucidation of the prime significance
of this usage, whether it was hygienic, functional or wholly symbolical in original intent. On the deepest inquiry into its origin and

practice, it seems that it is just another and precarious instance, as hinted, of the stupid conversion of purely figurative dramatism of a spiritual idea into an actual rite. Illuminated intelligence devised the dramatic depictions of spiritual truths; it remained for shut-eye stolidity of mind to convert them into assumed physical operations. On this basis there can be an understanding of the whole colossal record of religious ineptitude. It is religion's "Guide to Folly" indeed. At a fatal epoch literalism fell like a blight over the area of mind illuminated by the light of former ages and withered the fair verdure of esoteric cryptography into the sear leaves of dead meaning.

The rite no doubt was a purely symbolic portrayal of the idea of the soul's uncovering itself upon entry into the divine communion with the inmost power of the atom of matter. Likewise it could have been intended to convey the soul's divesting itself of its veil of matter near the end of each cycle of its life. It would thus suggest the complete severance of the spiritual soul from its union with body, the philosophically conceived cause of its fall and its "degradation." The cutting off the foreskin would thus have connoted the soul's final escape from the alternate covering and uncovering of itself as it entered or left the domain of matter, or its final emancipation from union with the flesh. If it holds any more profound esoteric significance than these direct intimations of its actual suggestiveness, it must be brought to light by the turning of a still more recondite key.

If it was intended to signify that the soul was no longer under the cycle of necessity, no longer bound to the wheel of involution and evolution (at least in the sort of bodies familiar to us) and free from further involvement in material limitation, it would carry much the same significance as that other practice—also a symbolic depiction carried over into wretched literalness by crazed ignorance —of holy men "making themselves eunuchs for the kingdom of heaven's sake." In such an expression is to be caught an inkling of the hidden import of these ancient formalisms. To render oneself a eunuch for any recondite religious purpose could only have stemmed from the idea that, with the body thus cut off from the power to generate its reproductive seed, there was exemplified the soul's final release from the necessity of uniting further with body. This was another way of suggesting its return to primal androgyneity, its pristine hermaphroditism, in which it lay in the time of its residence in nirvanic dreaminess. In this state it is the One and not the two-in-one, its polarity only latent, male-female in one, not male *and* female. In so far as "marriage" in its theologico-philosophical sense of the union of spiritual consciousness with physical mechanism is to be regarded as a hardship and an evil—as unfortunately it was so considered in great part throughout the whole religious development—its hazardous necessity was at last overcome by the soul's consummation of its victory, whereupon it could retire to its heavenly place and be free from further adventures in "matrimony." This inclination is understandable, in typology at least, for the soul is then approaching the last stages of her long cycle and yearning for the blessedness of the return to unity. She is nearing her heaven, where there is neither marriage nor the disposition for it.

The next observation of the modus of physical reproduction at the human-animal level is one that yields a great truth of philosophy when the analogical deductions are traced out. This is the fact that, as nature instructs us, there is required a pretty effective frictional contact between the bodily implementations of spiritual and material life to engender the sensuous response which both attends and produces the transplantation of the seed of soul into matter's soil. The schematism of life's methodology in this particular has not been sighted or proclaimed with sufficient succinctness.

Sense is the first and basic form of consciousness in its serial awakening and manifestation. Sensation is the first degree of awareness, and from it, as it yields pleasure or pain, emerges emotion, the next stage. From emotion arises thought and out of thought at last comes spiritual intuition. Consciousness would remain forever "unconscious," undeveloped, if spirit, which is consciousness in potential, and matter, its polar foil, were not brought into affective relationship in an interchange of their several influences. They must be brought together, not alone in naked intimacy, but with the effective vigor of frictional contact, to awaken the latent energies in both their natures. They must impinge upon each other with the natural force of their several opposing powers. Or the active energy of spirit must meet and wrestle with the inert and passive opposition of matter. The archaic scriptures picture the impingement of the two upon each other under a variety of typal representations. It is a friction, a tribulation, a bruising, a wrestling, a battle. These are all interesting and yield deeper meaning when followed down to their philological lairs. "Tribulation" is from the Latin *tribo*, "to rub." The tribulation which St. Paul says we shall have in this world results from the abrasions and the scuffing which the soul receives from its sharp and often painful experiences in the material world. The soul is knocking roughly against the hard coldness of the world of things and the necessities laid upon it by physical needs. Crudely stated, it must rub sharply against all that matter places in its path in mortal existence.

Then there is the figure of "bruising." With great vividness this is put before the mind in the great Biblical declaration that God would put enmity between the serpent (of the lower nature in man) and the seed of the "woman," and that this enmity should come to view in the reciprocal bruising of the heel of the son of the "woman" and the head of the reptile throughout the evolution of humanity. "He shall bruise thy head and thou shalt bruise his heel," said the Cosmocrator to the serpent. Here again is abrasion, friction, contusion between the two arms of the polarity. As the Christ in man stood above the low crawling serpent of the carnal nature, the point of contact and mutual wounding must necessarily be where the lowest extremity, or "heel," of the upper man came in conflict with the highest point of the lower self, its "head." This position of relationship was aptly designated in the ancient zodiacs, in which the feet of the Christ-child, held in the arms of the mother, the

Virgin (Virgo), rested just above the head of the gigantic serpent (Hydra) stretching across seven signs of the zodiac.

There are many versions of the wrestling and battling of the two forces, the chief archaeological one being that universally mistaken for a supposed future historical warfare,—the Battle of Armageddon. The name was derived from the Egyptian *Har-Makhu,* the name given to the Egyptian Christ figure, Horus, "Lord of the Two Horizons," and the later addition of the Hebrew *Adon,* "Lord." As the god who stood on the morning and evening horizons, Horus was depicted as the divinity in man that stands on the boundary line separating spirit and matter and there wages the eternal conflict with his twin, the power of darkness, Sut.

Under whatever form it is considered, the implication is that out of the conflict and clash of opposite polar energies there is engendered a heat and a fire which, like the potent rays of the sun, becomes the immediate productive agency of a new birth, awakening and calling forth energies till then latent. It is the heat that causes seeds to germinate. The release of generative heat by fermentation is one of the chief symbols in old systems. But the generation of life-giving fire by friction is another equally emphasized. From the warmth of the embrace between soul and flesh, from the heat of the battle between them, and from the fire of friction between the two poles of life arises the electric glow of inner consciousness, from incipient sense, through emotion and thought to spiritual love. This is one of the most revealing of all the vital truths imparted to early humanity by the exalted Sages who drew from their fund of near-divine mastery of knowledge. Out of the marriage and intercourse of spirit and matter in their incarnational relation the seed of new life is implanted in Mother Nature's body.

The rich accretion of philosophical wisdom to be drawn from this ray of phenomenal revelation is worthy of an extensive elaboration. The direct implications and points of instruction for systematic thinking are both striking and authoritative. To begin with, it underlies the absolutely indispensable role of matter in the cosmic economy. It thus strikes at the unconscionable absurdity of those philosophies which rain their barbs of ideological invective and contumely upon the innocent head of their Antichrist, matter. But chiefly it confronts the thinking mind with the practical imperative to understand that all man's values in the field of emerging powers of consciousness are brought to birth out of a constant tug of war, euphemistically dramatized as enmity, between the two poles of life. This broad facet of truth has been set forth in sufficient amplitude since the day of Plato, but it seems never to have been admitted into the structure of philosophy at any time with keen enough perception of its cogency to orient the academic mind in a correct posture toward the nature and important role of matter. It has never been evaluated with an appreciation adequate to lift the pall of odium off the head of matter in philosophical speculation. The opposition that matter puts up against spirit has not ceased to be signalized as a thing of evil import and to be decried as a cosmic mishap. Indeed the battle itself has been characterized as an unfortunate miscarriage of cosmic strategy due to the interference of an evil principle somehow permitted to invade the counsels of Infinite Good. Confusion and chaos have arisen in the theological arena because evil, misconceived in the first place as a principle independent of the total life of good, has been severed from any necessary relation to good and placed by itself in a world of hostile motive. Properly envisaged it should have been known as the twin of good and divinely activated to co-operate with it in the establishment of values that only by its opposition could be brought to concreteness. Good can never be established without the countervalence of "evil." And the values eventually won out of the conflict are beyond good and evil in their relative aspects in the phenomenal world. These forces are not two antagonists combating each other for the mastery of creation. They are the two components of one reality, as necessary to the stability of that reality as are inside and outside to any dimensional entity, or front and back to a sheet of paper, or right and left in any form. Indeed by an insidious tendency of the mind there has ever been the proclivity of thought to ally good with up, with front, with inside, with right hand, and evil with down, with outside, with back and with left hand. Our very word "sinister" is from the Latin word meaning "left hand," and the French word for "left," *gauche,* gives us in English "gawky," and *gaucherie* is "awkwardness." "Dexterous," a word of positive significance, is from the Latin *dexter,* meaning "right hand." But these are popular mistranslations into literal realism of what were purely dramatic modes of depiction of relative significances in ancient formularies. They are part of the exoteric wreckage which uncomprehending mentality makes of esoteric truth whenever it is handed over to the masses ruled by low intelligence. The ascription of "evil" to any part of the machinery of evolutionary movement is simply the work of man's limited perspective and belongs in the same category of error as the blunder that a simpleton's mind might make if he declared the brake on a vehicle to be evil because it obstructed the forward movement.

Likewise the aim of life is to generate the "fire" of creation, and the methodology requires the friction between mutually coordinated forces and mechanisms, but in seeming opposition. All that is needed for man to view the phenomenon with balanced discernment is to use this much of philosophical knowledge to correct the hasty misconceptions of naive judgment. The scriptures have again and again assured us that God uses the powers of evil for ultimate good, but unreflective habits of mind allied with superficial observation and judgment of experience have defeated the recognition of the truth.

Mounting even higher in the scale of philosophical edification is the next reflection to be adduced from the frictional phenomenon. It follows close on the heels of the item just amplified, and carries thought forward to a realization of one of the most potent of all truths. It springs directly as a deduction from the premises of the situation. It is the great truth that *only through the frictional relation with an actuality outside itself can the latent energies of spirit be born in the open field of manifest expression.* Almost universal is the belief that spirit is all-sufficient unto itself and able to produce or deploy its powers in independence of all extraneous physical relation. Let it be proclaimed with the most positive certitude that nature has negated this folly of shallow philosophy and arrant presumption by her presentment of truth in the creational procedure.

The method she utilizes under our observation distinctly attests that spirit is not all-sufficient to its own purposes, and that its growth and unfoldment into power can not be effected in independence of its relation with matter. Such has ever been the ideological predominance of spirit over matter in theology and general supposition that the legend of spirit's power to actualize its aims grew until it left the matter of a requisite mechanism for its successful work quite out of consideration. It has been a stupid miscalculation that spirit could function and blossom, so to say, *in vacuo,* and that it could sweep ahead to the evolution of its genius and powers without regard to any need to be instrumentalized or implemented by an organic vehicle. Philosophy has feigned to assume that it was something that could flash its decrees in empty air, or bring its aims to pass by a sheer fiat of its will, needing no localization in any scheme of organic development. It was conceived as something that can "blow where it listeth," without awaiting the slow provision of a structure of implementation. It was practically conceived as a power that could see without an eye, hear without an ear and know without a brain. Indeed so far was this presupposition carried that in religions it became a defamation of its character to speak of it as in any way dependent for its expression upon ignoble matter. In this overweening estimate spirit could disrupt and dissolve any material formation that sought to limit it. To make its manifestations dependent upon the organization of matter was to reduce it to an ignominious slavery under the thing which it were blasphemy to mention in the same breath with it.

This errant presumption in the case must now be seen to be shattered by the evidence life itself presents. Spirit will in its arc of predominance in the cycle gain the victory over matter. But it will not do so in utter independence of matter or out of relation with it. It will achieve its high purpose only by the help and through the agency of matter. It would, as already said, remain an unplanted seed, a chick *in ovo,* if its forces were not harnessed to physical mechanisms. Idealistic philosophy has long needed the balance of this simple realization to hold it steady against the extravagant fling of over-laudation of spirit as majestic lord of life.

It should have been more correctly formulated in philosophy that spirit's ultimate superiority over matter consists, not in its ability to manifest its powers in complete contempt of matter, but in its function of organizing matter into mechanisms fitted to give fullest and freest play to its energies. Spirit is not dependent upon matter for its being; it *is* dependent upon it for its manifest existence in the worlds. The amount of its potency able to be released and set to work in creative effort is contingent upon the capabilities of the organisms which alone can transmute purely potential energy into kinetic power. Electricity can not drive wheels and pull trains until it is harnessed to the requisite machinery.

Idealistic philosophy has justly earned this disdain of straight-thinking people because of its failure to concede the necessary value of matter in affording spiritual faculty its engines of accomplishment.

CHAPTER XXI

THE OIL OF GLADNESS

AN altogether signal determination of philosophical truth comes to view as reflection proceeds from its base in the known creative formula to wider areas of cosmic order. Not only is spirit seen to be dependent upon its linkage with matter for the actualization of its designs, but beyond that there is established the even more important fact that spirit can deploy its energic faculties outward in concrete development only in response to the call of outer material circumstance and pressure. This is quite elucidative of the meaning of experience *in toto.* It is of fundamental and critical strategic importance in the true living philosophy. It postulates experience as the indispensable condition of the unfoldment of consciousness. The great conclusion thus upbuilt is that *it takes a call, a challenge, a provocation from the world outside to draw out the hidden powers of the soul.*

That which is within in embryonic potentiality can not be brought out to actual energic operation except in response to a stimulus from without. *The slumbering inner divinity bestirs itself to activity only at the call of the exigencies of the world without.* There is in life's code a requirement that an intercourse between the periphery of sense and the interior hub of latent consciousness must bring the latter awake to awareness of its own nature and resources. Although it can not be considered a mere product of sensual experience, it yet owes its unfoldment into active power to the need of answering the call of the exterior world and its excitations. It will not arise of itself alone out of primal dormancy. The outer is the magician that evokes the reality of consciousness and all its faculties from out the apparently empty hat of first inchoate being. As Greek philosophy phrases it, it is the outward experience that 'causes the principles to arise." Mind can not exercise itself in thought, can not formulate its rules and keen perceptions of logic unless it has the substance and material of sense data as the ground of thinking processes in the first instance. Thought can not arise and take form in an empty heaven. It can not germinate until it has the facts of solid existential reality presented to it in the concrete and demanding to be dealt with. The mighty challenge they present is that they be dealt with according to the principles of truth and rectitude set by the all-ruling cosmic Mind. This lays on the creature mind the obligation to discover and follow truth as ordained by parent Mind. The soul's apprehension of truth can not evolve out of pure abstraction. Its base is concreteness. It must proceed from the concrete to the abstract. Roundness, squareness, tranquillity, whiteness are not possible conceptions to it until it has contacted round, square, serene and white objects. This by no means commits it to adopt a philosophy of sensationalism as the answer to the life riddle. But it does grant to sense the due measure of credit it deserves for its part in the genesis of consciousness. Sensual excitations do become the talisman, the magician's wand of power, which knocks at the door of inchoate consciousness to awaken it from the sleep of unconsciousness.

Hence all the hue and cry that has been raised in the ranks of philosophical and religious ideology for centuries against the life of sense, the world of experience, the flesh with its vilified lusts and the devil of the tempting lure of material things is seen at last to be the fruit of a delusion as groundless as it is chimerical. These influences emanating from the outward side of consciousness and impinging insistently upon the soul's attention in the early part of the cycle are in no wise hostile to the interests of the soul's growth, as pious religious persuasion has so long assumed. The only peril lurking on that side is that the soul, in the first blind confusion and distraction following its immersion under the host of motivations of the personal life, may give inordinate attention and undue

importance to their demands before its eyes are opened to a balan
view of their contributory service to the larger plan. As undue
valuation of sensual experience is indeed bound to occur in the
period of philosophical immaturity—and this is part and parcel of
the educative experience—the equilibrium between mind and sense
will be eventually regained. As in the case of the planets, chaos
and cosmic ruin are avoided by the exact maintenance of a neutralized state between the centrifugal forces of sense and the centripetal
pull of the spirit. Stability is won precisely at the point where the
two are balanced in equal counterpoise. If either soul or sense is
allowed to gain too heavy a preponderance, the safety of the embodied life is jeopardized.

Orgies of historical asceticism, actuated by the overwhelming pre-
possession of the desirability of crushing the carnal self in the interests of the soul's purity, have been a pitiable delusion, drawing in
their wake the sorrowful spectacle of self-mortification under the
lash of misguided pietism. A proper philosophy would have erased
or corrected the horror.

The sense experience is wholly salutary and absolutely vital to the
whole plan of spiritual advancement. The spirit is as dependent
upon flesh for its unfoldment of divine capacity as mind is dependent for its functioning here and now upon mortal body and
brain. The sense life is the lever by which consciousness is raised
from the depths of the underworld of unconsciousness. The evocative ministry of outward environment and its impacts on the organism are as the sun and genial air to the seed or young plant in the
soil, challenging hidden energies to bestir themselves. Always the
potential inner answers the call of the actual outer.

It is the *Upanishads* of that country which has most generally
been accredited with having produced the most subjective philosophical systems in the world, India, that present to us the true
doctrine of the schematic utility of the external life of sense. As
summed up in the sententious pronouncements of Radhakrishnan,
eminent Hindu Professor of Philosophy in Calcutta University, in

his two splendid volumes on *Indian Philosophy*, the doctrine is expressed in one of the most precious of all dialectic findings, as follows: *"To deny the world without is to destroy the God within."* This is the one final statement that goes to the root of the problem. In intensive study no declaration of similar trenchant conciseness upon this matter has been encountered. Its omission out of general philosophical discussion is tantamount to ignoring nearly half the problem which speculation faces. One half of the problem is the soul, whose kingly power, buried initially in the depths of the flesh —like the bees' nest of honey in the decaying carcass of the lion slain by Samson—is to come to full exercise in the processes of growth; the other half is the outer environment by contact or conflict with which the soul is to be polished and refined to the shining perfection of its nature.

It is the cry of all "spiritual" religion and philosophy, particularly of those schools that have emanated from India, that to contact God one must go within. Corollary to this is the idea that the discovery of one's inner divinity may be facilitated by shutting out as completely as possible the environing world. These presuppositions have been the conceptual background and nurturing soil of the great world movements and cults of ascetic practice, contemplation and systems of spiritual austerities generally. It has been presented as a matter of simple self-evidence that to find God one must go within where the deific power dwells in the depths of consciousness. The unexploited riches of divine being, of boundless knowledge, ineffable bliss, love and infinitude lie within. Within are the inestimable and inexhaustible treasures of grace, the measureless resources of magic and miracle. To find them has been the motive of the siren song of all the metaphysical and mystical programs of religion. Mysticism has dilated upon this theme without end; religion has baited its most fetching appeal to the loyalties of its millions of devotees with the lustrous hues of this subjective Eden and the roseate promises of its easy attainment. The theory embodies truth in the main.

The systematism of this entire work rests upon the postulation that a seed fragment of God's mind has been deposited within the inner heart of man's being to be awakened to growth through the repercussions upon it of the exertions of the outer personality. On that point there is agreement with the primary claims of mystical cultism. Divergence of view, however, arises the moment the first step is taken in the direction of an approach to utilization of the great knowledge. It is necessary to part company with the almost universal predilections and persuasions governing mystical practice, because of the shallow and unphilosophical assumptions that have led such practice into errancy and failure, not to add, enormous fatuity and wreckage. It is one of the most grievous chapters in the book of human cultural aspiration that the entire utility and advantage of holding the precious knowledge of God's immanence in man's heart has been almost totally nullified, and endless eccentricity, miscarriage and tragedy have been bred in the life of millions, by the failure of philosophy and religion to balance this cardinal knowledge with the complementary understanding that alone can guide devotion to sane usage. Measureless volumes of consecrated spiritual striving have gone into empty futility for the want of one item of dialectical intelligence that would have turned effort in the proper direction and rendered devotion effective for true gain. This priceless item of necessary comprehension is the knowledge that the God within man's being is from the start only potentially deific, and that his powers and genius lie dormant until they are aroused and brought to expression through the long experience of reaction to the stimuli coming in from the personality and the world without.

In the tersest possible terms the truth is that, while God dwells within, man can not find him there by abandoning the world without and withdrawing inward to cultivate the divine acquaintance. If it might be put with laconic bluntness, it has to be said that the God within is not available to man until he has been brought out and united with the human part of man. Always spiritual cult preachment has been to the effect that the human and personal part of man must be taken in or lifted up to be united with the higher or inner part. It is just as true to put it the other way around.

It can be rejoined, of course, that one must at any rate go within to find him in order to bring him out. But this is a mere sophistical thrust and does not controvert the main thesis that the whole success or failure, utility or damage, of human procedure in the matter rests on the mental conception of the difference of direction, so to say, in which man is to approach his God. It makes both immediately and ultimately all the difference in the world in the prosecution of the individual's evolutionary mission whether his orientation to the task is rightly facing the realities of the situation, so that the psychological forces in play may operate harmoniously, or whether his understanding and procedure based on it are all askew. There can be little question about the importance of the individual's knowing whether he is to turn his back, psychologically, on the world, to seek spiritual aggrandizement within the interior of subjective contemplation, or whether he is to throw his interest and turn his loyalties outward in a keen participation in the concrete actualities of life in the world. Hardly any situation with opposite alternatives could present the possibility of greater difference in results. The wrong choice in the issue has bred incalculable suffering among misguided zealots, all the more deplorable because it was gratuitous.

Philosophical insight has long predicated the presence of divinity in the human nature. The very doctrine of the Immanence attests the fact. But possession of the knowledge has ever failed to generate vital cogency in the life of those proclaiming it because it has not been held in rational mental balance. The feature always wanting to supply balanced comprehension has been the realization that the Immanuel in human life was not full-blown divinity, but godhood in its infancy, in its immaturity, in its potential form only. The posture taken was forever a wrong maneuver, based on an expectation that could never be fulfilled.

It was assumed that if one would but enter the deep sanctum of deity within the confines of the personality, deity would be found ready to hold court with human weakness and pleadings, and extend to the outer man its full resources of infinite wisdom. It seemed incompatible with earthly estimates of divine character that the god within should himself need education. Here is offered the solution of a riddle that has perplexed millions of eager enthusiasts in religious devotionalism from ancient times to the present. They have closed their eyes on the world and retired within the reported holy precincts of inner consciousness, expecting to be welcomed into halls of rapturous delight and regaled with conscious ecstasies. Instead they have found empty caverns of mental blankness and no welcome of joyous illumination. The god is there, doubtless; but he is asleep in his cradle. He is not yet grown to stature; he is still the largely unawakened seed; he is the Christ-child.

And what is necessary is not that he be approached and visited from without, but that he be invited to arise and come out, look upon the world in which it is his karmic obligation to be immersed, and "develop his powers," as Plotinus so clearly states it, by prosecuting his further evolution in the milieu of sense and outward event. His only chance of getting awake to reality lies in his attachment to a body open to receive impressions from the world outside. He will arise out of the dormancy of his initial stage only by his reaction to the impact of outer events upon his sensitive core. He will come to a realization of his innate genius only as it is challenged to exercise itself in response to the impingement of external occurrence or circumstance. God indeed he is, yet he must await the call of the outer world, the shock and brunt of physical experience, to unfold his latent capacities into conscious employment. In fine there is demanded the friction between germinal divinity and the concrete world to bring forth the seminal seeds of new and higher life.

Rightly do the *Upanishads* of India decree that to ignore the world without is to destroy the God within. And with equal pertinence does the *Talmud* declare that if we will know the invisible world of noumenal reality, we must open wide our eyes on the visible world of phenomena. The most supremely vital lesson of practical value needed to be mastered by philosophical studiousness at all times is that which springs from this investigation. It is the great truth that the inner deity in the human constitution deploys his hidden powers only in response to stimuli carried inward to its central seat from the world without. The inner answers the call of the outer. The soul dwelling within is there to meet the needs arising from its own body's contact with the world.

In general homiletics it has long been preached that the world is a school of training, in which the qualities of soul character were to be drawn forth and built up in the melee of active events. But this well-discerned common maxim of ethics has not cast its ray of enlightenment over into the area of philosophical theorization, nor introduced the lesson of its fine significance in that wider field. Had acumen availed to effectuate this transference, neither the fanatic effort to nullify the world's influence, nor the near castration, as it were, of man's natural proclivities, together with the suppression of wholesome enjoyment of nature's pleasures, nor the efforts to aggrandize the soul at the expense of the total extinction of the animal self, could ever have come to their baneful manifestation in the life of whole civilizations. Instead of these aberrant trends toward abject self-mortification, there would have been attained a more balanced relation between the natural man and the second Adam, or the Christ, as the golden mean of excellence found in the equilibration between the two natures would have been held in view and used as a sound gauge of philosophical ideology through the centuries. In that happier case history would have been spared the reading of that heart-sickening epoch marked by the devastating sweep of the rage for self-crucifixion and repression of all healthy instincts, bred from the mental disease of warped philosophical notions.

The nub of the great truth under discussion has been treasured in the core of the word "education." Its great pertinence has been glimpsed at times and lost again. It is a "leading out" of germinal capabilities into outward functioning. All skills and adeptness are to be viewed as having been drawn out from an inner seat of potential ability. Well might it be punned that "the mighty comes from the mite." Socrates showed that the unschooled boy taken at random off the street of Athens knew already the great mathematical theorems, needing only to have the knowledge "brought out." But nothing comes out of the tiny seed unless, after planting, it is played upon by the radiations of a higher vibrational force. The dynamic properties hidden in its deepest being will only display their strength in answer to the knocking of the outer life. Not too quickly can the world of intelligence assimilate this cardinal truth.

The fatally hypnotic obsession of mystical religion has chiefly been induced by the delusion that spiritual gifts and faculties could function by a sheer fiat of will and in total disseverance from any educative process, in which things and events played the part of the evocative agency. By the million men have called upon the spirit within to display its majestic power and glorious radiance, on the arrant presumption that one had but to invite it by the waving of a wand and it would parade forth its miraculous mastery. To a degree the whole paraphernalia of rite and mummery in religion has been designed with a view to the superinducing of the predicated supernal powers of the resident deity.

But the god is not to be summoned by mummery. He responds to the call of empirical reality. The actual experiences, the needs, rebuffs, the joys, griefs, hopes and strivings of the personal self in concrete life penetrate to the inner seat and arouse the god to put forth his latent strength. The very physical danger that threatens the personality from time to time is a potent magician to awaken the slumbering energies of the soul. The divine self-consciousness would never flower into beauty and bear its fruit in the empty regions of pure spirit. It must draw nourishment for growth from the soil of physical experience.

The tree—a notable exemplification of most cosmic truths—grows only by the effort it exerts to express new growth far out on the periphery of its form at the end of the branches. Life likewise grows by the effort it expends to propagate itself far out on the exterior boundaries of its material embodiment. The tree grows in stature by its new exertions each season in extending its reach further away from its heart. Similarly life gains by a correlative activity in pushing its conceptual formations fully out into concrete manifestation. Activity remote from the central heart of being redounds to the enhancement of the innermost nucleus of conscious life. By a mystery the deepest center of being receives an increment of growth as a repercussion from the contactual experience of its physical extensions far out on its frontiers. The fruits of empirical living are by a magical process carried back to the inner granary and harvested there for perennial use. Both the tree and the permanent inner counterpart of life in man grow by what each does in the outer leaf of personality. Their work in the personality, even though that personality perishes in the autumn, builds up the central deposit of accrued gain at the end of each cycle in the imperishable part. Deep within the organism the ego of both tree and man reaps and garners the fruits of what it labors to produce out on its farthest limbs. Periodically life swings outward to plunge into concrete experience; in the same rhythm it swings back again, carrying with it the harvested fruits from the fields and gardens of objective history. Each gleaning of product is added to the permanent store of wisdom and faculty. It plants its seed, enriched in potential capacity, over and over again, and each time that it consummates its cycle of added growth it redeems a further portion of nature's subconscious life to spiritual self-consciousness.

The planted seed, or soul incarnated, is the light which God sends out to do his will in the worlds. He plants himself potentially and the germinating and burgeoning of the grounded seminal essence in the course of the cycle's growth localizes the execution of his will in the outer rim of the creation. He makes himself operative in the outer soil of sensuous existence. The divine light is borne outward in the seed, a hidden deific fire, destined to come to glowing flame in the round of unfoldment. God, at home, gains by what his emissaries, his "children of the light," win and bring back from their conquests far out on the frontiers of spiritual dominion. The common poetism that falls so often from the lips of spiritual cult addictions—"we are sparks from a central divine fire"—is apt in its delineation of our nature in relation to the One Creative Force. But equally relevant is that other description: "We are seeds from the tree of Life and Knowledge." The living energy reposing in the bosom of the seed is verily a fiery potency, merely lying dormant till aroused by the touch of vivific rays. The two metaphors blend into one in the finale. A seed is the embodiment of pent-up fire, as the Chaldean Oracles declare that "all things are the product of one central Fire, every way resplendent." The central Forge sends out its sparks, emits its light, darts its thunderbolt or shoots its rays to the outermost boundary, where they throw inert matter into activity, organize structural growth and in the end return with accrued gains to the primal hearth.

Well does the scripture say that the Tree of Life is planted on both sides of the river of water, for its roots are watered by the stream of moving life that flows on the border between spirit and matter and are nourished equally by the sustenance they draw from both the physical and the spiritual sides of life. As the *Book of the Dead* writes it, the soul "cultivates the crops on both sides of the horizon," where the realms of sense and soul have their frontiers in common, and man can cultivate both the wheat and the tares, to be separated in the harvest.

Once planted, the germ of sentient life finds itself confronted with the special conditions that environ it. Its first task is to send its roots as deeply as possible down into the soil, that it may be able to draw thence the elemental energies and the physical sustenance it requires for the establishment of its position firmly in the kingdom below it. Only thus can it maintain itself in security against the perils that threaten it. Under the pressure of the forces playing upon it, the life spark exerts itself to neutralize, parry or overcome the influences that might destroy it. This is its answer to the outer call. The necessities laid upon incipient consciousness to fend for itself are its educators. They are the provocatives of evolution.

It has become a recognized principle in modern biological science —one of nine new formulations since Darwin's day—that unfoldment of growth only brings to manifestation a pattern of structure predetermined and germinal in the organism from the start. Environment does not determine either the direction or the form of the development; it simply provides good or poor conditions for the unfoldment of a pattern already set. Therefore it is seen that evolution's course to a divinely known, because divinely conceived, end is the coming to form of the ideal structure planned in deific mind *ab origine*. The part played by environment, less vital as determinant of form, but all important as agency for the actual deployment, is the provocation, so to say, of the latent energies of growth to active exertion. The inner nature only unfolds itself at the challenge of the outer world.

Here again it becomes apparent that an intercourse between inner spirit and outer matter is the essential methodology at work. Inner life's effort to accommodate itself to peripheral forces and conditions provides incentive to exertion, by which self-consciousness and self-knowledge are won. When at an advanced stage the inner self comes to clear perception of its nature and its mission, it gains the power to initiate action, from which point onward it learns more skillfully to manipulate environing conditions to its own behoof and for its own rational ends. The day on which consciousness steps over the last boundary between unconscious automatism under nature and conscious self-determination under mind, is the gala day in the life of Self. For then mind assumes control of the "seven elementary powers," and begins to superimpose directive will upon their activities. Thus the whole order of creation is made anew—

a new heaven and a new earth are brought into being. For creation
steps from the realm of the subconscious habitual over into that
of the consciously different. The order of the elementals, under
whose control St. Paul says we live until we adopt the mind of
Christ, is ended and the order of mind begins,—at the symbolic age
of twelve. The Christ then comes out from under the rule of his
Mother—Nature—and turns his attention to the Father's—Mind's—
business.

It is Nature's office and prerogative to mother the seeds of spiritual implantation. Her duty is to produce life prolifically. The
declaration of Isis on the statue at Sais is: "I am the goddess Isis,
the mother of all living; no man hath lifted my robe, and the fruit
I bore is Helios,"—the suns of mind. In nature's ample bosom the
very suns are born. So also the sun of divine intelligence is born
in her lap, in the physical body and brain of man. Her work is to
bring forth. And so ubiquitously does she perform her function
in every nook and cranny of the organic worlds, that she was given
the opprobrious name of the Great Harlot. She was everywhere
yielding up her body to impregnation for life's purposes. Ancient
philosophies designated her efforts to produce living birth even
before the gods had fecundated her with the seeds of their mental
creation as the Great Abortion. Nature unaided by mind was
destined to fail. But when she received the germs of deific mind,
her abortion was stopped. Then she bore the sons of God.

It would seem as if nothing could render plainer or more cogent
the analogical conclusion written all through the phenomena of
creational method. Inner values, faculties, powers, are to be drawn
out by excitation from the outer rim. Outer man is not to retire
inward to commune with inner man, for inner man is not yet
awakened. He must be aroused from sleep and summoned forth
to meet outer man in the affairs of the world. He must germinate
and grow, as any seed, under the stimulating goad of impacting
forces. God sent his sons into the world not that they should keep
their light hidden under a bushel, but that they should bring it out

and set it aglow on the hill of open manifestation for all the world to behold. Infinite chapters of morbid delusion in world history would have been more sanely written if this true view of man's approach to divinity had not been beclouded by the heavy fog of nescience.

The repercussions of the phallic analogies so far considered have been little short of momentous for the correction of various philosophical theses by the native force of truth from the physical realm. One of the effects of such rectification of bad philosophies has been to redeem nature and the life of soul immersed in it from the intellectual contempt which a badly distorted religionism has thrown upon it for centuries. Not inimical to the highest interests of the divine soul, but performing a service of intrinsic friendliness in its behalf, matter is rescued at last from the preposterous contumely which misguided ascetic proclivities had heaped upon it from the earliest times. The actor's mask of villainous character has been torn off the face of the three dramatic figures, the world, the flesh and the devil, and the trio stand revealed as friends acting under a sadly misleading disguise. Matter, the eternal target of piety's obloquy, has been shown to be no more deserving of religious contempt than is one's mother. And the procreative mechanism of animals and humans has been revealed in a new light, as being the instructive analogue of all creation.

But still higher service is provided for introspective vision as a deeper view of the natural process focuses reflection upon some of the most vivid and dramatic ideological intimations that can come under human inquiry. Indeed these more searching analogies point the mind at last to the final answer to the supreme riddles of human thought, to the location and character of that ultimate reality toward which consciousness is striving. Anything which promises so much as this is worthy the utmost consideration. It will be seen that a reverent attitude toward the teaching of nature in this great field will not fail to bring a reward of precious edification.

It is hardly conceivable that any doctrine of Christian theology could have so incredibly misled the minds of millions for centuries as the doctrine of "the shed blood" of the Christ has done. Taken in its literal and historical application to a man of flesh, whose physical blood was allegedly drained out on a wooden cross to save from sin millions already dead and other millions yet unborn, the teaching has reduced the mental view of generations to maudlin idiocy. How such a local and personal transaction could have repercussions beyond its own circle of cause and effect and radiate an influence both past and future affecting the destinies of countless millions of mortals entirely apart from their own exertion or merit, had been a conundrum of ecclesiastical manufacture whose idiosyncrasy has been matched only by its total dearth of intelligibility. Flatly it has been alleged that God's wrath at man's waywardness, disobedience and sin could be appeased only through the satisfaction of his divine blood lust by the bleeding death of his "only-begotten" Son in a physical body, suffering vicariously for the true culprit. The promulgation of a doctrine of this sort, instinctively repugnant to the human sense of right and reason, has afflicted untold myriads of minds for long ages with downright dementia. Yet in the same breath it can be said that, like all other doctrines adopted by early Christianity from pagan sources and frightfully distorted by literal translation, it is in truth a sublime presentation of veritude. Its real significance is only to be reclaimed from senselessness by consideration of its implications on the ground of phallic symbolism.

In the venerable literature of old Egypt there is a passage occurring several times in a slightly altered form, which must stand as the clue to the profounder meaning of the idea of man's salvation through the "shed blood of Christ," or "of the gods." In one place it is the great God Tem who is spoken of; in another it is Atum, and elsewhere again it is the "beetle-god," Kepher. In any of these cases it is God, the Creator, the divine Cosmocrator, who is referred to. In *The Book of Knowing the Evolutions of Ra and of Overthrowing Apep*, the God, Neb-er-tcher (the God in his totality), makes a long declaration to the effect that he came into being in the form of Khepera and that he created all things from out of Nu (limitless space and primal matter), emanating at last the two deities, Shu and Tefnut, brother and sister. The significant statement he makes is that "I had union with my closed hand and I embraced my shadow as my wife . . . and I sent forth from myself issue in the form of the gods Shu and Tefnut." These two in turn brought forth Seb and Nut (earth and heaven), and these latter finally produced Osiris and Isis (God and nature) and "the whole multitudinous offspring in the earth." (At one place the symbolism is changed to the creation of living things from the tears that fell from the eyes of the God in weeping.) But again the reference is to *blood in seminal form* in the passage in which it is said that the God Kepher rolled his phallus about in his hand, and from the *drops of blood* which fell upon the earth were formed the Gods Hu and Sa (spirit and matter), the progenitors of mankind. With still greater directness the symbolism confronts us with the inescapable obviousness of its reference, when the account recites that "the God Temu once in Heliopolis took the form of a man who masturbated. He thrust his phallus into his hand and worked it about in it, and two children, a brother and a sister, were produced, Shu and Tefnut."

The abstruse but clear and positive significance of this cryptic allegorism of ancient Egypt has not been discerned. It is nothing short of momentous for the understanding of cosmic process in creation, or at any rate for man's approach to an intelligent view of it. Symbols and figures are designed primarily to aid the dull mind of man in formulating thought about things that lie in dimensional apperception beyond his knowing range.

It is a beginning of understanding if one considers the gender which the word "hand" has been given in most if not all languages, primarily, Latin, Greek, Hebrew, French, Spanish. Is it surprising that the word is feminine? Not if it is reflected that what is really represented in the Egyptian cryptogram is virtually an intercourse between male spirit and female matter—as always. If the phallus is male, the opposing frictional agent, hand, would fall into the female categorization. And so it is found to be. This is wonderful enough.

The God Kepher(a), the "beetle-god," whose hieroglyph was the sacred scarabaeus, was styled often "the masturbating god." Before prudery raises its hands in pious revulsion at the designation, let it be understood that the Egyptians faced nature frankly and used her forms and phenomena as types of things the loftiest the human mind can cognize or aspire to cognize. Thus they used the physiological possibility of self-extraction of seminal seed to typify the lofty conception of God's ability to reproduce *from himself* the seeds of creation. Further to picture this abstruse procedure they used the Egyptian scarab or beetle as a living symbol, because, strangely enough, this beetle was declared by them to reproduce by the male alone without the participation of the female. The male scarab ensconced himself in the earth near the edge of the Nile waters and in a moon cycle of twenty-eight days came forth reborn as his own son. Archaic literature speaks voluminously of the sons of God as being "mind-born." The myth of the generation of Pallas Athena, Goddess of Wisdom, directly from the forehead of Jove, carries the same connotation. For the production of archetypal creative ideas the God-Mind needs no immediate implementation by matter. The Father produces his mental children directly from his brain alone. (This chances to be the nub of the great "Filioque dispute" over which the early Christian movement split into Greek and Roman Catholic Churches.)

What must be contemplated in the Egyptian depiction in the broadest general view is the great fact here accentuated in unmistakable clarity, that the deific being exercises creative function by means of a frictional intercourse between the two focal nodes of his life, the spiritual, represented by his phallus, and the physical, typed by his operative hand. It aids in the reduction of all creative process to a formula which gains enormous elucidative force by its reference to known creative method on the human plane if this prime principle is kept forever in view. Cosmic creation, precisely like the human, is engendered by an intercourse between male and female, from the highest plane to the lowest. God, spirit, and matter or nature, marry and beget their offspring, the universal family of worlds. God and Mother Nature are in sexual relation for the ends of creation, but at such a level of elevation and magnitude as it is impossible for the feeble mind of man to follow. All it can do is to conceive cosmic operation in the general terms of its own realistic grasp of creation as known in its experience. But it is an immense gain if man is intelligent enough to conceive cosmic creation as of the same nature and pattern as that which he knows and in which he participates.

But shining out in the most glowing splendor is the revelation in the Egyptian glyph of a great and elusive mystery of meaning never divined by Christian theologians in the phrase, "the blood of the Gods," as the propitiation offered for man's salvation. Never once in the eighteen centuries of theological lucubration has it dawned upon the darkened minds of scholars that divine "blood," as the agent of human redemption, was to be understood as blood *in the seminal form.* The common recognition that male seminal fluid is the concentrated essence of the blood, had never once occurred to any mind as the clue to the esoteric meaning of the word. And this befell in spite of many allusions in the Old Testament to the blood as containing "the life of the soul." The Israelites were more than once enjoined to refrain from killing and eating the animals "that have the blood in them," for "in the blood is the life of the soul."

What, then, is the "shed blood of the Gods" and of Christ, and what the meaning of the theological dogmas in which it is the central element? A world's history would have run in different course had this clarification been held beyond the third century. Alas! it was swept away in that flood tide of ignorance that overwhelmed the Christian movement from the third century onward.

Picture the difference between the true and the false conception of the meaning of "the shed blood" as man's savior! In the view of ignorant literalism it came to mean the few pints of holy gore that were drained out of the limp body of the man Jesus on the cross on Golgotha! Can one adequately visualize the stultification of mind necessary to accredit the concept that those pints of liquid, shall we say gathered in a bowl, were efficacious to save the mortal race of beings on this planet?

But if we look at the earlier conception, framed with esoteric subtlety, how the picture comes all aglow with intelligible and sublime meaning! The blood of Christ is now analogized as the *seminal life essence of divine beings,* drawn or projected forth from their own natures as the procreating seed of life for their children, the living products of God's eternal renewal of his life in successive generation. As the blood, in seminal concentration, carries the life-engendering powers, the self-ejection of the young gods' divine seed into the body of Mother Nature was their act of expending, sacrificing, shedding their own sustaining blood so that through that oblation the "sons of men" might also have participation in the eternity of divine nature. The gods poured out their "blood" that men, too, might have eternal life. From this the human men were debarred until the sacrifice of the higher divinities opened the way by forming a link of relationship between their lower status and the higher deific being by the implantation of the latter's potential seed in the lower forms. Thus they became the "children of the promise," and "heirs by adoption" of the divine life theretofore removed from them by an unbridged and impassable gulf, but now made viable by the Gods' outreaching hands. The sacrifice by the sons of God of their own generative seed-blood bridged the abyss, so that, as the Roman religion aptly allegorized it, they became the Pontifex Maximus, or "Chief Bridge-Builder" between God and man.

Not for a moment, however, should it be overlooked in what precise way the Gods drew out their seminal essence of blood. It was not by an act of sheer fiat of mind, but by the operation of an intercourse, frictional in nature, between polar opposites within the range of total life. The ejection of deific creative substance was generated in the first instance by the interior repercussions arising from the frictional contact between the organ of spiritual sensibility and the active physical hand of God. Always it is spiritual energies in intercourse with material opposition that educes the creative germinal powers.

Further corroboration of the interpretation of "blood" as seminal essence, the condensed and distilled electric life-power of the blood, is found in other mythical "stories" of creation and allegorical structures narrating "the creation of mankind." In many of these accounts it is set forth that mankind was created from "the blood of the Gods" mixed with earth. Literal stupidity could go no farther in the interpretation of this genetic formula than to take it as meaning the mingling of divine blood in some substantial form with physical earth. But it seems incredible that in all the centuries there has never been mental astuteness sufficient to see that the moment a literal meaning is read into such portrayals in the scriptures of old the sense is wrecked and absurdity stalks through every page.

The mixture spoken of as generating humankind was compounded of the life essence in the constitution of the Gods which *corresponds* to blood in human bodies, for the divine contribution, and of the earthly elements in the body of man, making the mortal addition. The "blood" of the Gods is that electric fluid essence that carries the unthinkably high voltage of dynamic mental and spiritual powers. This may still be a totally inadequate description, but it is about the best that language can do in the effort. It is at any rate to be conceived as a substance more ethereal than air, yet actual substance, whose highly charged streams of current are capable of carrying the incredible voltages of vivific power and intelligence ranging far beyond electricity. The Greeks called these currents of living force "rivers of vivification," and they indeed are streams of divine energy flowing from the throne of God. The "blood of the Gods" is an infinitely refined sub-atomic essence in and through which the life principle of the Gods darts and flashes, as currents of a cruder electricity course through the blood stream of mortals. Yet it is literally the "blood of the Gods," but from our point of view, it is blood raised to exalted powers of sublimation and vivification.

The scriptures several times iterate that the "fire" of spirit, brought down in mythology and theology by Prometheus and Lucifer, went down into the sea which is on the borders of the earth and turned its waters *into blood.* Here is another great symbolical treasure chest of biological meaning that has eluded the comprehension of savants for ages. The statements are symbolic references to the zoölogical fact that the blood in man's veins is the resultant product of ages of evolution of what was originally sea water! All earth life began on the seashore. The plasma in primitive life bodies was salt water. As the line of evolving life worked from the water out into the air on land, the interior sea water lymphs and fluids gradually took the form of what is now blood. It is still of the same chemical composition as sea water, chemical analysis now announces! And precisely this "sea" in human veins and tissues is that *"Red Sea"* which the sons of God, his children Israel, had to "cross" in their immersion in it during their long residence in bodies composed of it in incarnate life.

The production of mankind from the mixed blood of the deities and earth would resolve the original meaning given to the name "Adam." It is everywhere given as meaning "red earth." Earth mixed with blood would be red earth. It is purely a glyph for the creature compounded of the two elements, divine "blood" from heaven and gross matter of earth. Originally that is precisely what man is. One part of him, the physical, is of the earth, earthy; the other, the incorporeal, is of the life or "blood" of divinity from above. The mixture is *"the* Adam," as the Hebrew puts it. It is therefore the name which correctly defines the nature of man, who is both symbolically and really this "child of earth and the starry skies," as described in the Orphic wording. And this is why Jesus, as type of perfect man, was at the same time son of God and son of man in his composite being. It is told in old Egyptian and Chaldean accounts of the formation of mankind that the Gods poured out seven thousand gallons or pitchers of their red wine, to be mixed with the dust of the earth for the formation of humanity. Elsewhere the figure represents God or the Gods as molding man out of clay mixed with divine blood. A slightly varied form of the same allegory is seen in the Gospels, when Jesus, seeking a substance wherewith to anoint the eyes of the blind man, stoops down and mixes his spittle with the clay of the ground. Spittle here is a mild substitute for the stronger "blood," although, as coming from the head, it carries a measure of the symbolic meaning of life essence. Wine, as the "spiritized" blood of the grape and capable of giving man a divine intoxication, became a cognate symbol with blood. So that the miracle of Jesus changing water into wine at the marriage feast in the Gospels is another dramatization of the same deific transformation undergone by man the human by transfusing his blood with the divine wine of immortal being.

CHAPTER XXII

MY CUP RUNNETH OVER

IT remains now to approach the climactic portraiture of philosophical adumbration in the scope of sexual symbolism. The task is faced with a keen sense of the inadequacy of means and expressive resources to limn the vast chart of significance that is suggestively outlined in the pursuit of symbolic determinations. It seems next to impossible to catch and hold for steady reflection the overpowering flashes of interpretative light that coruscate from the surface of the symbolic mirror as the mind moves over it from one angle and perspective to another. It breaks upon thought almost like a veritable sun of truth, into whose dazzling effulgence one is not able to concentrate the gaze, yet by whose radiance one sees and knows things in their myriad forms of truth. These final aspects of creative phenomena release such a brilliant flood of light upon ultimate conclusions in philosophy that the former dimness of speculative vision in the search for truth must by contrast appear most lamentable indeed. It turns out that philosophers have searched and pried into every dark corner and recess of speculative inquiry for the answer to philosophical problems of ultimate meaning and ultimate reality, when nature has been holding plainly before them all the while the direct and positive outline of the truth they sought afar.

It is necessary to start from known creative process in the human. From the great fundamental fact that the generative seed is emanated as the result of frictional movement between polar opposites, the examination proceeds to note the next significant detail in the creative formula. It is the transcendent fact that the seminal seed is generated and produced as the climactic outcome of a relatively long series of involutionary and evolutionary passages in the frictional movement and is projected forth for incubation in the body of matter *by an orgiastic transport of bliss.* Nothing less than tremendous are the analogical implications flowing from these ground data.

The first formulation in the analysis is a determination that needs nothing to enhance the perception of its weighty bearing on evolutionary rationale. There is at once in view the observation that as it requires friction with matter to awaken dormant powers of spiritsoul, each successive dip of spirit into involution and return through evolution increases the strength and vividness of the awakening powers. Scrutiny of the processes of growth everywhere discloses the fact that advance in the stature and unfoldment of latent capacities in both the range and intensity of conscious life accrues by successive rhythmic stages. Hence it can be predicated that there will be a deepening intensity of enjoyment or sharpness of realization in consciousness at each infusion of the soul into body and resurrection therefrom. Each new try at life in the flesh should schematically yield keener delight and more zestful appreciation of living reality for the perigrinating soul. This is in all probability the case, although the soul, at least in early stages, does not possess a sufficiently conscious memory of past events to have a basis of comparison with present experience. It is rational, however, to assume by the force of omnipresent analogy with the growth of conscious faculty in all life process, that each stage of ongoing carries the expression of a successively higher note in a continuous crescendo. On its evolutionary side life never presents a diminishing, but always a rising swell of conscious realizations. It is indubitable that Creator-Mind designed life to grow ever sweeter at each succeeding step in its rhythmic dance.

This broad generalization has been seen and dilated upon in philosophy, poetry and sentimental religionism, yet rather mystically than dialectically. What has just as definitely not been seen, however, is the fact lying a little farther ahead in the analogical perspective, that the successive enhancements of living zest and delight in the whole evolutionary march are bound to go on to a culmination of rhapsodic transcendency in a final paroxysm of blissfulness that terminates the whole serial order with the projection of the seed. *The expulsion of the seed by the force of ecstatic consciousness closes the cycle of the creational period.* Nature must keep her rhythm, and rapturous consummation must be followed by recession of life forces into conservation and recuperation to build up for a succeeding expression in course.

Never has the human mind envisaged this schematism of life method with sufficient reflective discernment to draw from it its overwhelmingly cogent suggestiveness for determination of truth. There stands before the mental view the mighty graph of the natural truth that *the production of the seed of future life is conjoined with the supreme ecstasy of consciousness.* In the first flush of realization of this fact arises the recognition that nature must hold *the creation and planting of seed as the supreme and climactic end of her exertions.* She has indicated the pre-eminence of this function in her economy by the inescapable demonstration that she accompanies it with the one overpowering transport of bliss in the whole of man's experience, with the obvious intent of making it impossible of failure. The one thing with which the Creator-Mind could take no chances of miscarriage or failure was the provision for continued reproduction of living forms, to give conscious units their abundant chance at experience. The generation of new life must be put beyond any possible thwarting. Hence the lure to its fulfillment, the sheer delight of it, was made sensationally powerful.

The instructive function of the examination of these particulars is great indeed. The supreme deductions for both religion and philosophy flow from the implications of the premises. In the first place the essential constituent of the answer to all the pressing philosophies of pessimism and doubt, cynicism and despair, is immediately provided. That the living stream moves on to expanding volume and heightened zest in consciousness is at once the rebuttal of the whole case for a negative view of life. Life is moving steadily forward, even in spite of jolts and apparent recessions, to more abundant and joyous values. It even can envision a goal, ever nearing, of unspeakable bliss. The philosophy of doubt rests on want of reflection on nature's ways. Nature moves consistently toward sweeter delight and a crowning denouement of happiness. The scriptures have been in line with this pronouncement of nature and have encouraged the faltering spirit of mankind with their publication of its sure fulfillment in the latter days.

Then the patent inferences from the data in view swell to voluminous refutation of the lugubrious doctrinism of errant religious piety, that this life is for the most part not only a labor and a sorrow, but even a deception and dream hallucination of the soul, and that the mortal human must count on sin, sadness and suffering as the normal lot of the believer as he sojourns in this vale of tears, looking beyond to that other world of the after-life for the true joys and eternal happiness denied in the life in body. This negative view of life, generated by a maudlin and morbid misconception of sanctity and miscarried philosophical ideas, is decisively rebuked and flouted by the principles exhibited in nature's teachings.

A religion that can not localize the value of life in the living experience of it, but builds only on its negation and postpones realizations to its end, the while decrying and suppressing the divine instinct for its enjoyment, is in nature's court adjudged a false and pernicious system, if it is not already denounced by the negative fruit it has always borne. A true and salutary faith is one that places affirmative value in the life it essays to explain and beautify. The human mind is already committed to defeat in its dialectical enterprise if it is not able to rationalize affirmatively the experience it lives through, but must seek escape by denying reality to the experience itself.

It seems unthinkable that a philosophy of skepticism which turned away from earth in denial of its values and taught millions to reach forward to a hypothetical heaven of roseate coloring should have gained a nearly universal vogue for centuries. Yet such in fact has been the extraordinary outcome of ages of a jaundiced religiosity. Reason and logic yielded at last to the promptings of a twisted and melancholy view of earth life, with the fateful consequence that myriads lived their lives under hard philosophical durance, refusing validity to the actual experience, and thus losing earth while courting heaven, and delaying heaven by failure to lay the essential foundations for it in the life here. It was a case of the crow losing the piece of cheese already in his bill in his foolish effort to reach and grasp the shadow of it in the water.

The grand apical truth that now gleams forth to intelligence from the principia of creative function is the stupendous certification to thought that all living values accruing to ego consciousness throughout the long course of earlier vicissitudes are brought to crowning height and supreme intensity of realization in a tempestuous sweep of ecstatic fulfillment which alone is able to project the seed from the interior depths of life's secret reservoir. The great aeonial struggle and intercourse between spirit and matter ends its cumulative course and terminates the cycle of effort in triumph, with the exultant outburst of exuberant joy, as if for victory won in the generation of the seed for the next more radiant cycle.

The outer consciousness of the individual ego may not have overt knowledge that his every experience along the way is a moment and a movement in his progressive march to the mount of final rapture. Nevertheless the inner soul has a dim sense and a steadfast intuition of cumulative value won at each step. It has vague yet unquestioned presage and heralding of the coming consummative event. But since this inward guidance is for a long time inarticulate to the outer mind, the Sages of antiquity took pains to inculcate the ground fact of it in their sacred books, and portrayed their philosophical structures of evolutionary truth in the open language of phallicism, so that none could miss nature's instruction. Some grandiose attainment to crown the long ordeal of earthly striving the mass mind has seized upon, for the expectation of a heaven of bliss at the terminus of earth's path is the highest promise in every religion. Under its semi-delusive persuasion the confident expectation has for centuries been harbored that the gala day of rapture beyond any known on earth will supervene after the demise of the body and in that other world where faith awaits sorrow's end and joy's perennial reign. The original true knowledge that the heyday of bliss is to be attained here on earth in the last of the soul's visits to the planet has been submerged under the confused ideas that gained a foothold among the masses when nature's method of life renewal was lost out of common ken.

It was designed by the Sages that the human mind and heart should be fortified with a basis of courage and cheer in threading its way through the tortuous labyrinth of earthly life. To this end there were incorporated in the scriptures assurances of a surpassing reward at the end of the march. The glory that men shall attain at the "end of the age" (viciously mistranslated the "end of the world"), when they shall rise as gods among the immortals and shine in robes of solar raiment, is constantly held before human eyes. But only in meager measure has this assurance come home to recognition as an actual possible achievement of our future. That a great and glorious "Day of the Lord," as the Christian Bible phrases it, is to dawn for all men in the consummation of their growth to deity, is the religious persuasion of all. But so vague and nebulous, so vacuous and tenuous is it, that it has not borne realistic fruit in the life of intelligent people. It has sunk to the level of sentimental poetism and pietism, and has commanded little serious credence and no sure trust. It is little more than a sanctimonious tradition.

But however lost now from realistic grasp, it was originally a stable acceptance grounded on instinctual sense of truth. The great and ineffable Day of the Lord is coming to all, but it will come to each in the last phases of his incarnational sojourn in the body. It will come as the climactic culmination of the whole series of lives on earth, bringing the ripened fruits of the whole career of effort in mortal bodies. It will be the rhapsodic consummation of all values sought and cherished in the life struggle, as if all value were concentrated in one moment of transcendent bliss.

There is little possibility of the finite mind's gaining a lively realization of the actuality of this stupendous event crowning all experiential significance, save through the help of phallic analogy. Each contact of soul with matter's inertia and each retirement from the immersion in sense brings an enhanced keenness of rich experience. Life grows more intense and vivid with each turn of the wheel of outgoing and return. As virtue gains sway in the motivations, as the apperception of beauty, truth and goodness deepens, as brotherly charity ripens into sweetness, as human compassion grows ever more tender, the whole psychic nature of humankind will rise ever nearer to the point of climactic strength, at which there will ensue an access of blessedness and completion,—a "painless orgasm," as Plato termed it, ending the human cycle. The soul will in that culmination end its earthly career and enter the kingdom of the gods and the heavens, as *Revelation* says, "to go no more out." The night (of incarnation) may be filled with weeping, "but joy cometh in the morning." The long night ends as the day of the new light and love breaks upon the world of liberated consciousness.

This is possibly as much as pen can do to state the oversweeping tide of living elation that swings in upon consciousness as the divine impulse rises from greater to greater strength in mind and heart, and finally breaks all bounds in a swell of enchanted blessedness that overflows the brim of the mortal cup of being. It is as if all life united in a paean and transport of delight to celebrate the creation of the seed of future life. This indeed is the great oblation, when the gods, through paroxysms of compassionate love, pour out the essence of their life-blood that countless hosts of new children of God may receive the germ of immortal life and the nucleus of divine mind for their eternal benison, and that life may be multiplied for myriads of its creatures. This sacrifice bears no connotation of giving up happiness already won. It means the "making sacred" (*sacra,* "sacred," and *ficio,* "to make") of life that had not yet been elevated to immortal status.

Long and sedulously has the philosophical quest been directed to locate the thing called "ultimate reality." Earnestly it has sought through the maze of sensual, emotional and intellectual states for that which bears the stamp of true, as against false, being. Persistently it has striven to lay hold of that which is not fluid, is not evanescent, not subject to change and decay, that which, as Heraclitus put it, "abides amid the flux" of things that pass. In the world all things are in process of change into something else. Where and what is that which changes not, that abides in stable unity with itself? When that can be grasped and held, then will God, true being and the ultimate reality be known. Always it has been assumed that when this final real is apprehended man's evolution back to Deity will be accomplished, his struggle ended, victory won and an eternity of Nirvanic bliss assured.

To this fatuous persuasion of shallow philosophical thinking the phallic analogue gives a quite definite negative. It proclaims an opposite philosophy which, if viewed aright, becomes the solvent of all such questions of ultimates, finalities and reals. The brain of man has long been harassed, or obsessed, with the naive assumption that there will come a time, at the apocalyptic end of the cycle, when blessedness will be established for aye. The movement of growth and advance will come to a halt and all things will rest in static fixity; man will reach a final condition of rest and beatitude and remain therein forever.

Phallic symbolism points to a different story. It tells of no *final* achievement, no *ultimate* eternal. What it bespeaks is a climactic attainment at the cycle's end, but no abiding state of everlasting rest, all evolutionary effort at an end. *Life is never going to renounce its privilege of electing to move forward to larger dimension.* Larger rounds will follow smaller. But at each round's end, it must pause to recoup its spent forces, retiring into the inner arks for sleep and inactivity to gain its rest. What nature tells the reflective mind is that the cycle will end in a crowning achievement of rapture, a transport of ineffable joyousness, which will fulfill every instinct of divine aspiration in the high tide of complete realization of all that the cycle can offer, and in the production of the Christ-child consciousness of a new order of being, which will be the seed for the next higher stage of life's endless gamut. Not an eternity of static rest, but a moment of ec-static bliss crowning the long frictional intercourse between the opposite poles, will be the soul's guerdon for its well-fought battle and trial of the cycle's history. Then a long sleep and an awakening on a new morn for cosmic adventure in worlds transcending those it has conquered. The soul will never sigh for other worlds to conquer; it will always have them ahead. Nor will it ever sink to ignobility in the inane perpetuity of static inactivity. In the swing of the eternal rhythm between active conscious labor and struggle to the equally delightful interlude of rest and sleep at each cycle's end, the immortal soul goes onward in life's dance. Work and rest, waking and sleeping, summers of growth and winters of hibernation, youth's high adventure of the morning and age's pensive reflection at eventide, onward moves the fragment of God's conscious being in the everlasting shuttle of birth and death.

Not until the human mind wins a grip on the knowledge that life does not reach a haven of high attainment to stop and dwell there forever, but that it ends each effort at hill-climbing in a moment of triumph to rest a while and then begin a still higher effort on the following morn, will its inner counsels be blessed with perennial gladsomeness. To contemplate the successive ends of the cycles in consummative bliss will be health to the navel and marrow to the bones of the adventuring spirits of God. But to contemplate the final ending of the cycles themselves with the close of this one, would be to quench the native ardor of divine mind for new conquest, higher advance, further growth, more thrilling self-discovery and increase of life zest to endless time.

And this sad fatality is indeed what has befallen the race of mortals in the long period since the third century, when the vista of continuity in the individual's unit of conscious life was obscured and the view shortened to the single stretch of this one day. Philosophy is indeed the critical determinative in human history. Tragedy attends every slightest misconception. The greatest of all historical tragedies was the fatal plunge of the mind from ennobling philosophy into the rabid zealotry of fanatic faith from about the third century. Its catastrophic consequences still harass and defeat us.

And now the great philosophical answer as to where supreme reality resides in the human sphere of effort or attainment rises also out of the milieu of phallic indication. All the while philosophies were seeking this answer in strained dialectic and rational questing the reply was being flaunted in front of them in the orgiastic culmination of the creative act. As the tentative delightfulness of lovers' first tender approaches point to a fulfillment in a moment of climactic ecstasy in the union to come, so the partial and tentative pleasures and joys along the way point to a grand denouement of rapture in a conclusive experience. The "value" of any experience is to be appraised or rated according to its place and contribution, its part and function, in the scale of rising powers of appreciation,—what it contributes to the generation of that climactic exaltation. Even as an insignificant skirmish in the early indecisive part of a long war receives its final estimate of value in victory in the weight it contributed to the final triumph, exactly so the allocation of value to any experience along the way must be adjudged in measuring its part in the cyclical denouement. All minor events win their value not as isolated units, but in the context. Their worth is fourth dimensional and must be sought in the view of whole processes. As Aristotle so clearly showed, value is inwrought, even hidden, in the entelechy, the revelation of perfection at the cycle's end, toward which all effort, even failure, is pointing and striving throughout. The rash essay of the human mind to locate finalities, perfections and ultimates had better yield at last to prudent understanding. The attempt to fix on final goals, or a final goal, is philosophically futile. "Final" can apply only in a relative and tentative way at any time, and only in reference to each cycle's conclusion. There is no absolute "final." The mind had best disabuse itself of this fatuity. The value of any experience is in what it contributes to the enhanced character of the next experience, and that to the next. As John Dewey sententiously has written: The meaning of growth at any stage of it is to be found *in more growth later on.* And Tennyson has voiced it in his line in *In Memoriam,* that life ever goes "from more to more."

The place to look for values, then, is in the immediate experience itself, but understood as tentative in present appearance and awaiting succeeding events to disclose its fuller significance, awaiting indeed the cycle's culmination to have its highest meaning unveiled. In every event there is something that, while the event itself seems to pass without particular distinction into the flux, lives to determine the shape of all succeeding experience. Its value lies in what it is at the moment, evanescent as that may seem as it flits by, but viewed in the light of what its moment hands on to the future and the climax. It is a stone in the structure, but that structure considered as building through a movement.

The one supreme gift promised the creature by his Maker is eternal life. In the building of what life becomes every moment is a real accession. Eternal life is the one promise haloed with more than golden glory. It is the climactic reward. It is all of what life can offer its children. And each circling of the movement is promised to be a growing experience of joyousness, to be capped by a veritable apotheosization of consciousness.

As the highest note in an octave on the piano strikes the first and lowest note in the octave next above its seven, it is possible to see here, by analogy, a quite important elucidation for systematic thinking. To an octave on the instrumental keyboard would correspond a range of life covered by a creature in its given cycle. And this would again parallel a power or range of consciousness of a given extent or manifested in a given dimensionality. Humanity functions in what is commonly considered a three-dimensional consciousness. The fourth dimension is predicated, described and declared a possibility of the future as consciousness expands through unfoldment of hidden capacity. It seems altogether likely, then, that when the run of development in the human cycle has reached its culminating point and strikes the apical note in its series, it rings the first bell in the series next above it. This is to say that the consciousness expressed in a given cycle reaches a high point at which it is projected over into the introductory stage of the next higher dimension of awareness. The climactic surge of being in each cycle gives the conscious unit a foretaste of the higher blessedness it will become capable of knowing in the next round.

There is yet to be accentuated the law of life that makes rhythm the method and modus of all progress. The final running over of the cup of supernal ecstasy is the last of the whole long series of rhythmic beats. Sexual phenomena accurately match, and therefore are truly symbolic of, cosmic procedure in the large. Life is rhythmic in every pulse and movement; sex is likewise rhythmic in every manifestation. The zest, the poignant sweetness and the transport increase, not in a steady heightening, but in alternate ebb and flow, culminating when the highest wave matches the superior tone of life on the upper level and merges by that affinity into its nature.

From the implications of this observation philosophy may profit immeasurably. For the analogical shadow falls over into the larger zone of creature life and limns for us the broad truth that the experiences of the life period—as well as of the whole cycle of life periods through which the individual consciousness must pass—themselves unfold according to a rhythmic measure, both of time and pitch. In large part the individual is not openly aware of these pulse-beats, the alternate diastole and systole, or ebb and flow of qualitative surge. He may be aware of periods of depression alternating with times of exaltation, but he is not likely to be mentally cognizant of the pattern of successive beat to set measure running throughout his career. But the whole of human and other life is set to rhythm; and so it is to be expected that the structure of a time movement will be manifest in sex, the basic analogue. Such in verity is the case, and hardly anywhere more obviously. The access of delight rises in successive tides, each higher swell following a momentary recession, to break at last on the beach of consciousness in a long sweep of delirious abandon.

This is the story of man's incarnate existence. Each life carries the wave one note higher in the scale, followed by cadence, until the last tone catches up the blend of all the antecedent notes in one grand harmony, and the cup of human gladness floods over the brim in unbounded largesse of being.

The chart of creational action dissolves the errant philosophical dream of a final static heaven of bliss forever enduring in unchanging sameness. It teaches rather the flowing river of life's tides in an unending stream, with each forward surge lifting the consciousness a tone higher in the scale of happiness, as each season's crowning ecstasy draws forth the seed of the next cycle. It must be concluded that life does not sustain high bliss at a constant even pitch. Apparently such unrelieved intensity of vibration would exhaust its vital reservoir of strength. Life's song of gladsomeness is not one sustained note, but a melody of successive notes, for which again our music is an apt and accurate analogue. Instead, it gives itself in and through the creatures that embody it one climactic moment of exuberant joyousness after another, the succession of such high moments revealing the structure of the melody. To the limited consciousness of lower life whose reach extends over the long-drawn ring of but one note, the grand overture of the ensemble is not known. Yet even it is made aware of the presence of structural pattern in the successive notes through its knowledge of the scale in minor gamuts in nature and in its own world. For larger notes are themselves composed of whole scales within their arc, wheel within wheel. Each wave, large or small, rises to its crescendo of bliss and breaks into foam with it.

Life is thus an endless succession of surges, beats, breaths, throbs, pulsations, each of which is itself both an involution from the world of noumena into that of phenomena, and an evolution in reverse order, with an accumulative sum of gathered bliss overflowing the golden goblet at each cycle's end. At each new consummation of a round life feels its head anointed with the oil of gladness and its chalice brimming over.

In the Greek word which gives us our "ecstasy" there is a fine hint of deep relevance. It is from *ec* (*ek, ex*), "out," and *stasis,* "standing." It is quite definitely a reference to the actual experience of the soul in its culminative event on earth. Its transport of joyousness is exuberant beyond all bounds, because it is caused by its release from the body, so that it does literally "stand outside of," or beside itself, with joy. Likewise the same connotation goes with the Greek word for the "resurrection," *anastasis*. It is the "standing up" (*ana*) or the rising of the immortal soul out of the encasement of the body.

The soul's joy in this final act of leaving the shell of life, which during its sojourn here had been its prison, tomb and sepulcher—at the same time that it had been also its womb of a new birth—is so rapturous that it verily becomes a "transport" that carries it into higher worlds.

Implicit in the phallic symbolism also is the answer to the great query,—why does God create at all? Why does he bring into existence worlds in which evolution proceeds from one glory to another, but through deep valleys of pain and conflict? Standing firmly on the ground of the sexual analogy one perceives the obvious answer to the great Sphinx riddle. The grand motive of deific creation must be the analogue of man's own motive in parenthood, but magnified and exalted beyond any reach of the human's circumscribed powers of realization. God's creations must be to him acts of parenthood, of like nature with those of his children, if on a scale and at a height unthinkably prodigious. The throbbing contact of his own spirit with his material hand yields overmastering delight to him as to his children, who are made in his likeness. All arcane tomes of wisdom assert that God creates for *"Lila,"* delight, pleasure, play, "the sport of the Gods." And sport and play constitute, even in our tongue, "recreation." And here is the amazing linkage of the key ideas in the whole matter. In the rapturous delight of creation, it is true that God, life, is re-creating itself. Puritanic severity will still, perhaps, flout the idea that God may be considered to take recreation, enjoy himself, find pleasure, in his paternal acts of creation. Yet here is obviously one case in which pagan philosophy kept a healthy attitude and Christian religionism took a morbid view. If men are gods in miniature or in the making, their instinctual motivations must give clues that hold for greater gods. If man finds growth, pleasure, delight in play and recreation, so, too, at his unimaginable level, must God. The climactic transport of the phallic analogue sets its inviolate seal upon the correctness of this fundamental archetypal principle.

In its high cosmic sense the consummative bliss figured in human creative method is that grand coronal, "that far-off divine event to which the whole creation moves" of Tennyson's illumined forecast. If the entire process of world formation, carrying on the long intercourse between spirit and matter, is an act of creation, it can confidently be expected to have its sublime denouement in its one consummate moment of procreative sacrifice, else the most meaningful pronouncement alike in the Hebrew, the Egyptian, the Greek and the Christian scriptures is a falsity. Man is made in the image of his Designer, who could not negate the cardinal *archai* of his own nature when he generated from himself his limitless progeny. Man is the likeness of his Parent, and he carries parental life on into new manifestation. What he experiences, the Generator experiences or has experienced, in grander dimensions, at more elevated heights. And out of this dialectic of ancient premises of knowledge comes to view that other crucial ingredient of the wisdom formula, that the ineffable and transcendent being of the Father can be known only to those to whom the Son reveals him. No man hath seen or will see the Father. No man can look upon the face of God. To human eyes it is given only to see the likeness of the Infinite in the character of the finite revelation. What the meager powers of the human mind permit it to know of universal creative method must be divined by an act of adumbrative genius which can see the parental nature in the filial counterpart or reflection. Therefore man's apprehension of cosmic creation must take its departure from study of his own progenerative functionism. And standing on this ground it is impossible not to assume that *the Father's boundless creation is an act of intercourse between the male and female elements of his own being.* Egypt was content to announce out of its files of secret wisdom that Deity drew forth the seed of its life by acts of frictional relation with matter, and left it to the developing genius of the race to understand at what an inconceivable pitch of transcendency above human procreation the cosmic intercourse was to be raised in contemplation. He who would come forth to charge that the predication of similarity of method between the known human-animal creation and the unknown act of the eternal Father blasphemes the divine nature by traducing it to the mean level of the lower, is merely wanting in imaginative power to lift the analogy from gross to supernal plane. It is the human type of creation, but is not at the human level. It must be conceived, as best finite mind can, at heights of majestic apotheosis and transfiguration. At such an exalted level the whole conception becomes transfigured from base imputation and evil ascriptions into reflections of unthinkable purity and beauty.

Plato speaks of the philosopher's ability to rise to a point of realization of divine order, harmony, beauty and joyousness in the contemplation of the works of the Cosmic Mind at which he sinks into the ecstasies of a "painless orgasm." And he also calls the exalted raptures of high contemplation which possess him who thinks God's thoughts after him "a divine mania," which he says is better than staid reason. The enlightened philosophers of the Greek tradition knew they were speaking of divine raptures and transports in the image of phallic phenomena.

Likewise the Orphic-Platonic references to separations, partitions, exsections and mutilations of the Gods carried out in the implications of the myths of Kronos, Saturn and Jupiter, in which the allegory represents Saturn as dirempting his Father, Kronos, of his creative organs, and Jupiter performing a like "exsection" in turn upon his Father Saturn, all bespeak phallic foundation. Fathomless as must in reality be the esoteric import of such a mythic construction, it is at least apparent that the figure carries high truth. It can be taken as a delineation of the passing on of creative power from generation to generation in the upper hierarchical order of divinities. Doubtless deeper mystery is involved in the imagery. In Egypt, Sut, the power of darkness, steals and swallows Horus' eye. Likewise in altered figure he plucks away Horus' genitals. Here again the creative power passes from spiritual over to material grasp. We have seen how in the *Timaeus* of Plato the Demiurgus, Jupiter, passes his generative power on to us his creatures. We are instructed to fabricate animal beings, using the power that he used in our generation. We are to procreate as he created. Our creation is in the image of his.

Each lower rank of beings was endowed to carry on the work of endless creation at its plane and station and in the likeness of *its* own superior progenitor. All creation is of the same pattern and manner. The seed of life from the range above is deposited in the material matrix of the range below and is there mothered in its growth. There can be no progenation without the union of the two polar energies. The matter or mother side lies barren and unproductive until fructified by the father's, or spirit's, bestowal of fecundation. The woman could pour out her life-blood and bring down the egg of new life in each cycle; but it was a wastage and abortion, until she received a life-giving essence flowing out from the side of spirit, the seminal blood of God. She remained virgin until fructified by the power of the Holy Spirit. The sacred scriptures, in which these primordial *archai* of truth were embalmed in myth and allegory, fell under the dark ignorance and the feeble intellect of mass religionism and suffered the corruption of their luminous meanings into dark enigmas and silly caricatures. The darksome shadow of human ignobility, too, flung its sinister pall over the scene, until the pure light that should have made lustrous the mind's grasp of essential truth and increased the sum of happiness by its radiation of purity and beauty, was defiled in a murky cloud of sin and evil.

Thus was brought into human life the tragic element of discord between wholesome natural delight and lugubrious religious sentimentalism. No system of spiritual culture would take down the bars of discipline and moral control of the animal propensities exercised in their restraint by the will enlightened by a knowledge of the laws of temperance. But neither would a true religion, countenancing a healthy naturalism, crush the normal free expression of life in happiness. Too slow has been the awakening of reason from the hypnotic sleep inflicted upon it by early centuries of morbid pietism. Too crassly has every instinct on the natural side been classed as "pagan" and tainted thus with the stigma of unholy and "unchristian." Only now is it coming to the light how grievously the massed imputation of evil to the whole of sex has bred an infectious malady throughout the body of mental life in the world. Clearly discerned it is now that an errant philosophical quirk, even a mere mishandling of ancient symbolic imagery and writing, has thrown the whole mentality of the West under the obsession of a noxious fixation. In the clutches of that morbid delusion vast areas of conscious experience have been inundated with the miasmatic effluvia of gloom. Natural lightsomeness and buoyancy that should enchant the soul in its visits to the gardens of the world have been sternly crushed under the pharisaical poses of warped pietistic tradition. The healthy mind of mankind has been deplorably distorted into false conceptions wh'ch have bred in-harmony and disease.

The emendations in broad philosophical ideation that are indi-cated by the inquiry must be made. A new start must be under-taken by flinging off at last the fetters that have bound the mind in a posture of hostility to phallic symbolism and by bringing the mind to confront reality and envisage nature in friendly spirit. The pall of evil and sin must be lifted from the body of sex, while of course franker treatment of it is kept healthy by purity of mind and discipline and balance maintained in all handling of it. What-ever labels of lowness and intrinsic baseness may have become agglutinized to sex from its detached sensual connotations in the purely profane mind must be torn off its front. Instead of accepting the character of meanness fixed upon it by secular ignobility, a certain measure at least of the high sanctity that aureoles it in the light of lofty philosophical understanding and phallic analogy, must be enticed downward and made to envelop it again on the plane of common thought. And the asserted impurity attaching to it in social view should be dissipated by the downward sweep of the vision of purity gained from contemplation of its cosmic essence on the more exalted levels. Such perhaps was the high intent of the Sage formulators of the phallic analogies at the outset in remot-est past time.

In the eyes of ancient wise men the physical body of the mortal was a perfect copy, miniature and epitome of the cosmic structure of life and creation. Hence both it and its functions were considered to be the one true clue and key to life's deepest mystery. Standing at the core of the organism of life, phallic phenomena had there-fore to be placed in a central position in every system of philosophy or religion that aimed at harmonizing the human mind with the realities of the living process. No more direct and effective psycho-logical stimulus toward an inner esoteric grasp of the cosmic *elan,* the divine libido, was seen open to the genius of mankind than the presentation of truth in local aspect, as incentive and magical goad to the pursuit of truth in eternal manifestation. Surely nothing could be conceived and formulated with the design of awakening slumbering insight to living reality more radically suggestive and theurgically dynamic than the impartation of the primal knowledge that man's own body was in itself the world in miniature, the microcosm, and that its processes prefigured in entirety the great economy of the universe. Flowing from this code item in basic systematism was the immediately significant deduction that in the sane and temperate exercise of the bodily functions man was imitating the life of the Gods. In short the aim of phallic symbolism undoubtedly was to help the human mind apotheosize the bodily function with the reflected light of cosmic significance.

Much would be gained for general wholesomeness of life, for dignity and purity in social consensus, throughout the long range of racial evolution, if a posture of greater reverence were traditionalized by release of the enlightening involvements hidden in the analogical purview. From the mires of unholy brutish sensuousness, from the smudge of low human motivations, from the wanton revels of bestial grossness, into which the sacred procreative instinct and function have been dragged by the sweep of the carnal mind of the unawakened creature, redemption of general cultural purity could be vastly advanced by the inculcation of the knowledge that *in the activity of sex man is enacting over again the sublime ritual of divine creation.* It is likely true that only as the ordinary exercise of the creational prerogative is elevated, purified and sanctified by the deeper apperception that it is life's holiest ritual, enacting at man's level the highest work of Godhood, will it be exalted above sheer animalism in tone and quality. Only thus will something of diviner sacredness enshrine it.

High romantic poetry, the lyric dramas of love, the enrapt philosophies of cosmic grandeur have at least embroidered the fringe of the cosmic vision. And in these moments of uplifted understanding, all sex is seen as the ineffable drama of cosmic creation. The very Gods pour out their life-blood to project the seed of future life and they do it out of their unutterable love of the worlds their oblation aims to redeem. Only the knowledge that the happy exercise of the function is a holy ritual imitative of the identical prerogative of the Gods themselves will sanctify the enjoyment. Happy the world of humanity if in the exercise of its creative power it knows itself to be repeating, at its proper place in the hierarchy of being, the great sacrificial oblation of the Gods!

OTHER BOOKS BY THE SAME AUTHOR

THEOSOPHY: A Modern Revival of Ancient Wisdom. The Academy Press, 227 Murray Street, Elizabeth 2, New Jersey. 2nd Edition, 1944. 351 pp. Index, Bibliography. $3.00. This work, issued under the imprimatur of Columbia University, New York City, stands as the only accredited academic work dealing with the great renaissance of ancient Oriental Esotericism in the Western world in modern times. It was the author's thesis presented for the degree of Doctor of Philosophy in Religion and Philosophy and was the second volume of a projected series of publications undertaken by the Philosophy Department of Columbia University under the title of *Studies in Religion and Culture,* designed to present a luminous history of every religious denomination, cult or movement in the United States. It was reviewed in highly favorable terms by periodicals both in this country and abroad and is regarded by both Theosophists and non-Theosophists as perhaps the most judicial treatment of the subject yet presented. Its digest and analysis of the great principles of the Esoteric Wisdom of antiquity has been lauded by discerning students as the clearest and most perspicacious so far given.

THE LOST LIGHT: An Interpretation of Ancient Scriptures. The Academy Press, 227 Murray Street, Elizabeth 2, New Jersey. 1940. 611 pp. Extensive Bibliography. $3.00. This work is regarded by many, among them leading clergymen and university teachers, as the one true and correct interpretation of the Christian and other Scriptures made at any time. With keys drawn from ancient Egypt's wisdom it pierces through the outer veil of Bible literalism and alleged history and reconstructs the long-lost structure of sublime arcane meaning, retranslating the "lost language of symbolism" in which the books of archaic wisdom were written.

The author's enlightened insight and amazing scholarship have combined in this work to establish the epochal fact that the Christian religion can no longer be considered a product of Judea in the first century A.D., but is of remote Egyptian origin. The correlation made between the Christian Bible and the long antecedent religious

343

literature of Egypt is a scholarly achievement of absolutely epochal significance. It is the virtual documentary proof of the truth of Augustine's statement that "that which is called Christianity existed among the ancients and never did not exist . . . from the beginning of the human race . . . until it was called Christianity in our day." The evidence amassed demonstrates beyond cavil that the Bible is a reprint of old Egyptian texts, whose meaning can not be grasped without the keys of understanding discovered in the Egyptian writings.

It is not too strong an assertion to state that it floods the entire area of hitherto dark and doubtful interpretation of Bible meaning with a veritable radiant light. It is considered by many to be the indispensable corner-stone of the "religion of the new age" so devoutly prophesied and awaited.

WHO IS THIS KING OF GLORY?: A Critical Study of the Christos-Messiah Tradition. The Academy Press, 227 Murray Street, Elizabeth 2, New Jersey. 1944. 492 pp. Index. $3.00.

As *The Lost Light* reveals *what* was lost, and restores it, *Who Is This King of Glory?* tells the thrilling story of *how* and *why* the Light was lost. And this revelation of the truth of history that has never before been made common knowledge constitutes undoubtedly the most significant and gripping story ever told in the history of religion. More than that, this story becomes the key to the understanding of the world situation in religion today. This book is the narrative of what happened back in the third century of Christian history, when the Christian movement passed over from the hands of the Philosophers of the Greek world into those of the unphilosophical and worldly minded Romans and suffered the total extinction of its original light of esoteric spiritual meaning, the historical result of which was the sixteen centuries of the Dark Ages.

The book is dedicated to the thesis that the saving divinity, the Christos, is a spiritual principle within the heart and mind of man. The whole great and immemorial tradition of Messiah's coming to redeem fallen humanity is in this work handled with a historical perspective, with an impregnable array of scholarship and with a consummate insight into the truth that will rank this volume as the crowning work of sanity in religion.

Back of the great wars of modern times are the mighty clashes in religious ideology. Unquestionably what is happening now is but the long shadow of what transpired in that fatal debacle of spiritual truth in the third century, and this incredible story is told for the first time in this work. The book is the natural companion and complement of *The Lost Light*. The two make a mighty team, pulling together to lift the car of religion out of the mire of superstition and bigotry onto the highroad of intelligence and luminous meaning.